1986

On the Uses of the Humanities: Vision and Application

INSTITUTE OF
SOCIETY, ETHICS AND
THE LIFE
SCIENCES THE
HASTINGS
CENTER

On the Uses of the Humanities: Vision and Application

A REPORT BY THE HASTINGS CENTER

The Hastings Center
Institute of Society, Ethics and the Life Sciences
360 Broadway
Hastings-on-Hudson, New York 10706

Library of Congress Cataloging in Publication Data

Main entry under title:
On the uses of the humanities: vision and application.

    1. Humanities.   I. Hastings Center.
AZ103.049 1984   001.3   84-22445
ISBN 0-916558-20-7

Contents

Preface

What is the cultural mission of the humanities? How directly can their knowledge and perspectives be brought to bear on public policy issues? What civic purposes can—and should—the humanities serve? Does the humanist's vocation lie in the public realm of action and practical affairs, or in the private realm of contemplation and detached scholarship—or some delicate combination of both?

Those old questions have had no historically fixed answers. They have been asked and answered in various ways, first in ancient Greece, again during the Renaissance, yet again in the nineteenth century, and once more in our own times. How those questions are posed and answered over time reveals the dynamic nature of the humanities, providing as well an insight into the exceedingly complex relationship between the humanities and the social, cultural, and political contexts within which humanistic inquiry takes place.

In the last decade, questions about the social role and future prospects of the humanities have arisen with renewed force and urgency. Scholars and teachers in philosophy, history, literary studies, and the other humanistic disciplines have been reassessing their intellectual and educational role. Humanists* working both within academic settings and outside the university have been seeking new ways to address the social issues of our time by drawing on the special insights and resources of their fields of learning. They have begun directing the knowledge and methods of their disciplines to contemporary social issues, not only in traditional classroom settings and in their published work, but also by working directly with policymakers and professional practitioners. Public policy issues, scientific and technological developments, and the social role of the professions are all topics that raise questions of perennial human concern—questions of ethics, history, cultural meaning, and individual self-identity that are woven into the increasingly complex fabric of our common life in modern society.

The humanities have tried to illuminate such questions by drawing on the cultural traditions of the past, by critical reflection, and by imaginative creation. The new challenges posed by modern society make the need for that illumination all the more profound and urgent. The issue is not whether the humanities will be used and applied, but how wisely, rigorously, and well their application will be carried out.

Since its founding in 1969, The Hastings Center has worked to shed light on the ethical and value issues arising out of recent developments in the biological, medical, and behavioral sciences. Its work has ranged over ethical problems of death and dying, population limitation, genetic counseling and engineering, behavior control, health policy, and professional ethics. In these areas and others, the Center has sought to bring humanists, scientists, lawyers, physicians, and policymakers together for dialogue and interdisciplinary study. Throughout, the Center's work has been guided by a firm belief in the enduring value of the humanities to the civic life of our society and by a desire to find a more satisfactory relationship between the sciences and the humanities. In the late

---

*By "humanist" we wish to identify those who work, teach, or write in the various fields of the humanities. We are not referring to that historical and cultural movement called "humanism."

1960s, the Center was something of a pioneer in the field of applied ethics. Before long, however, we were jòined by a rapidly growing number of individual scholars and research centers working on related topics of applied and professional ethics. The fields of applied and public history emerged during this period as well. By the late seventies, many private foundations, the National Endowment for the Humanities, and the state humanities councils were actively supporting such work. What we will be calling the "applied humanities" had come into their own. But that emergence has not been without confusion and controversy. The time has come to attempt a general assessment of the rapidly growing applied humanities movement in this country. That is the purpose of this document.

In the spring of 1981, the Center began a two-and-one-half-year research project on the Applied Humanities and Public Policy, supported by a grant from the National Endowment for the Humanities. That project gave us an opportunity to take stock of the applied work now underway in several fields, to assess the circumstances under which applied studies in the humanities tend to flourish and make productive contributions, and to identify the problems and pitfalls that, in some instances, have made applied work in the humanities less illuminating and rigorous than it ought to be. More generally, we stepped back from a consideration of our own ongoing work to ask some basic questions about the relationship between disciplinary scholarship and applied studies in the humanities, and about the models of "application" that seem most pertinent to the humanities. Those questions quickly led in turn to other, equally perplexing issues about the nature of theoretical knowledge in the humanities, as well as to identifying appropriate standards for evaluating work in the applied humanities. Along the way we found it useful to compare the latter with applied work in other fields, such as the natural and the social sciences. We also explored the linkages that do—or could—exist between the humanities and the biomedical, social, and policy sciences.

From 1981 to 1983 we surveyed the literature, held six extended conferences, conducted a number of discussions and interviews, and commissioned more than thirty papers. The papers explored the goals and methods of applied studies in the humanities, the history of efforts to formulate proper roles for the humanities, and the intellectual standards that scholarship and educational programs in the applied humanities should meet. Our meetings produced lively and sometimes heated discussions. They brought out clearly the tensions and suspicions that still exist between "disciplinary" and "applied" humanists, and they revealed some interesting differences in perspective among those doing applied work in various fields. If we did not eliminate these tensions, we believe that we did succeed in focusing and placing them in a clearer perspective.

The report that follows is an outcome of that work. It sets forth the issues we found to be central to an assessment of current work in the applied humanities, presents a general survey of the nature of applied work in a variety of disciplines, and offers our main conclusions and observations about how high-quality work in applied humanities can be nurtured and supported in the future. We did not attempt to achieve a tight, precise consensus among ourselves, only a general agreement; no member of our project would necessarily agree with every sentence in this report. We felt we neither could nor should lay out hard-and-fast prescriptions for work in the applied humanities or for educational programs designed to prepare students to carry out such work. But we did study the issues carefully, talked and argued at length for over two years, and developed what we believe to be the first general analysis ever undertaken of the applied humanities as a whole. It is that analysis that we present here. The various boxed passages, examples, and quotations are meant not only to help flesh out an occasionally general and abstract text, but also to convey some of the flavor that has accompanied recent debates. The various citations in the footnotes should enable the reader to find adequate further reading.

This report draws upon many sources. Perhaps the most important among them are the various papers and studies commissioned for the project, a number of which will appear in a companion volume, *Applying the Humanities*, edited by Daniel Callahan, Arthur L. Caplan, and Bruce Jennings (New York: Plenum Press, forthcoming, 1985). They pursue in greater detail the issues that can only be summarized or alluded to here.

We would like to thank the National Endowment for the Humanities for the support that allowed us to conduct this study. In particular we extend our thanks to Ms. Arnita Jones, Program Officer at the Endowment, for her helpful advice, generous encouragement, and constructive criticism throughout the course of this enlightening, but sometimes exasperating research project.

A special debt of gratitude is owed to James M. Banner, Jr., Otis L. Graham, Jr., Fred Nicklason, Martha Nussbaum, and Bruce Sievers for their special services as an editorial committee in preparation of this report. Herbert Fingarette provided a most helpful set of comments on an earlier draft.

Ellen McAvoy, Mary Gualandi, and Eva Mannheimer deserve special praise for their skillful and good-natured assistance in typing and retyping the manuscript.

Finally, we would like to thank most heartily those who attended our meetings, wrote papers, and served as critics and commentators on the papers written by others. None of them are to be held responsible for any errors of fact or judgment that may appear in this report. But we hope they will be willing to take partial responsibility for whatever insight the report may contain.

The following list of contributors to the project includes those who were permanent members of the group that carried out this study and are responsible for this report, those who wrote papers, and those who took part in at least one of the meetings we held.

DANIEL CALLAHAN   ARTHUR CAPLAN   BRUCE JENNINGS
Project Co-directors

Contributors to the Project on Applied Humanities and Public Policy

MEMBERS OF THE HASTINGS CENTER PROJECT ON APPLIED HUMANITIES AND PUBLIC POLICY

Those listed in this category are responsible for this report:

CO-DIRECTORS

Daniel Callahan, *Director, The Hastings Center*

Arthur L. Caplan, *Associate for the Humanities, The Hastings Center*

Bruce Jennings, *Associate for Policy Studies, The Hastings Center*

EDITORIAL GROUP

James M. Banner, Jr., *Scholar-in-Residence, American Association of Colleges*

Otis L. Graham, Jr., *Professor of History, University of North Carolina, Chapel Hill*

Fred Nicklason, *Professor of History, University of Maryland*

Martha C. Nussbaum, *Professor of Philosophy, Brown University*

Bruce R. Sievers, *President, Walter and Elise Haas Fund; former Executive Director, California Council for the Humanities*

PROJECT PARTICIPANTS AND CONTRIBUTORS OF PAPERS AND STUDIES

Robert Belknap, *Professor of Slavic Language and Literature, Columbia University*

Robert N. Bellah, *Professor of Sociology, University of California, Berkeley*

Daniel Callahan, *Director, The Hastings Center*

Eric Cassell, M.D., *Professor of Public Health, Cornell University Medical College*

Otis L. Graham, Jr., *Professor of History, University of North Carolina, Chapel Hill*

Kathryn Hunter, *Professor of Family Medicine, University of Rochester Medical Center*

Bruce Jennings, *Associate for Policy Studies, The Hastings Center*

Richard F. Kuhns, Jr., *Professor of Philosophy, Columbia University*

Bruce Kuklick, *Professor of History, University of Pennsylvania*

Edwin Layton, *Professor of Mechanical Engineering, University of Minnesota*

Ruth C. Macklin, *Professor of Community Health, Albert Einstein College of Medicine*

Mark C. Miller, *Director, Writing Seminars, Johns Hopkins University*

Fred Nicklason, *Professor of History, University of Maryland, College Park*

Martha C. Nussbaum, *Professor of Philosophy, Brown University*

Bruce Payne, *Professor of Public Affairs, Duke University*

Kenneth Prewitt, *President, Social Science Research Council*

Jerome B. Schneewind, *Professor of Philosophy, Johns Hopkins University*

Peter Stearns, *Professor of History, Carnegie-Mellon University*

ADDITIONAL MEETING PARTICIPANTS

Philip Appleman, *Professor of English, Indiana University*

Henry Aranow, M.D., *Lambert Professor of Medicine Emeritus, Columbia University*

Diana Baumrind, *Professor of Psychology, University of California, Berkeley*

Ronald Bayer, *Associate for Policy Studies, The Hastings Center*

Howard Becker, *Professor of Sociology, Northwestern University*

Walter Capps, *Professor of Religious Studies, University of California, Santa Barbara*

Carleton B. Chapman, M.D., *Professor of the History of Medicine, Albert Einstein College of Medicine*

Jack Crossley, *Professor of Religious Studies, University of Southern California, Los Angeles*

Strachan Donnelley, *Professor of Philosophy, The New School for Social Research*

William Dray, *Professor of Philosophy, University of Ottawa*

Colin Eisler, *Professor of Art History, New York University*

Joel Fleishman, *Vice Chancellor, Duke University*

Renée C. Fox, *Annenberg Professor of Sociology, University of Pennsylvania*

Lorraine Frank, *Executive Director, Arizona State Humanities Council*

Bruce Fraser, *Associate Director, Connecticut Humanities Council*

Amnon Goldworth, *Professor of Philosophy, San Jose State University*

Samuel Gorovitz, *Professor of Philosophy, University of Maryland, College Park*

Herbert Gutman, *Professor of History, City University of New York, Graduate Center*

Alice Kessler-Harris, *Professor of History, Hofstra University*

Martin Hoffman, *Professor of Psychology, University of Michigan*

Ellen Huppert, *President, Institute for Historical Study*

Terence Irwin, *Professor of Philosophy, Cornell University*

Arnita Jones, *Program Officer, National Endowment for the Humanities*

Albert R. Jonsen, *Professor of Ethics in Medicine, University of California School of Medicine, San Francisco*

Bruce Kuniholm, *Professor of Policy Sciences, Duke University*

Sanford Lakoff, *Professor of Political Science, University of California, San Diego*

Al Louch, *Professor of Philosophy, Claremont University Graduate School*

Ernest May, *Professor of History, Harvard University*

Ernan McMullin, *Professor of History and Philosophy of Science, University of Notre Dame*

Robert K. Merton, *University Professor Emeritus, Columbia University*

Kai Nielsen, *Professor of Philosophy, University of Calgary*

Roy Harvey Pearce, *Professor of English, University of California, San Diego*

James Quay, *Executive Director, California Council for the Humanities*

Richard Rettig, *Professor of Social Science, Illinois Institute of Technology*

Nancy Risser, *Director of Community Relations, CBS, Inc.*

1. Introduction

To imagine a human body needing neither food nor water requires a difficult feat of imagination. It is no less difficult to imagine a civilized human culture not needing history, philosophy, and literature. Those fields, and the humanities more broadly, provide cultures with the intellectual nourishment necessary for their survival and vitality. To be sure, any culture can suffer from a corrupting history, or from values that warp and debase its civic life, or from a literature that poisons the imagination. Yet a culture cannot endure at all without a historical memory, a set of values that gives coherence to its activities, and a literature that is expressive of its conscious self-conception, its unconscious fantasies and desires.

In their absence, there is no meaningful human life at all, and certainly nothing that can be called a society or a community. That remains true even in the face of a powerful scientific ethos and a bureaucratic state. For all of the social impact of the sciences, their meaning and significance cannot be determined until they have been critically interpreted; and the resources of the humanities provide a way of doing so. For all of the potency of the bureaucratic state to shape behavior, it is historical context, evaluative and expressive interpretations, and the restlessness of the willful imagination that will set public goals and give color to its civic flesh.

This is only to articulate once again the enduring case for the humanities and their centrality in a shared political and cultural life. Yet for all the permanent validity of that case, it needs continually to be explored afresh. In recent years, as in their long past, the humanities have all been subject to internal strife and competing self-definitions. At the least, they are not identical with, or as narrow or tightly compartmentalized as, the academic disciplines that encompass them. But what is their scope and role? This report addresses a question in the humanities that is at once new and yet filled with echoes from the past. *To what extent, and in what way, and with what voice, ought the humanities to address our social, political, and economic life?*[1] To put the issue another way, does it make any sense to speak of an "applied humanities," one whose intent is not only personal insight or theoretical knowledge, but practical and prudential contributions to matters of social and public life?

Those questions are as old as ancient Greece and as fresh as the charges leveled by the Heritage Foundation in 1980 that the National Endowment for the Humanities (NEH) had betrayed the humanities by trying to force them to address political topics.[2] The context of our interest in the subject is both personal and professional. Most (though not all) of those who joined us for our inquiry were trained in one of the disciplines of the humanities, but have in recent years focused some of their work on matters of public policy or general social concern. As often as not, their intended audience has been not only their academic peers in the humanities, but physicians, or lawyers, or legislators, or the general public. Their chosen topics of study or teaching or writing are not what Richard Wasserstrom has called the "set problems" of academic scholarship,[3] but issues of more immediate public concern—health and illness, crime and punishment, war and peace, poverty and affluence. Many in the humanities have found that kind of work congenial and enriching. It has promised and often provided fresh stimulation for those concerns and problems that drew them to the humanities in the first place. The desire to bring humanistic resources to bear on questions of public concern and social policy is an invigorating challenge.

But a desire to get at such questions in a fresh and more direct way raises some basic issues about the nature of work in the humanities. Is it the case, as some have charged, that those humanists who work on social and policy questions have trespassed on issues well beyond their professional training and competence?[4] Or simply trafficked in the faddish? Apart from those accusations, is it nonetheless possible that many in recent years have tried to do with the humanities that which is better left to other fields? At times some of our own colleagues have said that, but just as often the criticism has come from bemused policy analysts or legislators. Moreover, early efforts to join the humanities and public policy were not always successful. During the mid-1970s, the NEH instructed the various state humanities councils to give priority to public policy issues in making their local grants. That ruling led to considerable confusion.[5] Just what exactly do the humanities have to contribute to urban housing problems, or transportation tangles, or the provision of health care? It led as well to at least some projects that were simultaneously neither of great use to public policy nor wholly faithful to the humanities.

Those who took part in our project have at times felt chastened by their own failures, embarrassed by the ineptitude of some speaking in the name of a still immature field, and often uncertain how best to characterize and justify what it is they want to do. An adequate historical account of the emergence of this new direction in the humanities is often no less rough and groping.

It is tempting, for example, to explain the recent developments in terms of the much-discussed "crisis" within the humanities during the past few years. Its dimensions encompass a bleak job outlook, declining enrollment in humanities courses, the lack of a collective self-consciousness in the humanities, low public (and often private) self-esteem, and a distressing resurgence of vocationalism and preprofessionalism in the colleges. Yet the actual origins of such relatively new fields as biomedical ethics, or public history, or the teaching of literature in graduate professional schools antedate that crisis. And while some humanists have found employment in such formerly unlikely places as medical schools, legislatures, and corporations, their number is insignificant in the face of the generally dismal employment situation in the humanities. For all of the media attention given to the fact that some philosophers now work in medical schools and hospitals, their nationwide number is probably less than a hundred.

Our own interest in the subject, in any case, focuses on the nature of the humanities and their potential for direct application to practical life or public policy. The economic situation of those in the humanities may well have served as a stimulus to the notion of an "applied" humanities. Yet it is no less likely that repugnance at a widespread professionalization of the disciplines—a desire to give them more breathing room both within and outside of the academy—has been a no less important influence. Whatever the reason for the interest, however, it is the validity and future of that development that are our principal concerns. Inevitably, many of our examples in this report will be drawn from the fields of history and philosophy. Comparatively speaking, they have seen the most activity. However, other fields, particularly literature, show every sign of similar stirrings.

The phrase that we have used to open this discussion—"applied humanities" —is by no means graceful or felicitous, nor is its meaning self-evident. It might at once be argued that the humanities do not lend themselves to making, say, a distinction between "theoretical" and "applied" as is commonly the case in scientific disciplines (and that is an issue we will take up). Nonetheless, we found it useful to employ the term, at least heuristically, as a means of focusing attention and analysis on the ways in which the humanities may or could more directly contribute to social inquiry or public policy. The virtue of the phrase is that it helps to specify a set of interests and predilections for which no comparable traditional phrase exists. One could also speak of a "public humanities," that is, a humanities directed to a public rather than academic audience; or a "practical humanities," that is, an interest in immediate, pragmatic problems. Those phrases convey some of the currents that circulate in the field and capture different, though by no means exclusive, emphases.

Yet no single phrase seems quite adequate to encompass the full range of activities now carried out in the name of the humanities. The range encompassed by these various purposes can be illustrated by simply listing a sample of them: using literature in the education of medical students; employing historical research to defend Indian land claims; testifying as philosophers or historians before congressional committees on risk/benefit analysis, genetic engineering, immigration policy, health insurance plans, nuclear waste disposal, and welfare policy; using techniques of literary interpretation to analyze the language of the law; teaching courses in medical or public policy or environmental ethics; writing corporate or local histories, or serving as a historian to the U.S. Senate; analyzing concepts of "autonomy" and "responsibility," "guilt" and "culpability"; organizing a local history exhibit to illuminate a land-use controversy; serving on an institutional review board to examine research on human subjects.

The characteristic focus of the humanities has been on understanding and interpreting human life, whether historically, culturally, philosophically, or linguistically. While such understandings and interpretations will often have implications for behavior, their explicit purposes have not ordinarily been seen as directed toward action. Instead, the humanities concentrate on preserving and interpreting the literature of the past, on analyzing questions of the general nature of values and morality, and on understanding the meaning and signifi-

Joining the Issues

. . . a contemporary phenomenon [is] the rash of moral philosophers who are ready to solve contemporary problems for us—ready to resolve issues concerning vegetarianism, animal rights, nuclear deterrents, and our obligations to future generations, among others—by means of arguments that, so to speak, prove too much. These arguments are typically aprioristic in style, and yield conclusions far stronger than any consensus reasonable men and women are able to arrive at today. I share a deep distrust of this style of moral philosophy.

Hilary Putnam

Students spend less time thinking about technical questions of meta-ethics and more time grappling with the moral issues of the day. Courses in ethics are more "relevant" and students are more "involved." It may even be true that these courses are doing some good; perhaps students learn something; perhaps their powers of analysis are improved. (Probably not!) But students in such courses are not really studying philosophy.

Gilbert Harman

. . . it is possible "for philosophers to detach themselves so completely from primary materials that they no longer offer commentaries on science or law or education but instead merely give us commentaries on the commentaries on the commentaries. Philosophy then becomes an exchange among members of a closed club who live by taking in one anothers' laundry and have forgotten the original business—human inquiry, human practice, human choices and hopes—that once aroused their common attention."

Charles Frankel

How did the fresh attention that philosophers began paying to the ethics of medicine, beginning around 1960, move the ethical debate beyond relativism and subjectivism? In place of the earlier concern with attitudes, feelings, and wishes, it substituted a new preoccupation with situations, needs, and interests; it required writers on applied ethics to go beyond the discussion of general principles and rules to a more scrupulous analysis of the particular kinds of "cases" in which they find their application; . . . and, finally, it pointed philosophers back to the ideas of "equity," "reasonableness," and "human relationships," which played central roles in the *Ethics* of Aristotle but subsequently dropped out of sight.

Stephen Toulmin

I am disposed to agree with what has been surmised by others, that the opportunity which my official position gave me of learning by personal observation the necessary conditions of the practical conduct of public affairs, has been of considerable value to me as a theoretical reformer of the opinions and institutions of my time. . . . the occupation accustomed me to see and hear the difficulties of every course, and the means of obviating them, stated and discussed deliberately with a view to execution; it gave me opportunities of perceiving when public measures, and other political facts, did not produce the effects which had been expected of them, and from what causes; above all, it was valuable to me by making me, in this portion of my activity, merely one wheel in a machine, the whole of which had to work together. . . . I was thus in a good position for finding out by practice the mode of putting a thought which gives it easiest admittance into minds not prepared for it by habit; while I became practically conversant with the difficulties of moving bodies of men, the necessities of compromise, the art of sacrificing the non-essential to preserve the essential.

John Stuart Mill

cance of the human historical record. The humanities, as is often said, are principally concerned with the great texts of the past,[6] though one can think of many aspects of the humanities that would be no less concerned with present questions and contemporary texts. But even that latter point is still a long way from entailing that the humanities can provide direct assistance in solving current social problems, or in proposing future political or even cultural directions. Many in the humanities would specifically reject that role.

From a variety of perspectives, then, the idea of an applied humanities can seem both odd in itself and a threat to what many take to be the central work of the humanities. There are a number of important questions that need to be pursued in trying to unravel the problem. What does or might it mean to "apply" the humanities? Is there something inherent in the nature of the humanities—if they are to remain true to themselves—that should make them resistant to the notion of application? Or is there a sense in which they have always been applied? If an "applied humanities" is not a self-contradictory term why, then, has there been considerable resistance to the idea, or at least uneasiness about it? Is that resistance simply a historical accident?

In trying to answer those questions, it is also informative to compare the relative acceptability of applied work in the humanities with its place in other fields. One cannot, for example, help being struck by the stance of the scientific community toward applied technological inquiry. While work in theoretical science has a higher academic status than is the case with, say, engineering, the sciences have long learned to live with, and positively embrace, the idea that science is

appropriately both theoretical and applied. Quite the opposite seems to be more characteristic of the humanities, where many believe that a space, a careful gap, ought to exist between the humanities and the practical solution of political, social, and cultural problems.

Yet even if that gap can be bridged, a further question arises. What would be acceptable disciplinary and other academic criteria for an applied humanities? A considerable source of uneasiness among those resistant to an applied humanities is that its practitioners may do harm to the humanities by diluting scholarly standards. Can that danger be avoided? Moreover, if there is to be a successful applied humanities, would that have implications for the training of those who propose to point their career in that direction? The answer would seem to be yes, but the practical implications of that intuition are by no means clear.

While we want to analyze the notion of an applied humanities for its own sake, we believe it to be important also to open some extended discussion with representatives of those disciplines that have long taken it to be a central part of their mission to deal with (and often to solve) social and political problems. We start with the premise that those from the humanities may have much to contribute directly to policy questions. But perhaps they can make no less significant a contribution (though of a more indirect kind) by working closely with other fields more traditionally oriented toward such matters, such as the biological, the social, and the policy sciences.

There is, we believe, no good reason why the contributions of the humanities to exigent national problems ought to be overshadowed by other disciplines. At the least the question can be asked whether that is a mere quirk of history or a valid sorting out of potential contributions. There is also no reason in principle why those from the humanities should feel diffident or insecure in the face of rising requests from the policy arena for a greater participation in policy analysis. The important point is that those possibilities should neither be rashly embraced nor precipitately declined. Everything will depend upon the way in which the humanities might or could or should be brought to bear. That range of possibilities will, in turn, be a function of the history and traditions of the humanities and the judgment to be passed on the various efforts now underway to join the humanities to national concerns.

2. Historical Conflicts and Conceptions

In legislation creating the National Endowment for the Humanities and the Arts in 1965, Congress declared the following as principal purposes of governmental support for the humanities:

. . . a high civilization must not limit its efforts to science and technology alone but must give full value and support to the other great branches of man's scholarly and cultural activity in order to achieve a better understanding of the past, a better analysis of the present, and a better view of the future . . . democracy demands wisdom and vision in its citizens and . . . it must therefore foster and support a form of education designed to make men masters of their technology and not its unthinking servant.[7]

That formulation is noteworthy because it blends together in a brief compass several potentially competing conceptions of the humanities and what they can do. Congress, it appears, envisaged the humanities as a bridge between our past and our future, and charged them with apparently consistent, but in fact often conflicting, tasks. In one guise, they are the custodians of our cultural traditions and memory. They help us understand who we are in light of who we were. In another, they are the analysts of our present reality and predicaments, charged with the task of illuminating how the present is a unique and specific human moment, as well as how it is continuous with the past. In yet another guise the humanities are the educators of our utopian and critical imagination. They must nurture our aspirations for human progress and betterment. They must lift our attention above the confines of past practices and above the practical limitations that the need to cope with immediate problems imposes. That technology is singled out as a special problem hints at a long-standing tension between the humanities and the sciences, particularly that "applied" science which is technology.

The vision projected by Congress is correct and telling. The humanities encompass today, as they have in the past, a volatile blend of traditionalism, pragmatism, and utopianism. They are distinguished from other branches of knowledge by their persistent recourse to both the backward-looking orientation of historical inquiry and the forward-looking orientation of prescriptive, normative aspiration. These varied impulses often pull in different directions. While each no doubt exists in every generation of humanistic discourse, each also tends to vie for dominance. Thus the tone and temperament of the humanities varies, becoming now conservative and tradition-regarding, now revolutionary and *avant garde*, and now dedicated to the Platonic (or Nietzschean) mission of turning the world upside down. While Congress acknowledged the legitimate place of all three of these elements, it either mistakenly assumed that they could naturally and serenely coexist, or else wisely decided that it could not establish priorities among them.

In its formulation, moreover, Congress touched upon a second source of enduring tension (and vitality) in the humanities, that between their civic and their private mission, their outer and their inner concerns. The civic orientation is sounded first by placing the role of the humanities in the context of democratic citizenship, echoing in the political vocabulary of our own age the *leitmotif* of the Renaissance tradition of civic humanism. But this aspect is quickly muted by the central theme of two different traditions, liberalism and romanticism. There the humanities' principal contribution to democracy is said to be the preservation of human autonomy against the encroachments of technology,[8] that most social and visible of modern forces. In setting individual autonomy and protection against "unthinking servitude" as goals of the humanities, Congress echoed the traditionally private vocation of the humanities—the refinement of personal sensibility and insight—that also grew out of Renaissance humanism and its Stoic antecedents.

That brief congressional passage typifies the complex of meanings and emphases that reside in all of the most serious and thoughtful discussions of the humanities today. Defenders of the applied humanities naturally tend to select out a few of those emphases in order to orient their own work within a more general received understanding of what it means to be a humanist. They no less commonly tend to emphasize the pragmatic facets of the humanities with their orientation toward the distinctive and soluble problems of the present. They are inclined at the same time to stress the traditional civic, outward-looking vocation of the humanist.

Given this complex of meanings, it is not surprising that critics of the applied humanities are to be found across a broad spectrum of value commitments: critics on the right who emphasize the traditionalist face of the humanities, critics on the left who want its utopian, critical face to predominate, and those critics in the twentieth-century mainstream of the humanities—professional scholars who have inherited the liberal and romantic commitment to the humanities' private, inner-regarding vocation.[9] The tensions and the critical perspectives those critics generate are not new. They have always been a part of the gradually evolving understanding of the humanities in Western culture. The basic features of our own current debates first took shape during three particularly important historical periods.

Greek Roots

The first and in some ways most influential development took place in ancient Greek thought in the fifth and fourth centuries B.C., where debate about the meaning and value of *paideia* gave shape to many elements in later Western conceptions of the humanities.[10] The traditional educational system of the Greek *polis* was built on an assumption that the basic purpose of education was to subserve the ends of the city. The young male in this culture received a rigidly controlled training in music, poetry, and athletics. The manifest purpose of this instruction was the cultivation of patriotism and civic virtue. No Athenian poet, dramatist, or historian could avoid the need to justify his work or art in terms of its contribution to these ends and, ultimately, to the well-being of the community as a whole. The idea that the arts, philosophy, and history exist for their own sake, or for the sake of some separate nonpractical pleasure they provide, was entirely unknown at this period. We cannot even speak here of an "application" of these studies to public life. Application presupposes separation, and we see here, instead, a thoroughgoing fusion of study with public life and public ends.

Patterns for many of the later tensions in the humanities began to be found at the end of the fifth century. In the political and cultural crisis that beset Athens during and after its disastrous involvement in the Peloponnesian War, the basic conception of civic education was transformed, largely through the influence of Socrates and Plato.[11] In their work are the roots of subsequent debates, pitting arguments about the *instrumental* value of the arts and humanities against arguments for their *intrinsic* value.

For Socrates and Plato, philosophical inquiry and other parts of education were valuable as ways to practical ends set up and articulated from outside by the city. They were valuable in further ways as well. They also contributed to the inquirer's ability to deliberate about the ends of human life themselves, leading him to a more refined or more cohesive account of the values basic to a living of the best human life. To restrict philosophy to a merely instrumental role would be to deprive it of one of its most significant practical contributions, its assistance in pressing, and answering, our deepest questions about who we are and how we ought to live.[12] These inquiries were valuable additionally because they were themselves constituent parts of the good human life, having a value in their own right as excellent things for a

human being to choose to do. Building on Socrates' claim that the unexamined life is not worth living, and on his life-long practice of dialectical inquiry into the nature of the basic human values, Plato coherently altered the extremely instrumentalist and utilitarian conception of intellectual study held by his culture without wholly severing the connection of inquiry with broader social goals and purposes. He argued, indeed notoriously, that philosophers—just in virtue of their *paideia* and philosophical study—would be the best rulers for a human city.

This synthesis is preserved in a more complicated and ambiguous fashion in Aristotle's work. Like Plato he insisted on the usefulness of various forms of intellectual endeavor; and maintained that their value in our lives is not exhausted by instrumental usefulness. But in an important and influential break with previous tradition, Aristotle cast the question of intrinsic value in a new light by separating the forms of inquiry into two broad groups: those whose end is the improvement of some aspect of practical life (for example, medicine, literature, the study of ethics, politics, and history), and those that have as their end only theoretical understanding (mathematics, astronomy, the nonethical parts of philosophy). The former can contribute to practice both instrumentally and through their contribution to our understanding of our practical ends. The latter are constituent parts of the best human life, and thus practical in that sense; but they do not subserve any other ends outside themselves. To Aristotle, then, we can trace our modern idea of pure inquiry—and the problems of interrelation and application that arise with the birth of that idea. It is conspicuous that, for Aristotle, all the studies that we group under the humanities were of the practical and not the purely theoretical type. Nonetheless, his conception of scientific inquiry had a decisive influence on evolving conceptions of humanistic study at a later period.

By the time of Epicurus even this uneasy synthesis between the intrinsic value of the humanities and the quality of common life in the polis had broken down, giving way to the beginning of the modern privatistic and individualistic conception of the humanities. In Epicurus a humanities education once more assumed the purely instrumental value that it had in the eyes of the defenders of the traditional *paideia*. Only now the ends it served were not those of the city but those of the inner man, the private self.[13] In this way, as Martha Nussbaum notes, Epicurus inaugurated "a characteristic modern picture of educational activity; namely, that it goes on in a place that is a sanctuary from public life, protected from its stresses and its claims."[14]

The second pivotal juncture in the historical development of the humanities was, of course, the revival of classical learning that took place in the fifteenth and sixteenth centuries. During this period, the terms "humanist" and "humanity" came into modern usage to designate a separate form of study centering on the study of ancient Greek and Roman languages and literature, as well as ethical philosophy, rhetoric, grammar, and poetry.[15] Italian and European humanists in this period engaged in an enormous variety of activities, ranging from the production of accurate translations of classic texts to direct involvement in affairs of state; the latter were intended as direct applications of the humanities.

No simple account of the orientation of Renaissance humanism is possible.

The extremely eclectic humanists did not represent a unified movement or world view. But in this very diversity Renaissance humanism consolidated most of the tensions and cross-currents that we have noted in the classical Greek period. Some influential thinkers, like Machiavelli and Guicardini, were pivotal in reviving Aristotelian and classical republican political theory and refining the earlier tradition of "civic humanism" that later became transmitted through seventeenth-century England to have an important impact on the American Revolution.[16] In a different way, Reformation leaders like John Calvin stimulated the public activist orientation of the humanities. Other early humanists, reviving Epicurean and Stoic philosophies, developed the more inward and private vocation of the humanities that later found fertile soil among the great French humanists like Montaigne.[17]

The concept of "vocation," as Ernst Troeltsch and Max Weber noted, is very different for Renaissance and Reformation thought.[18] For many Renaissance thinkers, attempts to bring humanistic knowledge and learning to bear on power and wealth, or to approach them with religious and moral prescriptions, were not seen as appropriate. By contrast, it was—as suggested by Calvin's *Institutes of the Christian Religion*—a part of the Christian vocation to bring religious and moral reflection to political and economic life. The Reformation thinkers held in suspicion an "aristocracy of culture," contemplative self-indulgence, and a learning not immediately directed to daily life in the world.

Given the historical diversity, then, it is risky to attempt an overall characterization of the ways in which the conception of the humanities developed during the early modern period. At the least it is fair to say that it was complex, dynamic, and contrapuntal. In general, though, by the end of this period the main division and tension of emphasis between the public and the private vocation of the humanities was firmly established.

Individualism and Tradition

At the same time, the social thought that emerged after the Reformation in the West in the seventeenth and eighteenth centuries broke sharply with older Western traditions. The conceptions of human action contained in its ideology became part of the common sense of the more developed Western societies in the nineteenth and twentieth centuries. The new philosophy saw individuals not primarily as members of a community, as had the older religions and political traditions, but as separate bits of matter in motion, each driven by will and passion, especially the fear of harm and the desire for comfort.[19] This new way of thinking was radically subversive of older conceptions of social order. In the new conception, society lacked any organic value. It was merely an association created by contracting individuals to further their own quite heterogeneous ends. This new philosophy is the classical form of liberalism, the ideology of economic man, what can be called utilitarian individualism.[20]

A reaction against the harshness and narrowness of utilitarian individualism set in quite early, already by the eighteenth century. This movement called, in its early phases, Romanticism might also be termed expressive individualism.[21] It accepted the individualistic assumptions of its predecessor but insisted on seeing something more in the individual heart than exclusive self-regard and the pursuit of self-interest. It recognized powerful emotions, feelings, and sentiments that created sympathy for nature and for other persons. It has accompanied utilitarian individualism, in a variety of forms, ever since, partly as critic, partly as complement. Particularly among the educated classes, utilitarian and expressive individualism have shunted aside older strands of the Western tradition—biblical religion and civic humanism in particular—though these latter have never ceased to carry some cultural influence. Science and technology (both present and future oriented) reinforce an antihistorical, antitradition bias.

The primary problem that the triumph of the individualistic ideologies raises for the humanities is our relationship to the past, to time and memory. All cultures outside the modern West have viewed the past—the source of sustaining tradition—as a primary cultural resource, probably *the* primary cultural resource. Modern individualist ideologies are almost by definition antitraditional, inimical to memory. It is not that modern culture, certainly modern academic culture, wishes to remain ignorant of the past. We now know more or can know more about the past than anyone has ever been able to know before. But our relation to the past is different from that of traditional cultures. Traditional cultures remember the past in order to incorporate it. We seem to remember the past in order to abolish it; and it is perhaps no accident that the most advanced frontier of this tendency is located in the United States.[22]

The ethos of utilitarian individualism has, of course, for a long time been seeping into the humanistic disciplines themselves, however much humanists may initially have resisted the new tendencies. The most obvious influence is the questioning of all received opinion. Thus, even in the case where tradition itself is the object of study, as a living reality it is often viewed with suspicion and skepticism. Every text, every event, is to be considered on its own terms, so far as the investigator can get at it with the most sophisticated possible critical methods. If a scholar can overturn received opinion and offer a "revised" view, he or she has scored a great triumph. A relentless historicizing, beginning as early as the Renaissance, while increasing our knowledge, has pushed the past ever further away from us.[23] In remembering too much, that tendency has come close to destroying any practical memory at all.

Expressive individualism has exploded the past in a somewhat different way. It too works with the ideal of what Michael J. Sandel has called an "unencumbered self,"[24] but here the encumbrances to be eliminated are not restraints on the pursuit of self-interest but limits on the expression of authentic feeling. The great modernist writers were trying to free themselves from every constraint of convention and routine, to discover the depths of true individuality. Given this recent history, it is not hard to see why the humanities are in crisis and have difficulty producing wisdom or character.

Professionalizing the Humanities

The third key phase in the development of the modern understanding of the humanities began toward the end of the

nineteenth century and reached maturity during the first decades of the twentieth. This phase, the professionalization and institutionalization of the humanities, produced a clear differentiation of separate disciplines, each with its own special canons of rigor and methods of research and each firmly formalized in university curricula.[25] This professionalization tended to confine the humanities to an academic setting. Professional humanists then came to address their central activities of teaching and scholarly writing to other professionals and students in their field.

The rise of the applied humanities has begun to challenge and change this extreme, historically idiosyncratic situation. Of course viewed from the perspective of this most recent, atypical period, the concept of an "applied humanities" is an error. But when viewed in the light of the total tradition of the humanities in our civilization, it fits squarely within it—a return to the kind of diverse purposes and social roles that have characterized the humanities for most of their history. Yet by the same token, the applied humanities cannot offer a full expression of the humanities tradition either, because of the tradition's extreme diversity. They can, however, offer a way of keeping alive the energy, the tensions, and the creative ambiguities that have always marked that tradition. As a result of the long historical development summarized above, the applied humanities face a unique task. How can they cope with professionalization while at the same time not sacrificing the care and rigor it has often brought? For it is that professionalization, extending back for at least a half-century, that sundered much of the humanities from the larger social life outside of the university and that set the stage for the disciplinary narrowness that marks much of their work at its highest levels.

A number of sociological and intellectual signs identify this professionalization in the post-World War I period.[26] Academic associations and specialized disciplinary journals gained in importance. Standards of merit based upon an evaluation of published work began to replace the nineteenth century's dependence on social status or inherited position as the measure of success for an academic career. During the same period, criteria were established for tenure. Certain universities emerged as leaders in the various humanistic disciplines, and methods of training and apprenticeship were developed in philosophy, history, and literature for training new scholars in these areas.[27] Thus a range of criteria ordinarily associated with a profession—specialization, distinct methods, criteria for apprenticeship and promotion—emerged within the humanities in the late 1920s and early 1930s. On top of that, scholars in the humanities began to see their task in part as that of developing methodologies for the examination of humanistic problems akin to those utilized in the sciences.

The humanities retained their place in the curriculum relative to the emerging social sciences by stressing the importance of liberal studies in the production of public-spirited, service-oriented, open-minded civic leaders. That theme served to strengthen more traditional rationales dating from civic humanism and the Emersonian tradition. The study of history, philosophy, the classics, and literature was touted as useful for the kinds of applied concerns that dominated the curriculum in other areas of the modern university. Once the humanities had reestablished their credibility within the modern university, they then held their territory by defending the utility of the pure pursuit of inquiry. It was precisely their nonutility, the timelessness of their concerns, that was praised and supported as useful. The social sciences and the humanities continued in tension during the early part of the twentieth century; and these trends have, to a great extent, continued up until the present day.

3. Current Work in Applied Humanities

No single term or concept adequately captures the various manifestations and aspirations of the humanities. While this report assumes a tacit distinction between the humanities in a contemporary disciplinary sense and applied humanities, there are no sharp boundaries, either conceptually or in practice. Nonetheless, work in applied humanities has some characteristic features—family resemblances more than identical likenesses—that serve to give a different flavor and emphasis to its work. In part the difference may be in the audience to be addressed: either the general public or professionals from fields other than the humanities. Arguments, language, and deployment of examples will be different from what would be the case in dialogue with disciplinary peers. In part the difference may be the choice of issues to be addressed—those that exercise the larger society rather than specialists in a technical field; or addressing issues in a concrete rather than theoretical way.[28]

In short, no single characterization is likely to capture some "essence" of applied humanities; and any generalization will admit of exceptions. The borderline becomes perhaps most indistinct when moving between or among different levels of humanistic application and interpretation. Understanding and interpretation are central to any sensible construal of the work of the humanities. But that work can be done at the most broad and encompassing level, e.g., attempting to comprehend the drive for meaning and values in human nature; or much more narrowly, e.g., attempting to interpret the possible range of meanings in a complex passage of poetry. A public policy issue—for example, gun control—can with equal legitimacy be approached as a debate symbolic of competing strains in the history of American culture, or as an issue of the relationship between law and morality. While the two approaches need by no means be exclusive, they would most likely be explored in different ways and by making use of different humanistic methods.

In what follows we present brief surveys of the kind of work being done in what we would characterize as an applied humanities mode (even if many who do such work might not exactly so describe their work). Perhaps it is not surprising, but an important discovery for many who took part in our project was how little we often knew about applied work in fields other than our own. It was a healthy reminder of the extent to which the humanities have remained isolated, not only from the broader society, but from each other as well. It also became evident from our explorations that most of the interest in applied humanities is to be found in the fields of philosophy and history, though with pockets of interest here and there in literature, linguistics, and classics. We will limit our remarks here to the first three fields only.

Philosophy

Of all the humanities disciplines, philosophy has undoubtedly witnessed the most rapid and widespread development of applied studies. It has also thus witnessed a sharp shift in interest and focus, one that has revived a much older American tradition. During the nineteenth century, American philosophers routinely addressed their work as much to an educated public as to their fellow academics. Questions of practical morality, religion, culture, and politics were thought to be appropriate philosophical fare, and the course on moral philosophy was considered a central ingredient in undergraduate higher education.[29] By the 1930s, spurred in part by the rise of positivism and in part by the professionalization common to all of the humanistic fields, those earlier marks of the field fell by the wayside. Logic, epistemology, and the philosophy of language came to dominate the major university departments. As a background for understanding current work in applied philosophy, three factors important to its development need to be mentioned.

First, almost all the work that has been done thus far in applied philosophy has grown out of what may broadly be referred to as the British analytic tradition. That tradition has focused on the use of language, logical systems, and conceptual analysis. The predominance of the analytic approach in applied philosophy has given applied work a distinctive identity; and the contributions that applied philosophy can make grow largely out of the strengths of that approach. It is an open question whether the "continental" approach, principally phenomenology—with its stress on subjectivity, the structures of consciousness, and the "life worlds" within which consciousness is formed—will eventually produce its own variant of applied philosophy.[30] Through its contacts with sociology in "ethnomethodology," for example, phenomenological approaches have already provided some interesting insights on the dynamics of the professional-client relationship and the social construction of reality in clinical settings.[31] The revival of pragmatism (a more distinctly American phenomenon) now going on in some quarters may also serve to inject new philosophical orientations into applied philosophical studies.[32]

Second, the impetus for the development of applied philosophy grew out of major transformations within disciplinary philosophy that have occurred in the last decade or so. In the 1950s and 1960s academic philosophy was dominated by the philosophy of science and other highly technical areas of the philosophy of language and logic. It had almost self-consciously become a highly professional field, moving sharply away from social and political issues or guidance for individual lives.[33] Interest in social philosophy was at a low ebb, and ethics was almost exclusively concerned with the metaethical analysis of the meaning and justification of moral terms and arguments. The pendulum has shifted considerably in recent years as normative social philosophy and ethics have experienced an extraordinary intellectual renaissance.[34] The advent in 1970 of the influential journal, *Philosophy and Public Affairs*, conveniently symbolizes the shift. Work in applied philosophy, which draws heavily on these newly revitalized

The term "applied philosophy" is an enigma. Some view it as a redundancy; others as a contradiction. Some as indicating an important change in the focus of philosophical investigation; others as what philosophers have always been concerned with. And some view it as a welcome revitalization of the discipline that has stagnated; others as the eclipse of the queen of the sciences. Such differing views are neither unusual nor surprising, but they do point to the need to subject the notion of applied philosophy to careful scrutiny.

. . . The latter third of the 20th century is seeing a significant change in the Anglo-American philosopher's conception of his task. It began with the "rediscovery" of normative ethics. In their teaching and research philosophers started attending to the questions of personal morality that everyone faced in their daily lives. The extension of this focus into issues of social importance was given a tremendous lift by the publication of John Rawls' *A Theory of Justice*. And today sees philosophers both studying and teaching courses on business ethics, medical ethics, environmental ethics and the like. Moreover, this activity is no longer limited to the narrow confines of the academy. Philosophers are actively attempting to influence public policy on these issues by setting up "think tanks" to research and debate them, testifying before policy-making bodies, and offering themselves as consultants to professionals in a wide variety of areas.

On this understanding, then, applied philosophy involves focusing philosophical analysis and deliberation on issues of societal and individual import. Moreover, it insists upon addressing these issues in the context in which they arise, rather than constantly abstracting from real situations to ideal cases. In other words, rather than treating the facts of situation as variables that can be altered at will . . . applied philosophy insists upon beginning with the facts and sticking to them. . . .

Louis I. Katzner

branches of the discipline, now enjoys the kind of intellectual support from the discipline that did not exist in the fifties and sixties. Indeed, the rapport between disciplinary and applied studies in philosophy is closer than in any other field and provides an interesting contrast to the barriers existing between academic and public history.

Third, the subject matter and problem settings with which applied philosophy has dealt are more diverse and wide-ranging than those to which other fields in the humanities have been applied. Work in applied philosophy has ranged virtually across the entire spectrum of activities in our society, from the most global questions of environmental and biomedical ethics, warfare, and governmental foreign policy, through decision-making in business and professional practice settings, to the most personal and intimate issues of sexual morality and intrafamilial relationships.[35]

The current applications of philosophical inquiry are therefore exceedingly difficult to catalogue and classify. However, one distinction will help to sort out the two basic types of study done by applied philosophers. This is the distinction between *clinical decisionmaking*, or micro-decisionmaking, and *policy decisionmaking*, or macrodecisionmaking.

Purposive, rational human choice, or more simply, "decisionmaking" is a basic unit of applied philosophical inquiry. Philosophers working in an applied vein examine the reasons and justifications for human choices, and they bring ethical principles and other normative criteria to bear in the evaluation of the moral roots and consequences of specific decisions. They aim to clarify the reasoning behind decisionmaking, to explore neglected assumptions, alternatives, and options, and to assist in a process of justly assigning responsibility for choices that lead to human harm. This characterization fits applied ethics most directly, of course, but it also pertains to the application of other branches of philosophy. Logic and epistemology, for example, are also crucially involved in the assessment of the reasoning that goes into decisionmaking.[36]

The distinction between clinical and policy decisionmaking is useful because it identifies two types of choice situations that can in principle (and often do in practice) call for somewhat different standards of reasoning and criteria of evaluation. Moreover, it cuts across the two realms where most work in applied philosophy is done, professional ethics and public policy analysis.

Clinical decisions are typically limited in their scope, in the duration of their effect, and in the number of persons whose lives they affect. Most often they encompass face-to-face relationships. The limited character of these decisions, however, does not make them unimportant or inconsequential. They are often decisions about life and death, freedom or imprisonment, financial well-being or deprivation. Paradigmatic examples include the treatment decisions that physicians make for their patients, or the ways in which attorneys fashion a legal defense for their clients. Policy decisions, by contrast, set rules, standards, and administrative procedures that are relatively impersonal, affect an indeterminate number of people, regulate large domains of human activity, and often remain in effect for long periods of time. They can bear on housing, foreign policy, or welfare issues, and on the allocation of scarce resources, for example. They too have serious consequences, although the long-term implications are often difficult to identify precisely and

may not be immediately obvious. Policy decisions are made in both the public and the private sectors.

One of the most difficult tasks facing applied philosophy is to clarify the ingredients of rational, responsible decisionmaking in the realms of clinical and policy decisionmaking. Most work in professional ethics to date has concentrated on the issues involved in clinical decisions, while applied philosophical studies of public policy and business ethics (which grow out of political and social philosophy as well as ethics) have tended to focus on policy decisions. Increasingly, however, these two areas are beginning to merge, as it becomes clear that in our complex, technological society policy decisions shape clinical decisions and vice versa.[37]

Yet as important as is the interest in clinical and policy decisionmaking, it is no more important than a focus on key conceptual and theoretical questions that have a powerful impact of policy thinking and attitudes. The concepts of "rights," "health," "responsibility," and "autonomy" have a central role in policy, just as do questions such as "when does 'life' begin?" Conceptual analysis does not necessarily focus directly on decisions; but it is no less vital for policy thought and action.

On the whole, relationships between disciplinary and applied philosophers tend to be cordial and mutually respectful. Practitioners of applied philosophy generally believe that their analyses should conform to the same standards of rigor and argumentation that prevail in the mainstream discipline, even though they often must adopt different conventions of writing style and presentation. And, of course, many individual philosophers move back and forth between applied and nonapplied work.

Yet there is at present a lively debate among philosophers concerning the intellectual status of applied philosophy. Many participants in this debate—on both sides—believe that applied work is merely derivative and parasitic.[38] They cast applied philosophers in the role of mediators, brokers, or translators whose task is to transmit disciplinary knowledge to lay audiences or to apply general principles of theories to specific cases.[39] Others, however, are not so sanguine about the self-sufficiency and power of disciplinary knowledge. They argue that the abstract conceptual analyses and normative theories produced by the discipline often distort the human reality of the issues with which they deal.[40] They contend that the experience and insight accumulated by applied philosophical studies can and should creatively feed back into the discipline to improve the "basic" philosophical research that goes on there.[41]

This debate is healthy and productive. The overall legitimacy of applied philosophy is firmly if not fully established, and those who engage in applied studies should be encouraged to improve the quality and expand the scope of applied work. At the same time, disciplinary studies can be—and are being—enhanced by the philosophically creative work being done in the applied wing of the discipline. The debate over applied philosophy has now ceased to be a squabble over turf and has turned into a lively dialogue about the more fundamental issue of improving the quality of the work being done.

Applied and Public History

Applied work in history is somewhat more complicated than in other fields because it is made up of different intersecting components.[42] Many academic or disciplinary historians, beginning to reassert the broad public and contemporary relevance of their work, argue (as did Thucydides) that an accurate understanding of the past is essential to making decisions in the present. The nonacademic wing of the profession—those calling themselves public historians who work outside the university and engage in a wide variety of historical projects relatively unconnected to disciplinary research—has become much more organized, self-conscious, and active in recent years. Public history has become a vital sector of the history discipline, and its own self-definition and sense of mission greatly extends and complicates the range of possible meanings that application can have in the field of history.

In tandem with those developments, a subfield is beginning to emerge that concerns itself directly with the problems of policy analysis and policymaking in both the government and the corporate sector. Peter Stearns has suggested that we distinguish this third area of inquiry by labeling it "applied history."[43] Because applied historians often do their work outside of traditional academic settings and address nonstudent and lay audiences, they are akin to public historians. But since their work is focused specifically on policy analysis, they form a distinct category and have an orientation and agenda different from either academic historians or other public historians not directly concerned with policy issues.

That complicated situation forces the making of some cumbersome distinctions, and even among historians themselves, there is as yet little agreement on basic terminology. For convenience, therefore, we will mention both "the application of history" and "applied history." The former encompasses all of the components of the field mentioned above; the latter is pertinent when historians take part directly in policy analysis and the policymaking process. Recalling the distinction between clinical decisionmaking and policy decisionmaking introduced in the preceding section, we should mention that as yet no branch of history has been applied to clinical decisionmaking. Almost all of the applied energies in this field have been directed toward policy questions.

Academic or disciplinary history has begun to reassert its connection with public life in a number of ways. Traditionally, of course, it has always claimed public relevance as a core component of a liberal education. However, the growth of social history as a field of research and the increasingly close connection between historical and social scientific research have produced academic studies of clear policy relevance. This shift in the basic agenda of the discipline has also produced a new generation of historians equipped to participate in the curricula of schools of public policy and public administration. As a result of this educational cross-fertilization, more explicit attention has been paid to the contribution that historical training can make to the general and professional education of policy analysts and policymakers.[44] These contributions include the development of careful research habits, instilling a sensitivity to the processes of change, and developing a capacity to recognize the external factors that produce a social

moment when policy innovation will likely succeed or likely fail. In a more general way, academic research can have an impact on policymaking by correcting the mistaken assumptions about the past that policymakers hold.

Public history is a broad and diverse wing of the profession. Public historians often have specialized professional training in media, museum work, and the like. In general, public history makes use of history outside the academic context. It includes, for instance, the entertainment and enlightenment of public audiences through museums and historical site preservation efforts, media presentations, and the development of regional or other types of memorial histories that contribute to the special regional, cultural, and ethnic identities of particular groups. In many cases these activities of public history have policy implications. They may help to sensitize political leaders to the existence of unmet social needs, or they may assist in the consolidation of grass-roots movements. In general, however, public history is not primarily oriented toward specific policy issues or the task of policy analysis. Like academic history, albeit in different ways, public history is primarily devoted to an educational and public service mission.[45]

Applied history proper has complex ties with both academic and public history. Like the former, it is based on scholarly investigation and research; like the latter, it involves work outside the university and interaction with nonhistorians. Nonetheless, because of its focused orientation toward policy analysis, applied history has its own distinctive purposes and problems. It aims to make two principal contributions to policymaking in both governmental and corporate settings. First, it provides a usable institutional memory for corporations, agencies, and other complex institutions.[46] In this way, it enriches the temporal horizon and context of institutional decisionmaking and helps to preserve the distinctive traditions of the organization. Yet, too often in the past, applied historians playing this role have been employed to produce honorific documents useful mainly for public relations purposes. One important challenge facing applied historians today is to move beyond this memorialist function and to produce critical analyses of institutional history that can seriously inform policymaking; and some have begun to do so.[47]

Second, applied history also often aims to employ historical data and analysis in order to improve the definition of policy problems, to aid in the assessment of policy options, and to recommend the best available policy choices.[48] In pursuing these goals, applied historians join

Applying the Classics at the Naval War College

Lecturing to U. S. Navy captains on Thucydides, analyzing ancient Spartan battle plans with Marine Corps colonels, and debating the ethical limits on U. S. military responses to terrorist attacks are all part of a normal day's work for ALVIN H. BERNSTEIN, a classicist on the faculty of the Naval War College in Newport, Rhode Island.

After majoring in classics as an undergraduate at Cornell University, Dr. Bernstein spent a year at Oxford and then returned to Cornell where he received his doctorate in Ancient History in 1968. For the next fourteen years he taught in the history department at Cornell University, specializing in ancient military history and Near Eastern civilization. A lecture invitation first brought him to the Naval War College in 1980, and he returned there to spend the following year as a Distinguished Visiting Professor. Attracted by the unusual challenge of teaching the humanities to a student body comprised of high ranking military officers and civilian policy makers, he joined the War College faculty as a full-time member of the Strategy and Policy Department in 1982.

The combination of his conventional academic career at Cornell and his experience teaching at the War College has given Dr. Bernstein a special opportunity to reflect on the differences between "pure" humanistic scholarship and the role of the "applied humanist" in what is very definitely not an ivory tower setting.

The most obvious difference, in his view, is in the types of students he has to teach. Like its sister institutions, the Army War College and the Air Defense University, the Naval War College stands near the top of the military's internal education and career development system. Its student body is made up of senior military officers—Navy captains and Marine, Army, and Air Force colonels—and mid-career civilian executives from the Department of Defense, the CIA, and other federal agencies. These officers and officials are well seasoned, pragmatically oriented professionals, more accustomed to commanding ships at sea or battalions

applied philosophers, applied social scientists, and others in the domain of policy analysis. Their special purpose is to contribute the distinctive perspectives and concepts that come from historical inquiry.

Should applied history become a separate, autonomous discipline with its own training programs and its own standards of practice? A debate on that question has emerged, but we hope that such a separation will be restrained and limited.

The health of both the academic and the applied wing of history—as in the other humanistic fields—requires that intellectual channels remain open. Applied historians should not, and need not, weaken disciplinary standards of rigor in their research; that would run the danger of compromising their critical contributions to the improvement of policy analysis. Peer review mechanisms—not yet as common as they should be—are essential to monitor the quality of work on

---

in the field than they are to sitting in the classroom pondering the texts of Plato and Thucydides.

At first glance, this might seem an inauspicious environment for a classicist and an unlikely setting for a humanities education. Dr. Bernstein has found quite the opposite to be the case, however. As mature adults and experienced professionals, his students are far more serious about their studies than normal undergraduates or even graduate students. In teaching the latter, Dr. Bernstein often found that he had to convince them of the value of studying the classics; for them the humanities often seemed to deal with abstract and etherial concerns. But he rarely has to coax his War College students to take the classics seriously; most often he finds that the perennial human issues raised by these texts speak directly and tangibly to the life experiences of military commanders.

When discussing a work like *The History of the Peleponnesian War*, for example, Dr. Bernstein aims to familiarize his students with the mind and the sensibility that informs the text, and to study the nature—and fallibility—of human judgments that shape political and military decision making. This capacity to reflect on the process of judgment is then applied to concrete problems of military strategy and planning. This pedagogical approach is consonant with the Naval War College's traditional humanistic approach to military strategy, which is treated as an "art" rather than a "science."

More than anything else, it is probably this basic institutional philosophy that enables Dr. Bernstein to function effectively as an applied classicist at the Naval War College. After two years he has no regrets about his decision to move into that setting. He finds his teaching rewarding, and he has been able to pursue the course of his own scholarly research without difficulty. Above all, he still identifies himself as a classicist and believes that he is making an important contribution by bringing the conceptual framework of a trained ancient historian to bear on the contemporary issues discussed at the Naval War College. "My experiences at the War College," he says, "have reinforced my belief in the value of looking at the world through the humanist's eyes, and in particular through the classicist's eyes."

Tending to the History of the United States Senate

Few institutions in American society are more conscious of, or take more pride in, their own special history and traditions than the United States Senate. But for all its august sense of history, the Senate has a highly fragmented institutional memory and very few mechanisms that ensure long term continuity in its functioning. With a fairly high turnover rate among its professional staff, a Senate committee may well begin investigating a given issue without realizing that virtually the same issue was studied (perhaps by the same committee) fifteen, ten, or even five years before. Repairing the tatters in that institutional memory and helping to make the Senate's past better inform its present are just two of the tasks that fall to the Senate's Historian, RICHARD ALLAN BAKER.

In the early 1970s then Senate majority leader, Mike Mansfield, began the process of improving the preservation and use of the Senate's extensive archives. One outcome of that effort was the creation in 1975 of the Senate Historical office. In that year Baker, who several years before had served briefly as acting curator of the Senate's art collection, became the Director of the Historical office.

Coming out of graduate school in the mid-60s Baker had begun a conventional academic career. A specialist in American history, he had taught at a small college briefly while working on his dissertation. In 1967, however, he decided to leave teaching and took a masters degree in library science at Columbia University. Moving to Washington, he worked at the Library of Congress, and then spent several years with a private research firm until he assumed his present position with the Senate.

As Director of the Historical Office, Baker supervises a staff of six full-time and two part-time professional historians. The Historical Office takes on a variety

client-oriented projects. At the same time, the experience and findings of applied historical work can feed back into the discipline and improve the quality of its basic research and theory.[49]

The demands of working in policy settings will, however, require applied historians to accommodate their styles of investigation in certain ways. Like other applied researchers, they must learn to cope with time pressures and the need to do "quick and dirty" research.[50] They may also have to rely less heavily than the disciplinary historians on the narrative mode of presentation, highlighting instead the analytic conclusions and generalizations of their studies. They must on occasion be prepared to make specific policy recommendations. They will be less able than their academic colleagues to adopt the traditional tone of the detached observer or storyteller.

Literature

Applied work in literary study has, until now, been less vigorously and widely pursued than analogous work in

of tasks. One of its most important functions at the moment is to prepare for the celebration of the Senate's bicentennial in 1989. In addition, the staff undertakes a variety of archival and research functions, including writing a popular history of the Senate that will eventually be published as a textbook, editing transcripts of historically significant executive sessions of the Senate Foreign Relations Committee so that these important documents can be more readily available to scholars, and providing background historical research for the Office of the Senate Legal Counsel.

Baker sees his role as an historian employed by the Senate as a special example of the possibilities for applying the humanities in a governmental setting. He does not provide historical research directly related to pending legislation (that, insofar as it is done at all, is handled by committee staff members and the Congressional Research Service). However, he does serve as a bridge between the Senate as an institution and the academic community. One of his main goals is to make the Senate records and archives—a huge and largely untapped historical resource—more useful and accessible to scholars. In that way he hopes to foster better historical studies of the Senate and hence a better understanding of the Senate's role in the American political process.

Baker and his staff remain active scholars and historians in their own right, working (mainly at night and on weekends) on their own projects. They are active in professional groups such as the Organization of American Historians and the American Historical Association.

Reflecting on what he hopes to accomplish in the future, Baker observes: "There is a tremendous need for a better historical understanding of the U. S. Congress. There is also a deep well of interest in history among Congressmen and their staff, but in the past that interest has not been consistently articulated. The creation and development of Historical Offices in the Senate and the House are helping us place the activities of Congress in a better historical perspective."

philosophy and in history.[51] To a large extent this situation results from the relatively recent internal development of the professional study of literature. In an earlier generation, critics such as F. R. Leavis in England and Edmund Wilson and, later, Lionel Trilling in the United States made ethical and social commentary an integral part of the study of literary texts. However, in the fifties and early sixties the New Criticism—a movement distinguished by its emphasis on the literary text as an integral work of art demanding careful attention to the aesthetic dimensions of its language—tended to shift academic criticism away from this broader engagement with social, psychological, and political issues. While many of the founders of the New Criticism were deeply motivated by theological and cultural concerns, over time the movement did develop a somewhat narrow scholastic orientation.[52]

At this same time, and in connection with the ascendency of the New Criticism, doctrines of the purity of the aesthetic attitude and of aesthetic distance from practical interest (ideas that have a long and varied history) took on new life. This situation still prevails in much of the academy today. More recent critical fashions, for example, deconstruction, have overturned many of the tenets and practices of the New Criticism; but they have not necessarily returned criticism to a serious engagement with practical matters. The deconstructionist idea of "free play" and the deconstructionistic critic's mistrust of any appearance of order or system can lead away from serious, engaged ethical criticism.

There are, to be sure, some who would argue that deconstruction has important practical implications—as must any serious approach to interpretation.[53] Yet the prevalent idea that criticism is a kind of creative fictionmaking has appeared to many critics to license a kind of playful and clever writing that dissociates itself from the serious ethical concerns even of texts that have always been understood to express such concerns. And the arcane and self-referential style of much of this criticism does not readily lend itself to the sort of social dialogue that people working in applied humanities would like to generate.

It is possible, nonetheless, to point to several developments in current literary study that work against this pervasive fashion, promising a more fruitful connection between the study of literature and the understanding of practical problems.

1. The use of literary texts in applied ethics. Courses in applied ethics at many different levels (from the undergraduate introductory course to specialized courses within professional schools) have frequently included literary texts among their readings. Sometimes the motivations for this have been simply pedagogical: the instructor chooses these works for their power to present the ethical issues in an engaging and moving way. Sometimes the instructor also has theoretical reasons for the choice. Literary texts, for example, can make a distinctive contribution to a study of the issues that could not be made by philosophical works, just in virtue of their literary style and structure. They immerse themselves in the complex stories of human lives and evoke an activity of emotion and imagination not often cultivated by conventional philosophical texts.

2. The relationship between literature and philosophy. Closely connected with that enterprise is a growing interest in investigating the boundaries between philosophy and literature, especially on the part of philosophers. The issue is frequently raised concerning the treatment of moral issues; and its resolution is clearly of importance for the teaching and practice of applied ethics. Philosophers such as Stanley Cavell and Hilary Putnam have been raising questions about the knowledge of human life that we get from works of literature. Is it the same as the knowledge offered by philosophical works, or different in kind? Philosophers who began their work on literature by discussing the presence within literary works of certain familiar philosophical questions and arguments are now, increasingly, turning their attention to the closeness of the connection between style and content, asking whether there is a kind of insight that literature can give us precisely in virtue of its stylistic differences from philosophy.

This work—which has led to a more subtle and proper literary reading by philosophers of the literary texts in question—is now beginning to be of serious interest to literary critics as well. Increasing numbers of interdisciplinary symposia and journals are appearing as the two

An English Professor's Business

KATHRYN HUNTER was "minding my own business, an English professor's business," at a small liberal arts college when the decision was made by the college to begin a medical school. Among the courses she had taught was a freshman honors course called "The Evolution of the Ideas of Evolution," which biology students headed for medical school often took. That course led her to become acquainted with the science faculty, which resulted in her appointment to the health careers advisory committee, and, as the plans for the medical school heated up, ultimately, the chairmanship of the task force on relating the social sciences and the humanities with the medical school curriculum. "Because this was Morehouse College, we were particularly concerned with reinforcing medical students' commitment to underserved people, and a brief look at the American medical curriculum suggested that a dehumanizing education would influence the sort of practitioner that emerged from our program."

Edmund Pellegrino, M.D., then at Yale, visited several times on an NEH consultant's grant and persuaded her of the potential utility of literature in a medical curriculum. In the spring of 1977 she applied for and received an Institute for Human Values in Medicine grant to develop two year-long courses drawing upon literature, philosophy, history, anthropology, religious studies, and law. A few years later she accepted a position teaching literature at the medical school of the University of Rochester.

"From a mainstream English department point of view, teaching literature in a medical school is distinctly odd. But another view, mine, is that this job tests the value of liberal education. I teach the human condition. If the humanities have a life-long value, one that makes them worth studying and teaching to those who will not be humanities scholars, then it is here, as part of medical education, that they may be most useful."

She believes that her view of literature has been modified by teaching literature in a medical school setting. "I no longer read only "English." I am interested these days in absences, fiction and poetry that have *not* been written—about nurses who are ordinary but admirable women, for example, or about people living with genetic defects. Why these situations fail to engage the creative imagination suggests as much about our society as the stories and themes that can be found in literature. Above all, I am fascinated by looking at medicine, its characters and themes and stories, with an eye trained in literature and in literary criticism."

Among her failures she cites not yet finding support for more medical-humanities faculty at Rochester, not arguing well enough for the uses of literature earlier, and all those encounters where "I didn't understand Them and They didn't understand me."

On the other hand she ranks among her successes as an "applied humanist" contributions to the medical curriculum both at Rochester and at Morehouse, her informal teaching and learning opportunities with house staff, and, especially, her own enlarged intellectual life.

professions begin to acknowledge that each has something to learn from the other; and especially in the areas of ethical and social value most pertinent to applied humanities work. This trend will have important implications for the way in which both disciplines go about applying themselves to practical questions.

3. Literary theory and social thought and practice. Another recent development has been an increasing interest on the part of social and legal thinkers in communicating with literary theorists, in order to make progress on some important questions of method and procedure.[54] The complex controversies in recent literary theory concerning validity in interpretation, and the proper norm for interpretative practice, have been closely studied by legal theorists and lawyers. Their aim is to improve the theory and the practice of legal interpretation. The two professions have also discussed, with mutual profit, the idea of social convention in interpretation. A pioneering group in generating this discussion has been the Yale Legal Theory Workshop, led by Owen Fiss, which regularly invites literary theorists (as well as philosophers and social scientists) to speak with practicing lawyers. The legal philosopher Ronald Dworkin, for example, has recently argued that distinctions and arguments from literary theory can be used to support his view of constitutional and legal interpretation against its rivals—hence, to defend certain judicial decisions over others.[55]

Whatever the merits of this particular argument, there can be no doubt that the theoretical discussion of crucial legal issues has been rendered more subtle and more rigorous by the contact with literary theory (and the related areas of philosophy). And literary theory has been enriched and invigorated by this contact with important practical questions.

4. Socially and politically engaged styles of literary interpretation. Finally, there has always been a continous tradition of literary interpretation and teaching that has not been influenced by the New Criticism and its descendants, but has remained close to the social commitments characteristic of the ancient Greek study of literature. Prominent examples of this kind of criticism have been linked with distinctive political doctrines, especially to Marxism and existentialism. Each of these movements has thought it appropriate to ask of a work of literature how it influences the political lives of those who read it, or how it was influenced by the class background of the author. Each insists upon assessing and criticizing texts in the light of their practical contribution. Each movement has produced both criticism of the works of others and works of literature of its own, which exemplify its commitments. Although it would be relatively uncommon to find in the contemporary academy a self-confessed Marxist or existentialist literary critic, still the influence of both of these movements on the undergraduate teaching of literature and on the popular response to literature has been enormous, especially through the prestige of figures such as Brecht, Sartre, and Camus.

A major recent development has been the growth, in this country and in Europe, of a feminist criticism of literature, determined to examine literary works for information concerning women's lives and aspirations, the perception of them by others, and of their own self-perceptions. This criticism has insisted on maintaining (even in the face of skepticism from the professions) a vigorous connection between the analysis of texts and a confrontation with current social issues. Some of this criticism has affiliations with Marxism and some with varieties of psychoanalytic theory. Some of it is radical and/or utopian, while some is concerned more with the improvement of sensibilities than with sweeping political change. A common concern running throughout, however, has been to identify and to reform stereotypes of women that are perpetuated in myths, fairy tales, and even in linguistic usage itself.

In that way also this form of criticism aspires to transform in some fundamental ways the growing child's perceptions of gender difference. There is tremendous variety and vigor in this movement. It is one of the areas of humanities work that is most directly changing daily life in this country. As children are receiving a different, more carefully scrutinized first literary education, and as we are being urged to ask questions about our earliest and deepest myths, stories, and fantasies, we are seeing how immediate and how practically influential literary study can be.

In a parallel development, members of minority, racial, and ethnic groups are also subjecting the literary texts of the culture to critical scrutiny. They are demanding texts and courses that portray with sensitivity the variety and richness of the experience of their group. This social questioning has influenced the practice of authors (and filmmakers) by making once-common stereotypes unacceptable; and it has also had a significant effect upon the ways in which literature (and film) are talked about and taught.

4. *Models of Application*

As even a cursory survey of current work in applied humanities makes clear, there are numerous ways in which the humanities can be deployed. But are some ways more legitimate than others? One of the less valid attractions of an "applied" humanities is the implicit suggestion that they possess a body of knowledge that can—by translation, deduction, or transmutation—be superimposed directly onto social issues. Can the proper care of dying patients be immediately extrapolated from a reading of Tolstoy's *The Death of Ivan Ilyich*; or Central American policy deduced from an analysis of Thucydides; or child abuse laws from Mill's *On Liberty*? That is not likely. A deductivist notion of the relationship between the humanities and policy turns out to be highly ambiguous and, perhaps, seriously misleading.

Yet, if taken in the proper way, the relationship between science and engineering may present at least a partial analogue for the humanities. This analogy will be misunderstood if one assumes that engineering draws in a simple way upon the theories of basic science in order to build bridges, roads, and dams. The truth of the matter, as Edwin T. Layton, Jr., has pointed out, is that the relationship between basic science and engineering application is not that of simple deduction at all. He notes that "the theory provided by classical physics is neither adequate nor sufficiently accurate, and engineers have had to develop their own body of theory."[56] Moreover, the engineering sciences that were "evolved to bridge the gap between theory and practice cannot, in general, be employed by a more or less mechanical deduction from theory. Instead, the approach tends to be empirical and inductive rather than deductive and theoretical." The concept of "engineering design" is the most fundamental part of engineering work and cannot be reduced to a simple deduction from theory. It requires creativity, the use of scientific theories designed for engineering purposes exclusively, and a willingness to put aside idealized models of the way nature works in order to embrace the actual physical constraints of the real world.

Similarly, as many of those in the applied humanities have come to realize, they are able often enough to draw upon accepted theoretical principles, but just as often are forced to modify or abandon them altogether in the face of the particular social or policy issues being addressed. If they persist in rigidly trying to make use of principles not devised for practical application, they may deform them in the process, and may also say little of value about the policy issue in question.

The experience of the social sciences in trying to adapt their methodologies and findings to policy research is instructive (and perhaps a cautionary tale) for those attempting something similar within the humanities.[57] Beginning shortly before the Second World War, a concerted effort was made in the social sciences to bring them to bear on pressing national issues. That process was accelerated during the war and then blossomed considerably during the fifties and sixties. The attempt, however, to find the right fit between the social sciences and policy issues has been troubling and controversial. Considerable disagreement about the nature and validity of social science knowledge has been a fundamental stumbling block. The notion of "application" has been no less problematic. Efforts to simply deduce practical policy implications from large-scale social science theories have not been notably successful, even from the viewpoint of the most hopeful social scientists. From the side of those interested in making use of the knowledge, the efforts have not been that much more successful.

The sociologist James S. Coleman, in commenting upon the relationship between social science knowledge and policy problems, has written: ". . . A great amount of 'applied research' is funded which is neither discipline research nor very relevant to policy problems. . . . It is often a curious misapplication of the paraphernalia of discipline research outside the discipline: using excessively the jargon of the discipline; clutching tightly on to the most prestigious theories and theorists in the discipline . . . attempting to 'contribute to theory' (a theory which itself might be wrong, but is fashionable in the discipline), rather than address the problems in the real world; and other activities equally valueless except in their intended aim of increasing their author's standing in the discipline."[58] The same could undoubtedly be said for some recent work in the applied humanities.

One result of the various disputes has been the emergence of a number of different "models" of application in the social sciences. They provide a variety of suggestive possibilities for the humanities. Robert Mayer has nicely summarized four different models of the social science-policymaking relationship.[59]

One of the models is that of the "social engineer": "This model involves the social scientist working with the decision-maker in the direct application of existing theoretical knowledge to produce answers to policy questions. The engineer works on whatever problems are assigned or defined by the policymaker, leaving the selection of goals and objectives outside the utilization process. . . . In its most extreme form, the social engineer becomes a 'hand-maiden' or mandarin of the decisionmaker . . ."

The closest analogue to this model within the humanities might be that notion of applied ethics which sees its task as the straight-out application of prominent moral theories, drawn, say, from Kant, Mill, or John Rawls, to the moral dilemmas of policy or professional life.[60] There are a number of problems with this model in the humanities (as there are also in the social sciences). In its more debased form, it would not even try to make judgments about the validity of the theories; it would simply say, "if one is a utilitarian, then X would be the proper conclusion"; or, "if one is a deontologist, then Y would be the proper conclusion." That would lead to a type of "value-free" ethics, one likely to represent neither good ethics nor real neutrality. Equally hazardous would be the taking as a given the goals set by those outside of the humanities, as if there could be a sharp separation of ends and means. But such a separation would be a funda-

The Humanities and
State Legislatures

"I was a guest at the legislative scene; and though a guest would normally try to keep his best foot forward, I also had a job to do, a finite tenure, and had less than the normal bureaucratic self-interest at stake. I could be a kind of hit-and-run participant. Under these circumstances I think I was probably too well behaved, but I do not know that this opinion is widely shared."

This is how RONALD JAGER looks back on his two-year experience as a Humanities Consultant on the staff of the New Hampshire state legislature. From 1980 to 1982 Jager took part in a multi-state project sponsored by the State Legislative Leaders Foundation, an organization devoted to upgrading the institutional functioning of the fifty state legislatures, and funded by the National Endowment for the Humanities. This project supported a small pilot group of humanities scholars who served on the staffs of "sunset committees" in several state legislatures. Sunset laws call for a thorough evaluation of the mandate, effectiveness, and underlying mission of state agencies, boards, and commissions at regular intervals. The project organizers believed that these sunset evaluations were a facet of the state legislative process where professional humanists could make a particularly direct and valuable contribution. In addition to Jager, a philosopher who worked in New Hampshire, other members of the pilot group were: Toby Moore, a literary critic who worked in the Connecticut state legislature; Rob Watts, a specialist in religious studies who worked in the Georgia state legislature; and Jane Raible, a theologian who worked in the Washington state legislature.

Like the other participants in the project, Jager had pursued a traditional academic career, and self-consciously approached his activities in the state legislature as an extension and application of his professional humanities background. A Harvard Ph.D., he taught in the philosophy department at Yale from 1965-1977 and published widely in the areas of analytic philosophy and logic. He began to move in the direction of applied studies in the late 1970s when he left Yale to take up full time residence in New Hampshire, where he became a free lance writer and consultant and collaborated with his wife in writing books on the history of two New Hampshire towns. At the same time he continued his teaching as a visiting professor at the University of New Hampshire.

Jager was able to extend his activities as a Humanities Consultant in the state legislature somewhat more broadly than were the other project participants. He organized a series of seminars for legislators and staff members in which invited speakers would address particular public policy issues pertinent to the agenda of the legislative session then in progress. These seminars—which included such topics as the nuclear freeze, criminal justice policy, health care, and home rule— were broadcast on New Hampshire public television and gave legislators an opportunity to reflect on the broader historical and philosophical aspects of these issues. Like the evaluation reports prepared by the Sunset Office, which not only assessed the short term performance of various agencies but also analyzed their historical evolution, philosophical rationale, and institutional development, these policy seminars concretely demonstrated the contribution that scholarly humanistic perspectives could make to the legislative process.

Jager was also responsible for preparing several studies of the underlying values served by professional licensing and occupational certification procedures in the state. One such study focused on reforming the teacher certification requirements of the state's Department of Education.

By moving out of the Sunset Office and assuming these broader responsibilities, Jager found that he was able to loosen some of the constraints that the peculiar norms and customs of the state legislative environment placed on his activities as an applied humanist. Traditionally, in many state legislatures the functions of legislative staff members are quite limited. Staff members are expected to provide factual information to support legislative decision making, but they are not expected or encouraged to offer evaluations, advocacy, or political advice. Lobbyists and other associates of legislators provide that kind of input; staff members do not. Thus, not only Jager in New Hampshire but also the project participants in other states, all found that it was difficult to combine the role of staff member and Humanities Consultant. Policy analysis and procedural recommendations based on humanistic perspectives were not readily seen by legislators as simply informational contributions; applied humanistic analysis that had any bite to it spilled over into the realm of evaluation and advocacy and easily violated the norms of the staff role.

This situation hampered the effectiveness of all the project participants to some extent, and it illustrates a peculiar obstacle to applying the humanities in a state legislative setting. By moving out of the Sunset Office, Jager came to be seen more as a free floating consultant and less as an ordinary staff person. This helped lessen the role tension he experienced, and he found that by having a more ambiguous institutional identity he was able to function more effectively as an applied humanist. At least in the New Hampshire state legislature applying the humanities seemed to work best on a "hit and run" basis. Whether the humanities can have a lasting impact under those conditions, however, is open to question.

mental betrayal of the humanities. They cannot be a "handmaiden" to power without self-corruption.

Another possibility is the *"clinical model,"* first proposed by the late Alvin Gouldner: "In this model the social scientist interacts with the decisionmaker in all phases of the decisionmaking process. He assists in the clarification of goals and objectives, as well as in proposing appropriate programs and in evaluating them."[61] The analogue that comes to mind in the humanities would be that of philosopher-in-residence programs in hospitals, legislatures, or government agencies. This is a far more benign model of interaction, one that leaves the humanist as well as the policy analyst or decisionmaker with a full and free range of thought and action. To be successful, however, it requires a close and friendly relationship, with considerable give and take on each side.[62]

Still another alternative has come to be called the *"enlightenment model"*: it "is one in which the social scientist develops a series of broad scale studies of complex social systems. . . . These studies result in bodies of data and new modes by which society can evaluate its present goals and objectives and develop new ones. The impact of the social sciences is indirect rather than direct. While working on the same issues being dealt with by the policymaker, but independently of the latter, social scientists have a good deal of freedom to define problems and pursue inquiries on their own initiative." The humanities parallel suggested here is that of the scholar who chooses for his or her work some current policy issues, but whose study is conducted independently of a working relationship with policymakers or of observing the policy process at firsthand.

Still another possibility is what Robert

Professionals in the health field allegedly have moral obligations to their patients which override normal moral rules, especially moral obligations to treat the claims of persons equally. , . . "When should one's obligation to a client override one's obligation to society?" is not a question that can be answered by considering moral theory for an automatic answer. . . . Philosophers who make such professions their point of analysis in ethics cannot simply apply theory from the outside. To attempt to straightforwardly apply theory in this way would be an exercise in casuistry, and applied ethics is not casuistry. Rather, philosophers working in applied ethics need to begin from the perspective of the profession and engage in a constant interaction with theory and practice. As a result of that interaction, the theory will change. On this view, the applied philosopher has an important role to play vis-a-vis his/her pure philosopher counterpart. He/she tests theory and hence adds a unique and significant contribution to the evaluation of theory. It is this testing role which the traditional analogy with engineering/ physics overlooks.

Norman Bowie

Mayer calls the *"nonparticipation model"*: Here it would be "argued that social scientists should continue to write and do research as independent academicians. To the extent that their results are useful, they will be picked up in the policymaking process." This category can helpfully be amended by suggesting that the nonparticipation model would really encompass the work of those who have no special interest in policy issues at all. They would have no objection to a policymaker picking up their work, but would not seek it and would strenuously object if even a comma were changed. Their work would have to be taken pure or not at all. The humanities analogue might be the view that the humanities are essentially formally academic disciplines whose only task is to preserve and advance the tradition of scholarship and learning. They are independent of, and essentially indifferent to, contemporary social and policy issues.

Each of those models, in addition to its concept of how the social sciences and policymaking ought to interact, has often something implicit, but now and then explicit, to say about how the individual social scientist ought personally to interact with policy analysts and politicians. They run the gamut from paid handmaiden, through cautious, somewhat wary relationships, to a resolute refusal to have any dealings at all with workaday policy issues or people. At stake are different notions of what might compromise the integrity of their own field, commitments, and training. Social engineers sense no threat to integrity at all. They are glad to have the opportunity to put their field to the services of policy. At the other extreme would be those who do not think any noncompromising relationship is possible at all; one should just stay away. In between are those who believe one can work virtuously in the marketplace if care is taken to avoid occasions of sin. One need only mention some applied humanities analogues: working for a legislator, but resisting a denial of moral principles in the name of political expediency; or writing a corporate history and refusing to suppress unsavory parts of that history.

Of these various possibilities, only that of the "engineering model" would seem wholly unacceptable for the humanist. It combines two ingredients most at odds with the nature of the humanities: an indifference to ends and a concern with means only, and a willingness to forgo critical distance in order to play the handmaiden role. While the humanities may have helpful contributions to make, for instance, to the choice of prudent means of implementing a policy decision, their full strength will most naturally lie in examining goals and purposes, and in testing them against its understanding of human nature, history, and needs. If that type of analysis cannot be done, or is even partially suspended, the heart is cut out of the possible contribution of the humanities. Similarly, to forgo critical distance and to put the humanities to the passive service of political power is to commit a grave moral offense against the humanities. Just as it is of their essence to be focused on the human situation, it is no less a part of that essence to refuse to compromise that mission.

There is perhaps a fine line only between the enlightenment and nonparticipation models. The distinctive note about the former would be its interest in policy matters and a desire to make some kind of contribution to them. It would hope that some general knowledge could be generated that would filter through and helpfully illuminate policy. The nonparticipation model, if it bespeaks disdain for public policy matters at the working level, should have little to commend it to the humanist. That is not to say by any means that all, or even most, humanists should be concerned as humanists with policy. It is only to say that an arrogant, or disdainful, dismissal of policy issues as beneath the dignity of the humanist would betray the civic mission of the humanities; and it would be almost as arrogant similarly to dismiss those in the humanities who choose to make policy their special mission.

The enlightenment and the clinical models emerge as the most feasible and potentially fruitful for the humanist. The attraction of the former is that it is the most likely to allow the fullest scope to the training and insights of the humanities. It can take on policy matters, but without the constraints of meeting hard deadlines, doing the "quick and dirty" research that is a requirement of much policy analysis, or being unduly forced by political or practical constraints to rein in the imaginative possibilities. At the same time, it will not have some of the strengths of the clinical model, most notably the capacity of the latter to provide the humanist with direct access to decisionmaking settings and people, and to see at firsthand the consequences of trying to make use of knowledge drawn from the humanities.

Inevitably, of course, those who work in a clinical context will, in the immediate heat of moral struggles, often not have the time to do the deepest or best possible scholarship. Nor will they always have the same kind of freedom of expression, or possibility of elegance of expression, open to those who work at a greater distance from actual decisionmaking. That loss may be offset by the sense of immediacy and concreteness and by the possibility of making an immediate, palpable difference. There is, in any case, room for different personal interests and predilections, and thus no need for a forced choice among the various possible models.

Vision and Tradition

Whatever the model chosen it would be unfortunate if it slighted the creative and necessary tension between the past and the future, and between social constraints and social vision. That tension should be made manifest however the

humanities are brought to bear on contemporary problems.

Counterpoised against a too commonly narrow and highly technical humanities is a long-standing ideal of the animating force of the humanities. It evokes and instills a deeply rooted social vision, one grounded in tradition, alert to contemporary need, and aspiring to a viable future. The past was the starting point, and the traditional humanities, the locus of that vision, were based on a canon of classics.[63] They were not without inner tensions, but those classics did present the approximation of an integrated moral world view. Modern thought, by contrast, has produced anticlassics and an anticanon. Today there are many who see no basis for giving any texts a preferential status, or any tradition either. No integrated world view seems available or desired. At the same time, there is great anxiety as to what might count as a basis for the wisdom and character of which the humanities have so long talked. If the humanities are to help with social vision it may not only be through the application of humanistic disciplines to specific problems of social policy. It may be also and no less significantly through a reappropriation of a fruitful relationship between the humanities and the practice of life, a task perennial and never finished.

Perhaps the easiest role to see for the humanities is the critical one, for criticism is a central part of the ethos of contemporary intellectual life and the university. And the humanities can, in part, provide us with a critical perspective on our own culture by holding up to us the image of another culture, whether real or imagined. That image allows us both to see the limitation of our own culture and to envision other possiblities. Lionel Trilling suggested that a classical education—when in its last days it no longer had much connection with the practice of life yet still lingered on in schools and universities—played such a role. Of Freud, who kept his schoolboy diary in Greek, Trilling writes, "who can say what part in his self-respect, in his ability to move to a point beyond the reach of the surrounding dominant culture, was played by the old classical education, with its image of *the other culture*, the ideal culture, that wonderful imagined culture of the ancient world which no one but schoolboys, schoolmasters, scholars, and poets believed in?"[64]

Today there is no single "other" culture, no respected ancient world with which all educated persons are familiar—and not just with its dry contours, but with its myths, its heroes, its climactic historical moments—that stands in splendid difference and implicit criticism of our own. The student is inundated with other cultures that classicists, anthropologists, Sinologists, Indologists, and others are prepared to introduce to them. But the use of an elaborate critical apparatus may keep those cultures more distant than bring them alive. The enormous increase in our ability to reconstruct sensitively an extraordinary range of human cultures, both contemporary and historical, is certainly an important resource. Yet for all of its value it remains difficult for many to locate (or once located, to respond to) the roots of our own culture. How is it possible to have a sense of the continuity of those roots with our present life when the humanities become "disciplines" armed with "methodologies" and "critical perspectives" that frequently call into question the validity of any tradition? They cannot easily transmit a living memory; they often destroy it.

The modern individualist ideologies that dominate our consciousness and our universities can also be destructive of living memory and so of social vision. For the latter cannot be manufactured on the basis of present need or feeling alone, but always require an effort to discern what is good in itself and how that might be embodied. Tradition as living memory is not the mindless repetition of the past, but the creative reappropriation of the past in the context of present reality. Thus a sense of the past and a sense of the future are intrinsically related: if we destroy one we destroy the other.

One of the most demanding tasks for an applied humanities is that of finding the right balance between a useful response to present needs and the duty to put that response within the context of a tradition. Many of the most pressing social and policy problems arise in the context of rapid cultural and technological change. A popular, indeed predictable, feature of the ensuing public debate is that of a call for "new rules," a radical restructuring of past principles and perspectives.[65] A no less predictable counterresponse will be a fervent plea to protect the status quo, treated as sacred and unchangeable simply because it originated in the past.[66]

Yet no tradition can remain alive if it does not change over time. "New rules" cannot be viable unless they are permeated by those elements of the tradition that have stood the test of time and experience. An applied humanities would be a parody if it could do no more than generate new slogans and handy formulas. Its larger, more responsible task is that of enriching the present with the past, of complicating rather than simplifying reality, and of suggesting solutions that evoke complex and enriching visions.

5. Fields of Application: The Biomedical, the Social, and the Policy Sciences

In thinking about the various uses of the humanities, it is possible to envision and readily find examples of their direct application to individual social and policy issues. A no less important and related development has been a conscious immersion of many humanists into the work of fields whose characteristic focus has always been on such issues. There the question is not only how the humanities might relate to this or that discrete policy problem or issue, but more broadly how the general perspectives and methods of the humanities might best interact with the quite different perspectives and methods of other fields. It is possible to see in those broad interactions both an attempt to bring contrasting points of departure into contact with each other and to do so by means of the different "models" noted in the previous section. We will begin this section with relatively brief looks at the interaction of the humanities and the biomedical sciences, and the humanities and the social sciences. More extensive analysis will be accorded the field of public policy, or (as sometimes designated) the policy "sciences."

The Humanities and the Biomedical Sciences

For the past twenty years one of the most active areas of work in the applied humanities has been in the biomedical sciences. Scholars from philosophy, history, and literature currently teach in medical schools, conduct rounds and other educational exercises in hospitals and clinics, and engage in biomedical policy work at the state and federal levels of government.[67] There are programs in the medical humanities (literature and medicine,[68] bioethics, political theory) at a number of medical schools, and history of medicine departments have long been in existence at major universities.[69] The past twenty years have also witnessed an increase in the number of specialty journals and books devoted to topics in the philosophy of medicine and biomedical ethics, the history of medicine and nursing, and literature and the health professions.[70]

Medicine has long acclaimed the importance of the humanities in educating physicians and other health care professionals. At the turn of the century, distinguished physicians such as William Osler called for greater attention in the medical school curriculum to the humanities.[71] Yet, from the beginning of the twentieth century, the eventually triumphant attempt to professionalize medicine was at odds in practice with the notion that the humanities have a critical role in medical education. The 1910 Flexner report and subsequent efforts to root medical practice in scientific methodology worked as an important counterweight to any role that might be played by the humanities. While medical educators and practitioners had hoped that an undergraduate liberal arts requirement would enhance the role of the humanities, that emphasis has been undercut by the increasingly stringent scientific demands (or a perception of such demands) placed on those who enter medicine.[72]

Nonetheless, the humanities have more recently been able to work cooperatively with the biomedical professions at the graduate and postgraduate levels in part because many practitioners are acutely aware of the failures of their training in adequately preparing them for the humane dimensions of medicine. In the 1960s, moreover, a series of scandals pertaining to a questionable or simply unethical use of human beings for medical research—at Tuskegee, Willowbrook Hospital, and the Jewish Chronic Disease Hospital, for example—forced the medical professions to pay serious attention to both normative and regulatory questions about their own work. At the same time, many scholars within the humanities were becoming increasingly interested in medicine.[73] The power and prestige of the profession, its social and economic impact and the unusually rich

and complex set of historical and philosophical questions raised by technological advances, make it an attractive area of study (just as had been the case somewhat earlier with sociologists). This combination of circumstances produced a flowering of links between the humanities and biomedicine in research, teaching, clinical practice, and most recently the policy arena. In some places the medical humanities occupy departmental status within medical schools. At other schools single scholars have been appointed to do work in the various areas of the medical humanities. Many medical schools and undergraduate institutions have instituted specialized programs in philosophy, literature, or history that focus on biomedicine.

One of the most difficult issues is the degree to which those from the humanities ought to modify their traditional approaches to moral, valuational, or historical problems in light of the needs of biomedical practitioners. Many (but by no means all) scholars in the humanities are uncomfortable working by the bedside or in front of legislative committees, and this has led to intense discussion within the medical humanities about the appropriate styles and methods that ought be utilized by those working in biomedical fields.[74] Fear of co-optation or trivialism have led some scholars within the humanities to disparage teaching or research in the medical humanities (just as, analogously, some historians have avoided business history). Some medical humanities scholars themselves fear that a simplistic and mechanical application of moral theories to the problems that exist in medicine may distort the contribution that the humanities can make to the improvement of health care.[75]

Since medical educators often view the

Philosophy in a
Clinical Setting

. . . In an attempt to allocate my time most effectively, I limit my work mainly to a few departments: internal medicine, family medicine, the division of neonatology in pediatrics, and nursing. Within these departments I attend a variety of meetings on a regular basis—attending rounds, work rounds, morning reports, chart rounds, noon conferences, case conferences, et cetera—typically taking up a total of twenty hours or more per week. In some of these meetings I mainly observe; in some I respond to questions or raise them; in others, I lead the discussion.

. . . It is not always easy to be a philosopher among physicians. As any philosopher knows, it takes time to sort out and describe issues, to propose and examine possible answers. As any physician knows, time in a teaching hospital is scarce. How does one determine when to raise a philosophical question, or what to say when invited to comment? There are several problems.

In the first place, as a philosopher my understanding of the medical facts may be shaky. If I use the twenty-five-words-or-less to which I confine myself to get clear about the facts, then I offer nothing philosophical and slow down the proceedings for no one's benefit but my own. If I offer comments without getting clear about the facts, I risk offering irrelevancies. Although this problem diminishes as I learn more about medicine and its language, it does not disappear.

Where I do offer a comment, I am sometimes uncertain about how to focus it. Should I present a quick overview of the general philosophical issues at stake (with no time to show very clearly how they relate to the case at hand)? Should I examine a feature or features of a particular argument someone has already offered (with no time to show why such an analysis has an important bearing on the broader question, and risking the perception by staff that I am trying to make the arguer look foolish—with no time to show that this is not the point of philosophical criticism)? The possibilities are numerous, none of them entirely satisfactory. Any comment that focuses on the broader issues risks being so general as to seem like a platitude or truism; any comment focusing on the particulars of the case at hand risks a kind of triviality or, perhaps worse, a failure to bring in that systematic kind of analysis that should be one of philosophy's greatest contributions to such discussions.

Finally, whatever the level of generality, I find it also difficult sometimes to determine whether my comment presents something familiar to the physicians, even trite, or a new, perhaps quite strange way to view the issue. I have spent many years immersed in a discipline that asks different sorts of questions from the sciences and that pursues its answers in rather different ways. It is a challenge to learn where these ways of thinking coincide and where they diverge.

E. Haavi Morreim

humanities as a source of enlightenment and sensitization for medical students, there has been a tendency on their part to emphasize goals such as improved communication skills, a broadening of perspectives, and evaluative analysis as the object of teaching. There are some in the humanities who would disagree with these goals, or at least find them too narrow. They view their primary task as that of communicating the methods and rigorous substance of their discipline to biomedical professionals. They often stress the value of the humanities in helping students to think more clearly and analytically, in allowing them to understand the social and political context of medical practice, and in helping medical professionals to define better the normative and policy problems that they inevitably will encounter in the course of day-to-day practice. Their concern, in short, is less with "sensitizing" and "humanizing" young physicians than it is with helping to develop specific cognitive skills and social perspectives.

One of the most significant recent developments is the appearance of humanities scholars in clinical settings. Philosophers and historians are now acting as ethics consultants in some hospitals and medical schools. They also serve on institutional review boards and ethics committees, sometimes interview patients, offer advice to attending health care personnel, and write reports on ethical issues that arise. Yet, since there is very little professional training in the humanities that prepare scholars to do this kind of work, their appearance in hospital corridors has led to the worry that the theoretical emphasis of most humanities education may not be the most appropriate way of preparing them

Against Philosophical Authoritarianism

Finally, I refer . . . to the upsurge of interest in medical ethics among philosophers and to the proliferation of courses offered by them in our medical schools. I view these developments with approval, but also with much ambivalence. On the plus side, philosophers can perform a much-needed service by bringing medical students and physicians to query the authoritarian and paternalistic traditions of the profession, traditions that need modification but that can never be altogether' eliminated. But on the negative side, some philosophers fall victim to their own authoritarianism when they maintain that medical students and physicians can neither comprehend nor apply their professional ethic unless they are first drilled in the conventions, language and special methods of formal ethics. Apart from the practical fact that it is impossible to find a place in the already shamefully overcrowded medical curriculum for a detailed course in formal ethics, the conclusion that understanding of ethical matters can be achieved only by those who have traversed such courses is plainly specious.

Carleton B. Chapman, M.D.

Philosophy As Therapy

I participated in numerous informal discussions with nursing staff on hospital policies and procedures with . . . success. The first summer I was involved in several sessions exploring the legal and ethical ramifications of a controversial consent form recently adopted by the hospital; analytic scrutiny of the document assisted nurses to sort out different issues implicit in the wording of the form. During the second summer, a program on humanistic gerontology provoked some discussion of a problem which had arisen in the Long Term Care Unit; patients were being forced to eat in the dining room, even though many resisted this, preferring the privacy of their rooms for meals. An enthusiastic new assistant director of nursing had decided that it would be beneficial for these persons to eat in a communal situation, "to bring them out of themselves." Some nurses bridled at this patent paternalism which ignored the patients' individual belief systems, values, and self-determination; others thought the true reason was economic, since it would be more cost effective for the patients to eat together. This issue provided me with an opportunity to compare and contrast three health care models: benevolent paternalism, consumerism, and existential advocacy. Subsequent discussion with the new assistant director and the nursing director of the Long Term Care Unit proved profitable. The decision was made to deal with each patient individually, to attempt to determine with each patient whether eating in the cafeteria would, in fact, benefit him or her.

As a consultant to the hospital staff, I found—much to my chagrin—that a number of nurses and aides would ask me for advice on multiple aspects of patient care, assuming, I suppose, that philosophers are very wise and thus have answers to perplexing questions. I usually attempted a Socratic approach with such people, trying to help them realize they already knew what was being requested from me. I found this was most effective in nurturing their own sense of personal power and perceptiveness and in conveying a sense of what philosophy is all about. Initially, a hospital philosopher must devote considerable time and energy to educating staff members into the nature of philosophy, gently debunking some of the myths

to take part in medical practice.[76] At the same time medical staff and students often indicate that it is just this difference in background that those trained in the humanities bring to clinical teaching that makes their presence valuable.

While there is certainly room for disagreement about the value and impact of teaching the humanities in clincial settings, there is reason to believe that those in the humanities have been highly suc-

cessful at the policy level in influencing biomedicine policy and practice. They often serve on regulatory committees, national commissions and institutional review boards. They have testified before federal and state legislators, have been cited in court decisions, and have had a direct hand in the maintenance of various forms of institutional controls of the practice of medicine and the delivery of health care. The continued existence,

surrounding this esoteric discipline. This requires tolerance and considerable patience.

Finally, I was available, on a referral basic from attending physicians, to do "philosophical counseling" with patients and their families. Serious illness will often throw individuals into a questioning attitude regarding the meaning and purpose of human life. For some who have no traditional religious affiliation, a one-to-one discussion with a philosopher can lead to clarification of values and beliefs, a consideration of new conceptual options. Even those with conventional beliefs might profit from philosophical therapy. My function as a philosophical counselor was certainly not intended to conflict with the traditional pastoral counseling already available by local clergy but to complement it.

. . . Since the hospital had no staff psychiatrist, social worker or counselor during the first summer, I was occasionally called upon to deal with problems beyond the scope of my academic training in philosophy. Since I do have some rudimentary formal training in Gestalt psychotherapy, I was able to meet these demands in most cases. (I am currently pursuing a master's in social work to enhance these psychotherapeutic skills.) I am not convinced that the conventional bifurcation of philosophy and psychotherapy is correct. At its best philosophy serves a therapeutic, healing function, for it involves a clarification or an alteration of one's belief system, leading to richer experience and more efficient practical behavior. At one point I was asked to work with a young man who attempted suicide. Deeply depressed, he questioned the value of life, posing in an anguished way a perennial question of philosophy. We established rapport with one another, and he asked me to accompany him during the last week of my first summer to the state mental hospital to which he had committed himself. When he was released, even though I was no longer on the hospital staff, I continued to work with him— as did several psychiatrists, psychologists, and a hypnotherapist. He never was able to extricate himself from his torment. During the second week of my second summer's residency, he shot himself through the head with a pistol. Anyone who works in a hospital must be able to contend with this type of profoundly disturbing occurrence, even a philosopher.

Fraser Snowden

for example, of a national system of institutional review boards with oversight responsibilities for research on human subjects can be attributed in great part to persistent concern within the humanities. Humanities scholars played a central role in the work of the Commission for the Protection of Human Subjects (1974–1977) and the President's Commission for the Study of Ethical Problems in Medicine and Biomedical and Behavioral Research (1980–1983).[77]

The role of humanists in solving particular policy problems, and in serving as enlightened commentators on medical and health policy practices seems to have earned the humanities a degree of respect from social scientists, economists, medical administrators, and other traditional laborers in this area of policy-making. Certainly, those in the humanities have slowly learned to cope with the complexities of policymaking in the health care arena, and have begun to acquire the skills for doing work in this sector.

The Humanities and the Social Sciences

In many respects the humanities have a deeper affinity with the social sciences than they do with any other major branch of knowledge.[78] And yet, perhaps ironically, because of the close connection between their respective subject matters and concerns, there has almost always been a deep rivalry between the social sciences and the humanities. They have been sharply demarcated for many decades. Yet today there are signs that the intellectual segregation that has characterized their relationship is beginning to break down. New opportunities for cooperation and mutual enrichment are beginning to emerge. If this trend continues, interdisciplinary cooperation with the social sciences may provide one of the most fruitful avenues through which the humanities can regain contact with the important issues and problems of public life in our society.

Many obstacles stand in the way of this development, however, and the hopeful signs of cooperation between the humanities and the social sciences remain nascent promises yet to be fulfilled. The traditional tension and rivalry was produced by the historical development of the social sciences themselves and by the influence of positivism in both fields. The rivalry can best be understood if we recall that the social sciences, as separate disciplines and as autonomous modes of inquiry, were born out of a dissatisfaction with the humanities' inability to cope with the new social, economic, and political problems posed by modern industrial society; and out of a commitment to the positivist belief that it was possible to construct a nomothetic, predictive science of society and human behavior.[79]

Many of the early social scientists were humanists by training, but they abandoned the humanities in order to pursue a different mode of analysis and an investigation of much the same subject matter that the humanities studied.[80] Although a normative program of social reform was often the impulse that drove the early formation of the social sciences, eventually the positivistic tenets of value neutrality and scientific objectivity came to predominate professional self-identity. A fundamental division between the social sciences and the humanities settled on the basic distinction between descriptive and prescriptive inquiry.

In large measure, the new rapprochement between the social sciences and the humanities has been made possible by the decline of positivism and the attendant blurring of the hard-and-fast distinction between descriptive and prescriptive investigation. The interpenetration of the humanities and the social sciences that has so far occurred, however, has taken place mainly at the level of disciplinary study and theoretical investigation.[81] In the applied wings of the social sciences and the humanities much less contact has taken place. The applied social sciences remain strongly positivistic and quantitative in orientation (though that tendency has been much criticized of late).

While the applied humanities often draw upon social scientific studies in order to obtain a better sense of the

Social History and Social Policy

The historian's perspective on contemporary issues provided a sharp and vital sense of options, opportunities, and abilities to maneuver. As opposed to some social science research that appears better able to analyze the forces upholding a system than the forces that might promote change, the historians consistently analyzed the past record in ways that expanded the range of choices available to decision makers. In their work, the elements that compose the present situation appear to be far less determined and fixed. An aura of inevitability gives way to a sense of experimentation. Thus, the historian's sense of the contingencies that went into the construction of present policies and practices is a much-needed corrective to the more closed constructs of other disciplines. It is important that policy analysts and administrators recognize that the federal government funded a major health program in the 1920s, not because the precedent itself should be faithfully copied today but because the very notion of an alternative system is liberating.

To take this point one step further, historical analysis often serves to demystify a subject. It challenges one fundamental source of legitimacy—the notion that since an institution or practice has always been with us, it must necessarily always be with us. The dead weight of the past prompts inertia when survival comes to be confused with desirability. The historian can counter such an orientation, thereby stimulating attempts at change.

The historian's analysis is also well suited to explain the dynamics that shaped policies, to identify the critical elements in the decision-making process. Historians can work at the microlevel; sufficient records do survive in enough detail to provide historians with the necessary data on which to base such an analysis. Whether the case on hand be the organization of the hospital, the operation of a public pension system, or the presumptions that underlie urban design, the historian has much to tell the social policy analyst about the players, the strategies, and the rules of the game. To ignore such data is to miss some of the most illuminating and important moments in the implementation of social policy. . . .

Moreover, policymakers, in informed and uninformed ways, are already using history. But too fequently this history is an invented one; many administrators carry with them an image of the past that exerts a powerful influence on their design of programs. Both the long history of policy toward the black family and the short history of such a group as the Carnegie Council on Children demonstrate that, for better or worse, history is often integral to the formulation of public policy. Historians can, at least, help to make certain that policy people are using an accurate history. Furthermore, historians can bring their own sense of the past to bear directly on the framing of policy choices. It is simply not true that the nineteenth century was the golden age of family cohesion or that the black family totally disintegrated under slavery. And a policy that presupposes otherwise, may well be mischievous and counterproductive.

David J. Rothman and Stanton Wheeler

sociological and institutional context of the problems with which they deal, this often amounts to little more than the use of social science as a source of facts and information. Philosophers who work on professional ethics, for example, may familiarize themselves with the literature on the sociology of the professions, but they rarely integrate that literature into their work in any substantive or meaningful way. Applied historians, by contrast, are far more likely to do so. For their part, social scientists have been somewhat slow to recognize the value of normative analyses of professional ethics. They have consequently failed to investigate the way in which normative considerations and arguments have altered the concrete behavior of professionals in recent years. Hence, while the boundaries between social scientific and humanistic study are breaking down at the theoretical level, at the applied level the gap between these two branches of knowledge remains wide and yet to be bridged.

The humanities and the social sciences share a common subject matter and many overlapping concerns in their study of human activity. Both aspire to deepen and to broaden our insight into the multifaceted reality of the human condition. Both aim to expand the limits of our cultural horizons and to enrich our understanding of ourselves as socially and historically situated beings. Both take the realm of human artifice and performance as the primary locus of inquiry. They are thus both drawn to explore the meanings that adhere in the interactions among persons, the forms and conditions of those meanings, and the embodiment of ideas in texts and institutions which mediate the social relationships among individuals.[82]

In the pursuit of those common objectives, the humanities and the social sciences do of course differ in the categories they employ and in the themes they characteristically emphasize. The humanities tend to throw the particularity of individuals—their originality, their style, their creativity and causal efficacy as agents—into bold relief against a distant background of collective, historical, or material forces. For their part, the social sciences tend to highlight precisely those general background conditions and structures that both make individual particularity possible and serve to limit it.[83] Nonetheless, these differences are not so fundamental that they obviate the common ground that might link the humanities and the social sciences. Were this common ground better understood and more forcefully acted upon, the humanities' characteristic emphasis on human agency and the social sciences' characteristic emphasis on the context of agency might be reciprocally illuminating. That would allow each of these two families of discourse in concert to comment more intelligently on the human condition than either has been able to do separately.

Most, if not all, social scientific and humanistic disciplines have lately been caught up in a process of theoretical realignment and methodological turmoil, reflecting in part an uncertainty about the next steps in disciplinary development. We are entering a period of what Clifford Geertz has aptly called "blurred genres."[84] Disciplinary boundaries that once appeared firmly entrenched are beginning to break down, and new patterns of research are forming, based upon problems and metaphors that shuttle between and confound old dividing lines. Policy analysis, in particular, offers a fruitful common ground for joint work by humanists and social scientists.[85]

44

Public Policy and the Policy Sciences

The realm of public policy has perhaps attracted the most interest within the humanities during the past two decades. In part, that is because of a reaction against a technocratically based form of policy analysis and a desire to put something richer in its place; and in part out of a belief on the part of many that the voice of the humanities should be present in the wide-ranging national social, political, and economic debates that have been a mark of American life since the 1960s.[86] To this should be added a general perception that policy issues already reflect, and cannot evade, issues of meaning and value, history and future dreams.

A fundamental purpose of the humanities is to reflect upon the human condition, to explore questions of ends, meanings, interpretations, justifications, past memories and present purposes. How then can they fail to have something of value to contribute to the formation of public policy? A basic purpose of public policy is that of finding ways to devise a more human economic and political order, one sensitive to the demands of the past and its traditions, and to the future and its needs. How can that task not, in turn, be pertinent to the work of the humanities?

Yet those assumptions—of an ineluctable and natural bond between the humanities and public policy—have been challenged. That challenge has come from both the side of the humanities and that of policy analysis. From the side of the humanities, it has been said that they are not, of their nature, suitable for the resolution of the daily dilemmas of social, political, and economic life. The humanities seek not instantly usable practical knowledge of the kind needed to build bridges, balance budgets, or create jobs, but that deeper and different knowledge necessary for human self-understanding and reflected primarily in the great written texts of the past, whether historical, literary, or philosophical. As the principal vehicle by which tradition is kept alive, by which the ends of life are kept in the forefront, by which the heights and depths of human experience over time are kept before our eyes, the humanities speak to that which is most central and abiding in our life together. They do not speak to mundane policy issues.

Such a position—the argument continues—does not entail an indifference on the part of those in the humanities to matters of public policy. It only entails a distinction between the two spheres. The humanities cannot be true to themselves if they take on public policy issues, which are by their nature transitory, technical, and political. It is, moreover, pretentious and dilettantish for those in the humanities to believe they can effectively work with policy matters. They have neither the professional qualifications nor the practical experience to do so.[87]

Thus has a powerful argument been pressed by some in the humanities. The assumption of a fruitful relationship has been no less challenged by many within the policy sphere, though their stance is often more implicit than explicit. In a democratic system—so the argument goes—the political process determines the goods and values to be sought in society. While the question of what they ought to be is serious and basic, the role of policy analysis is to serve that system

> Literature can still help citizens to imagine what it is in public issues that they share: the personal basis for concern, the historical and cultural framework of the problems and values under consideration, the fundamental human qualities and purposes in disparate, even opposing views. Literature can help citizens to be thinkers-in-common; i.e., persons talking, however disparately, about an underlying set of values that derive from a common heritage and bear upon a common future. It can give words to aspects that will go on being important long after whatever policy decision under consideration has been made.
>
> **Richard Lewis**

by helping it to function effectively. That is essentially a technical task, not philosophical or theoretical. Once a commitment has been made, for instance, to devise a welfare program for the poor, or an incentive system for capital investment, alternative strategies must be weighed to determine which policy option would best achieve that end, how the chosen option could be financed and implemented, and what criteria ought to be used in evaluating its effectiveness once in place. Those are not suitable tasks for humanistic perspectives and methods.

Such essentially technical tasks do not imply indifference to the larger questions of the human good. They only imply that some should have the training and experience necessary to implement the concrete practical details of those goals that society chooses; practical, not theoretical, reason is needed. Inevitably, the analyst must live in a world of trade-offs (a term that is not despised), seeking not the larger truths—a task best left to the sciences and the humanities—but those smaller truths that result from the give-and-take, the clash of values and interests, that are the stuff of daily life in a well-functioning, pluralistic democracy. That, in essence, is one common response from the policy side to an expanded role for the humanities.

Both the humanities and policy perspectives, in short, could share the belief that they are engaged in different enterprises and that each, in its own right, is valuable and worthy. They can also thus believe that their mutual tasks are best kept separate. Neither field will gain by merging the two enterprises, and society as a whole will not benefit by confusing two distinct realms of thought and activity; the result will be neither good humanities nor good public policy.

There is considerable persuasiveness in that line of argument. Seen in its best light, it bespeaks a desire to preserve the integrity of different spheres of activity. It tries to embody a recognition that they serve different, but equally valid purposes. It attempts to take seriously the view that the humanities and public policy will of necessity have different standards of excellence and craft, different methodological criteria, and different, though complementary, roles to play in the culture.

Nonetheless, for all of its power, it is a viewpoint that does not fully appreciate the possibilities that a closer relationship between the humanities and policy could bring. It is, at the least, a distortion of the policy process to understand it only as a technical, instrumental enterprise. It needs values, tradition, and social vision as part of its conscious and animating apparatus; and it cannot, in any event, fail to be soaked in values, however much unrecognized or denied in the name of technical neutrality.

A first step in making some sense of the possibilities is to observe that the expression "public policy" is, in fact, much too loose to be of great help. Instead, we suggest that it is possible to distinguish among *public policy, public policy analysis*, and *public policymaking*.

Public policy can be understood as the aggregate collection of those actions undertaken by government, either by omission or commission, to advance the welfare of its citizens and the protection and advancement of its national interests. Those actions will embody social goals, purposes, and direction. In their totality, they encompass legislation, administrative regulations, court decisions, and other types of governmental action. Public policy can also encompass those possible actions that are deliberately omitted. While not everything that the government fails to do can be called a matter of public policy, there are a number of issues that work themselves into the public policy realm by virtue of the fact that a national debate, or a legislative or judicial ruling, determines that the government ought self-consciously to remain free of involvement with them. The debate over abortion, or other issues thought to be pertinent either to private morality or to the operation of the economic marketplace, would be examples here. In general, public policy will reflect the competition of values and interests, of tradition and modernity, of ideals and reality.

Public policy analysis can be construed as an analytical effort to devise the practical alternatives open to government in implementing public policy commitments. Its purpose has commonly been that of understanding the technical, bureaucratic, and legislative process by which policy is made, of studying the various possibilities of public policy initiatives, of exploring the potential consequences of different policy options, and of determining the most feasible means of achieving political, economic, or social goals. An essential purpose of policy analysis is to set the stage for policymaking. It is typically carried out by advisors or consultants to those who actually make policy.

Public policymaking is the actual act of making a policy choice, or of implementing a policy option. The understanding of public policy, or an analysis of policy choices, is not in itself to make or devise policy. Policymaking, by contrast, can be seen as the final outcome of understanding and analysis.[88] Decision, judgment, action, and choice are the dominant features. They will be part and parcel of the political process, encompassing struggles over different conceptions of the national interest and human welfare and reflecting the results of prior policy analysis. Policymaking will encompass bargaining, compromise, and a mix of high ideals and insistent reality.

Those distinctions concerning the realm of policy allow us to ask more specific questions about a possible role for the humanities. It might seem at first glance that the only, or most appropriate, relationship should take place in the arena of *public policy in general*. Indeed, it is at that level that the going is easiest and most congenial for those in the humanities. What ought to be the proper end of man and how ought public policy and government serve that end? What is a just society? How much freedom ought people to have? What ought to be the role of tradition in shaping political and social institutions?

At this level one can appropriately ask and grapple with the oldest, most enduring human questions, of equal concern both to the humanities and public policy. A notable feature of discussion and thought at this level is that there are, in principle, few if any constraints, political or practical. One is free to envision any kind of society, to ask the deepest questions with no restraint save that of logic and assumed values, and to set aside, if one chooses, anxiety about practical outcomes or possibilities. In practice, of course, policy issues will ordinarily be understood within the context of a set of political limitations and traditional values; yet imaginative initiatives are always possible.

With *public policy analysis*, one moves into a somewhat different realm. Here one must begin talking about and analyzing particular and concrete policies. The question is less the nature of justice in general, but instead, the specific ingredients of a just economic, or immigration, or housing policy in this society at this time in history. If economic growth is sought, would tax incentives to real estate developers be an effective means of attaining it? Would harsher sentences reduce crime rates? While discussion in the realm of public policy can be directed to all, citizen and expert, policy analysis will more commonly be directed to those with specific responsibilities, administrative or legislative (to legislators, for example, who can vote tax benefits for real estate developers or set harsher jail terms for convicted criminals).

A notable feature of public policy analysis is that, to be responsible, it must recognize the existence of constraints; those who devise policy must work within legal and political boundaries. Yet the need to recognize constraints can create a problematic situation for those from the humanities. Their fields invite an expanded imagination, a leaping over of boundaries. But public policy analysis is carried out in actual societies. It must ask not only what might be ideal, but what is feasible; not only about tradition in general, but about the pertinence of particular traditions to particular problems. It must move from the highest theory to a different level, and out of the past and into the present and future.

Inevitably, public policy analysis must also move a step closer to action and away from contemplation and reflection. The "is" and the "ought" begin to jostle each other more closely. If he or she would work in this realm, the humanistic scholar must understand not just the great ideas and deepest memories, but must also grapple with contemporary facts and data. If a fair immigration policy is being sought, how many immigrants might be admitted under a policy that favored reuniting existing families versus one that favored granting a legal status to those now classified as illegal? What is the moral import of that data? Yet the necessity of considerable intellectual flexibility, of balancing competing demands, and of constantly testing theory against reality is one of considerable value to the humanist. It helps to challenge a bifurcation of facts and theory or the creation of concepts notable principally for elegance rather than for credibility.

Policy analysis is not yet a fully developed discipline, but a collection of techniques and approaches—including various statistical methods, computer skills, decision theory, microeconomic analysis, and organizational psychology—designed to tell certain kinds of stories and to fashion certain sorts of conclusion. Their larger aim is to assist and improve governmental decisionmaking about complicated problems. Its constructions of reality are shared to some considerable extent with economics, and at a more general level with the other social sciences, and shared also with a substantial number of policymakers at various levels of government. Policy analysis is flourishing in the universities, with adequate enrollment of able students seeking governmental careers. Its professors consult widely; its students find jobs.

Those economists, political scientists, lawyers, and others who consider themselves policy analysts are generally optimistic. They expect that sophisticated techniques will be increasingly applied to complex problems, that careful estimates of social utility—of the efficiency and equity of public policy—will find a growing audience among the powerful. They also believe, on the whole, that the study of bureaucratic politics, and of organizations more generally, will identify removable or reducible obstacles to the intelligent deployment of public resources.

Yet for all its confidence, and its real success in improving the quality of governmental decisions, there has been continuing deep and thoughtful criticism of the dominant modes and attitudes of policy analysis. This criticism has helped open the way for the humanities. One of the main objections has been the narrowness of the approaches used. Utilitarianism is the dominant ideology among policy analysts, and this has in practice meant that cost-benefit analysis is a principal analytic mode. In such circumstances, economy and efficiency become almost privileged goals, chiefly because they are related to the most measurable aspects of people's needs and desires. Questions of equity concern policy analysts, but problems of definition and measurement tend to reduce the relative role of the former. Utilitarianism can account, perhaps inadequately, for legal or human rights; but it seems clear that dealing with these in cost-benefit terms is likely to distort and trivialize the issues.

Critics of mainline policy analysis often assert that the values associated with democratic political activity tend to be underemphasized, partly because of a reliance on markets in designing solutions of policy problems. Similarly, community values—especially those at odds with the national, rationalistic, and economic goals—are likewise said to be less often taken seriously by policy analysts. These problems are particularly evident in the courses on methods and techniques offered by the public policy shools and programs; and the humanities offer a potential corrective.[89] Serious substantive policy work, including courses that study policy problems in some depth, is ordinarily somewhat less narrow in its outlook. Members of policy faculties who have shared some or all of these misgivings have over the past several years moved to broaden the range of subjects and perspectives considered in the teaching of policy analysis. More policy problems have been studied in the light of relevant history, and a concern with ethics—little more than embryonic in most policy programs ten years ago—has won some measure of legitimacy in the field. The importance of values has been reasserted. As Garry D. Brewer and Peter deLeon argue, "human values are the crux of the policy sciences; problems for analysis are guided by the society at large, not the theoretical inquiries of the scientific disciplines."[90]

It is hardly surprising that work in history and public policy has been especially strong in the area of foreign policy. How could serious work on our relations with the Soviet Union proceed without reference to the memories that still shape policy, or to options chosen and those foreclosed by previous decisionmakers? Under the guidance of the historian Ernest May, at Harvard, faculty members in at least fourteen institutions have been developing and testing cases designed to sharpen the teaching of history in relation to policy. The "Uses of History" project has put the burden of its effort into foreign policy questions, but cases have also been written on decisions by domestic policymakers and political leaders. That kind of historical work has several values. It can give policymakers examples and images that will help them to recognize crises, to make more accurate and more careful use of historical analogies, and to envisage the costs of insufficient information and the consequences of some kinds of failure. Using real cases rather than hypothetical ones has an important added advantage. The information can help students develop some of the knowledge they should have, but usually do not, about American and world history.[91]

Historical cases narrowly focused on particular policymakers and their decisions may appear too limited, closer to the aspects of history claimed by the social scientists than to what is properly placed within the humanities. It seems, however, that in the hands of competent historians, the histories can have broad and surprising implications, challenging ordinary ways of thinking, illustrating dominant values, suggesting the uncertainties of choice, and showing the con-

The Risks and Benefits of the Historical Perspective

I am glad of the chance to speak to [this Congressional subcommittee] as a professional historian who has reflected a great deal about how history might guide policymakers in all areas of their responsibility, even in the especially complex area of immigration and population.

Though I am enthusiastic about this committee's receptivity to the historical perspective, I must begin with a note of warning. Turning to history for guidance is very likely to mislead you. That is not the fault of history, but of the way it is too frequently seen and used.

It is difficult to imagine a decision that any of us takes which is not shaped by certain assumptions about the past, but we normally take a very simplistic view of what history teaches, and lead ourselves into error.

Professional historians are hardly error-free, but we can tell you that when you ask what our past teaches about heavy in-migration to the United States, especially as that becomes a touchy political and policy question, the easy answers you are likely to get may be quite wrong.

. . . Two very widespread contemporary assumptions, probably valid throughout our historical experience, are now, it seems to me, untenable; things have changed.

The first of these assumptions is that the influx of additional population is beneficial to American society. . . .

The second assumption which our history implants in the contemporary mind is equally false. That is: those who oppose large-scale immigration, who

trolling influence of an ideology or a point of view. An overwhelmingly weak historical sense was evident in the first strong flowering of policy analysis. Its principal mark was a devotion to scientific and rationalistic methodologies; it sought precision and the authoritative backing of science. But there was a price to be paid for that predilection—a loss of touch with concrete human reality.

Yet policy analysis is "analysis" and not final choice or decisionmaking. It is still thinking and not acting. Accordingly, *policymaking* is the arena of action. Here elected and appointed officials fashion and make policy, pass legislation, issue rules, and pronounce juridical decisions. In one sense, that is the realm most remote from the work and traditions of the humanities. It is not at first glance the realm of scholarship, or great texts, or reflective interpretation.

But it is in this arena, finally, that one would most hope to see the cultural force of the humanities, to see whether actions taken reflect high values, display well-tutored moral and historical sensibilities and vision, and advance human welfare and self-understanding. Here "expertise" disappears or is subordinated to values and interests, ideologies and politics. Knowledge is important, but no less important are character and vision. If it is true, as sometimes said, that the people

raise the immigration issue as a subject for "viewing with alarm," must be today, as they were in the distant past, bigots and nativists who did not wish to make room for people different from themselves. But here, too, things have fundamentally changed. . . .

Thus, I would suggest that our history on the immigration issue is a poor guide for contemporary policymakers. The past is often misleading, if we simplistically assume that it repeats itself. . . .

But is there no more that the historian can tell you, beyond that some things have changed, and that the most prominent of these—the population/resource/environmental relationship and the source and nature of contemporary restrictionism—have transformed the issue and require us to look at it in a new way?

Yes, there is much more that can be derived from thinking historically . . . Among other things, the historian can tell you that immigration, unlike most aspects of life, comes to possess a sort of self-renewing momentum.

It tends to perpetuate itself, since immigration more than most human activities is a creature of habit, cuts grooves within which chains of families and friends spread the word that leads to uprooting and movement across national borders.

History most decidedly shows that national policy can interrupt these flows, but the longer one waits to impose resolute policy in this area, the more difficult it becomes. . . .

Thinking historically, rooting one's judgments firmly in a historical context, means much more than merely remembering a string of discrete facts in some chronological order.

The study of the past encourages a holistic view, the integration of isolated issues in the relevant context, and I would urge this upon you.

Otis L. Graham

get the kind of leaders they deserve, then their moral and social formation will show in the kinds of legislators they elect to represent them. If, in one sense, the humanities have the least technically to contribute at the actual policymaking level, in another sense they can have everything to do with the formation of the viewpoints, perspectives, and character of those who actually make the decisions. Those who teach the humanities will have a powerful opportunity to influence future citizens and policymakers; how their sensibilities and thinking are shaped will not be inconsequential for the future of a society.

As this brief survey suggests, there is no reason why there cannot be a plurality of legitimate ways and places for humanists to interact with policy questions and with those who will fashion policy. Yet some hazards must be avoided. The first is that they not play the handmaiden role. There must always be some critical distance between the humanities and the policy process. The second is that humanists not succumb to pretentiousness, either that of believing they have the final wisdom and that theirs is the purer life and vocation, or that of thinking that their disciplinary work has an elegance, thoughtfulness, and rigor that are infinitely superior to the muddling through of the policy process.

Those in the humanities who would grapple with policy issues need on occasion to gain a first-hand taste of political life. The purpose of this would not primarily be to gain credibility in the eyes of those who work out in the world of politics and policy (though that would not hurt), but in order to gain self-understanding and to test the limitations and possibilities of their own disciplines. Professors of humanities are among the few academics who rarely traverse much beyond the academy. Yet they should do so on more occasions, if only because they need to have their own imaginations and disciplinary potentialities stretched. A steady diet of confronting only students and their colleagues may leave humanists intellectually anemic, far more prone to note and comment on each other's work than on those larger human questions that usually provided the fundamental motivation behind their initial attraction to the humanities.

If it is true that much policy analysis and policymaking are in essence oriented toward action, then it is surely possible to agree that there are some basic differences between the sphere of the humanities and that of policy. Nonetheless, there are always two important contributions the humanities have to make. The first is that of the formation of character. The humanities have a central and indispensable role to play in helping by means of insight and understanding to form the traits and virtues necessary for citizens to make sound and sensitive judgments. If policymaking is an art, oriented toward action, then inevitably character, fundamental sensitivities, and basic human decencies will count heavily. The second contribution is that of providing alternative perspectives, frameworks, and vision. An inherent hazard of policy analysis and policymaking is to neglect the larger schemes and problems of human life in order to solve immediate problems and meet short-term demands. The humanities, by reminding citizens of tradition, of ends and purposes, can provide an important and necessary corrective.

6. *Academic Preparation and Disciplinary Standards*

If an applied humanities is to have a viable future, it will be necessary to devise more effective means of educating students to manage the difficult demands that good work requires. Many who now work in applied humanities have had to find their own way, usually lacking any special academic preparation for the applied part of their work; and they have ordinarily also lacked informal tutoring and collegial support. Effective work in applied humanities requires a variety of skills, many of which can seem to be in conflict with each other. As a minimal requirement, a solid education in a humanities discipline is necessary; and sometimes an education in two or more disparate disciplines. The applied humanist must simultaneously demonstrate disciplinary mastery of his or her own field, and yet be able when necessary or desirable to express that mastery in an idiom or way different from the characteristic of the discipline. His or her disciplinary education must be complemented by an understanding of the social, cultural, and political forces that provide the context in which applied humanities must be pursued in actual life and society. Sociological and psychological acuity and sensitivity are critical.

Many of those in applied humanities will move back and forth between an academic and a nonacademic milieu, and between disciplinary and applied work; some will work outside of the academy altogether.[92] There must, then, be an ability to maneuver in different worlds, and to adopt those stances and strategies appropriate to each. Inevitably, diplomatic, oral, and interpersonal skills will come into play for the humanist working outside of the university context—or working within it with those whose disciplinary methodology, and academic styles, are considerably different from those in the humanities. These various demands point to the need for graduate or other training programs that are not less, but more, demanding than for standard academic work in a humanities discipline. Considerable intellectual flexibility and emotional suppleness will be required. That can best be gained by a combination of standard academic training and internships or clerkships designed to impart a range of practical skills to complement intellectual ones.

At present the overwhelming majority of those teaching in applied programs are themselves graduates of traditional programs in the humanities. Many if not most have never been employed outside the university. For the most part they have had to acquire experience in applied work through self-training or interdisciplinary collaboration with colleagues from other departments and schools within their universities. That gap in faculty grounding may disappear within the next few years as more scholars begin to engage in applied activities such as consulting, contract work, and full-time employment for nonuniversity employers. In some programs special efforts have been made to hire new faculty members who are themselves graduates of applied programs and have therefore spent some time doing applied work. But the overall number of humanities scholars with this background is small. At least in the immediate future the bulk of teaching and research in applied humanities programs is likely to be conducted by scholars whose background and socialization in the humanities falls outside the scope of applied work.

The movement toward a greater emphasis on applied work in the humanities has already resulted in some changes in the curriculum of both humanities departments and professional schools. Carnegie-Mellon, Bowling Green State University, Georgetown University, the University of North Carolina, the University of California at Santa Barbara, the University of Colorado, and the University of Tennessee have all instituted programs that allow a student to obtain an advanced degree in applied philosophy or history. The Claremont Graduate School offers a dual degree program in business and one of the humanities (M.B.A. and Ph.D.).

Those programs usually require a student to take both standard courses in their discipline and specialized courses geared toward practical or policy work. To provide the student with first-hand experience they often also require students to particiate in internships for periods that can range from one to six months in a business, hospital, government agency, or private organization. The goal of these programs is to give students both theoretical and practical skills that will allow them to work either as teachers at the undergraduate or profes-

sional school level or, more often, as specialists in tandem with those in business and government. The programs are relatively new; it is thus difficult to know with any certainty whether graduates are in fact able easily to locate such positions.

Many additional schools are now considering instituting special graduate programs with their humanities departments. In some cases, the motive seems to be primarily financial. Yet shrinking enrollments in traditional humanities courses, and hopes for better job placement for graduate students, are not in themselves persuasive rationales for instituting specialized graduate programs in any area. The reality of the present economic situation is that there is for the most part little interest on the part of nonuniversity-based employers in hiring scholars trained specifically in the applied humanities. Moreover, there are no signs of an emergent stronger market in the universities. This situation would seem to indicate that, at present, no need exists for the creation of additional specialty programs in the applied humanities. Moreover, there are a sufficient number of such programs already in existence to afford those interested in pursuing studies in this area a number of educational options.

Some existing programs have tried to achieve a healthy balance between training in applied areas and traditional curricular offerings. Faculty members in many departments have stated that the creation of specialty programs on applied subjects has proven to be of real value for those students and faculty engaged in traditional work. Many in the faculty of the University of North Carolina's history department, for example, report that the creation of the program in public history has provided an opportunity for dialogue between faculty members doing applied and theoretical work that has been mutually beneficial to both varieties of scholars.

On occasion those involved with specialty programs in the applied humanities have been tempted to weaken course requirements in traditional areas in order to accommodate new offerings on applied subjects. But work in any area of the applied humanities requires that students be given a solid foundation in the basics of their discipline. Students ought not be asked to sacrifice traditional training in order to acquire practical skills. It would be preferable to add additional coursework and internships to the existing course of study already required of graduate level students. That requirement points toward the need to lengthen rather than to cut the amount of time spent in graduate training.

Practical experience of the kind to be obtained through participation in an internship in a nonacademic setting is also a valuable component of sound preparation for applied work. Since effective work in applied or policy work is often a function of more than academic qualifications, programs in all areas of the applied humanities should closely monitor student performance in order to help students develop the necessary social and communications skills requisite for such work in many settings. Faculty must realize and acknowledge to their peers and to prospective students that personality and interpersonal skills and, on occasion, intellectual entrepreneurship play important roles in determining who is and is not likely to fare well in applied work. (That, of course, would be comparatively more true of those choosing to pursue a "clinical" role, say, than that of an "enlightenment" approach.)

At the same time, the applied humanities should not be seen by faculty members as a dumping ground for those who cannot meet the requirements of traditional programs in the humanities. The applied humanities should be an acceptable option for those who show interest and aptitude. There are now many scholars devoting all or at least some of their research and professional work to issues in the applied humanities who would not be doing so if they had not encountered a course in this area during their graduate training. The quality of work available on applied topics in philosophy, history, and literature has surely grown to the point where every graduate program in the humanities ought to offer at least one course in this area.

Humanities departments also need to be open and flexible in order to accommodate students who are attempting to do advanced level work in applied areas. Since practical experience can play such a critical role in the education of those in applied areas, departments should be flexible in allowing students to take courses or internships outside traditional departmental settings. Flexibility is also necessary in order to help students design courses of study that meet both existing departmental standards and the requirements of interdisciplinary or interprofessional study. Many departments—such as the philosophy departments at Michigan State University, Brown University, Dartmouth College, and Case Western Reserve University—have constructed special programs and interdisciplinary committees to supervise the work of students who would like to pursue advanced studies in applied areas of philosophy.

While the focus of this report has not been on the employment situation of those employed outside of the university, we should mention a point that sur-

The Moralist as Expert Witness

Courts of law have permitted expert moralists to perform functions ranging from description of community mores, to metaethical analysis of terms and modes of argument, to substantive resolution of normative problems. In the past, this has occurred with little controversy and little recognition that such testimony might present unique problems not presented by more familiar types of expert testimony. It seems likely, moreover, that resort to expert ethicists and moralists will increase as advancing technology, especially in the medical and biomedical sciences, poses human problems never encountered before. Further acceleration may come from the increased readiness of other branches of government to assign major roles in ethical decisionmaking to individuals and groups believed to be expert at moral and policy analysis and from the general trend of courts and attorneys in favoring expert testimony of all sorts under the helpfulness standard. Thus, careful examination of the issues posed by expert ethical testimony is essential. . . . certain types of ethical testimony are far more problematic than others. For example, the law of evidence poses little obstacle to any type of descriptive testimony on questions concerning the morality or immorality of acts or policies according to specified ethical systems, the morality or immorality or acts of poli-

faced repeatedly during our project. Many of those unwillingly forced by economic circumstance to work outside the university report either indifference or hostility to their situations by those still within the academy. They are given neither sympathy nor support, and only rarely are they invited to maintain contact with their university colleagues (or would-be colleagues). Though a milder phenomenon, many within universities who have come to concentrate on applied work report coolness and sometimes scorn on the part of colleagues.

None of these attitudes are productive or helpful. Those working in applied humanities outside of the university need the support and nourishment of those within. Those doing it in the university need the help and standards of their disciplinary peers. Each has something the other can give; and they will be stronger working in a friendly way with each other than in working alone.

Academic and Disciplinary Standards

At the heart of the uncertainty about the uses of the humanities is that of appropriate standards of quality and discipline.[93] Can an "applied humanities" meet customary disciplinary norms? Ought it to try? If not, what might alternative norms be in the application of the humanities to issues outside of the ordinary disciplinary sphere? Many of those who have chosen to focus their efforts in applied humanities have sometimes felt the scorn and suspicion both of their disciplinary colleagues and of those outside the humanities as well. For their part, they often respond with ambivalence. They want to be taken seriously by their peers; and yet, at the same time, they often feel that the standards of evalua-

cies according to most or all moral systems, or the morality or immorality according to contemporary standards in given communities. Expert analysis also may reveal lack of agreement among moral systems about particular questions, leaving the court free to draw its own conclusions. Similarly, metaethical functions such as assisting the court with respect to moral reasoning or analysis seem relatively uncontroversial.

The case is much closer, however, with respect to the ethicist's normative functions—declaring certain actions or rules right or wrong absolutely or determining that one individual rather than another ought to be entrusted with making a moral decision. Review of leading schools of ethical and metaethical thought suggests that expert witnesses drawn from their ranks could serve as acceptable witnesses. Although these various ethical schools analyze moral problems differently, and at times come to disparate conclusions, lack of unanimity need not pose an insurmountable barrier. After all, courts continue to find expert testimony from warring schools of psychiatry, medicine, and art criticism helpful. Yet disagreement on moral questions may exceed that found in other areas, and for that reason, a court might well exclude normative testimony on "state of the art" grounds.

Richard Delgado and Peter G. McAllen

tion being applied to their work are not appropriate and can actually be highly unfair.

What, then, ought to be the standards in attempting to do work in the applied humanities, and in judging the quality of that work? An immediate difficulty in answering that question is that there are any number of possible roles that those with training in the humanities can and do now play. They can use their humanistic discipline to attempt to solve policy or other social problems. They can employ their humanistic background to provide, not solutions, but simply different perspectives and uncommon ways of framing issues. Humanistic training can be also used in a brokerage role, that is, by showing people outside of the humanities that there exist traditional humanistic resources capable of providing them some assistance; and then helping them to make use of those resources.[94] Occasionally, the humanities can be used to provide an antidote in the policy sphere to what seem to be excessively technocratic, or bureaucratic, approaches to problems. Here the humanities play the role of the critic, proposing not so much alternative ways of doing things as a different perspective on the way things are already being done. In short, just as there are a variety of ways for the humanist to work in a public policy or public arena, so too a variety of different standards will be appropriate to those different settings. No single standard is likely to be pertinent to all of them.

There is no doubt that an effort to take the humanities outside of the standard academic-disciplinary context encounters a number of problems and temptations.[95] There is a basic worry about whether there will be an erosion of scholarly standards and of an appropriate detachment. Work that is generated by outside clients or at the instigation of others, or situations in which advocacy seems called for, or where the desire for immediate visible and accessible relevance is strong, all can tempt one to dilute or adulterate the humanities. Inevitably, a philosopher discussing issues of medical ethics with physicians will be forced to speak in a somewhat different manner, and in a somewhat less technical way, than he or she might with his or her own colleagues in philosophy. At the same time, the philosopher could make very little contribution to the physician if there was an insistence upon exactly the same language and standards of rigor appropriate in an exchange with a philosophical colleague.

In part, of course, the same problem is encountered when someone in the hu-manities teaches, say, a freshman level course, where it is not possible or sensible to proceed in exactly the same way that one might deal with graduate students or at a professional meeting. In part also, those nonhumanities professionals who are the recipients of whatever the humanities may have to bring do not have exactly the same needs as a more general audience. Physicians are interested in knowing the contribution that the humanities can make to the care of patients, and policy analysts are often concerned with specific policy issues. Both groups will be concerned principally (as professionals) with the possibilities of application to the issues they encounter rather than the more generally enrich-

The Assumptions and Goals
of Work in the Applied Humanities

The philosophers who have addressed the moral implications of public policy issues have had several goals. At a minimum they have sought to provide intellectual clarification—resolving ambiguities and exposing unnoticed premises and assumptions that occur in public debates over moral issues. A more ambitious goal has been to provide moral arguments for particular positions on these issues, arguments that meet certain standards of coherence, consistency, and logic. These arguments do not necessarily differ radically in nature from those that might be put forward by scholars and other disciplines or might be encountered in journals of opinion, but they have tended to have certain unusual strengths: a critical and questioning approach to received opinion on moral principles; an interest in insuring that the moral premises used in a particular argument cohere with other basic beliefs and hence are part of a unified moral outlook; and a relative lack of partisanship and stridency. These qualities are nothing more than standard virtues of good scholarship; what is unusual is their presence in writing on ethics. The shift in philosophical practice has been premised on the thesis, now somewhat more widely accepted than it was a decade ago, that logic and reasoning are as important in moral debate as in science or other scholarship.

Moral philosophy, then, has endeavored to improve on intuition and sloganeering in an attempt to justify moral views on other than an ad hoc basis; when successful, it has provided rationales rather than rationalizations. These efforts have, however, met with considerable skepticism, both from critics outside of phi-

ing aspects of the humanities that might interest them in their lay role. This is not to say that those in the humanities may not simultaneously stress the more enriching aspects. It is only to say that, in order to make the contribution that can be made, they must inevitably find a way to speak in terms, and with a focus, pertinent to the needs of those to whom they talk.

Arnold Eisenberg, in his introduction to a reissued version of John Dewey's *Theory of the Moral Life* noted how Dewey managed to move back and forth among different levels: "Some passages, befitting the difficulty of their subjects, are more difficult than others; some, too, are exceptionally difficult because De- wey has not seen quite through his subject; but all alike, and in equal measure, represent a student talking to students, a philosopher to philosophers, and a vexed human being to his fellows."[96] That is a tribute of a kind to which anyone working in applied humanities could well aspire.[97]

A good deal of applied work requires the crossing of disciplinary lines. Thus the interdisciplinary character of the work means that some hybrid set of standards often needs to be developed, drawn from those fields to which the humanities address themselves, and from the fields of the humanities as well. Inevitably, it is far more difficult to devise standards for a mixture of two

losophy and from philosophers who were never convinced that the turn to practical issues should have taken place. . . . [Among these doubts] is the feeling . . . that philosophical work on these issues is simply too far removed from mundane reality to have any practical import. Even when engaged in "applied" work on social questions, philosophers typically make numerous idealizing assumptions, speak at a high level of abstraction, and close up shop before spelling out many practical implications of their arguments. The policymaker or interested citizen may be left with the conviction that reading the philosophers' essays cannot effect the decisions and judgments routinely encountered in professional or civic life. . . .

The very qualities of philosophical [writing] that prompt these doubts may also, however, be seen as strengths. Philosophical writing on moral issues aims to improve, in certain respects, on day-to-day ethical reasoning. The chief difference is that we ordinarily take no special pains to insure that our moral judgments are systematic. On occasion we back up our moral views by reference to moral rules, such as the doctors' "First, do no harm." Rarely do we try to defend these rules, or to resolve a conflict among rules, by referring to higher order principles. This is ordinarily just as well, for most of us would quickly find that our moral outlook is not organized according to any consistent principle or set of principles. The assumption underlying much philosophical work on current moral issues, however, is that a reasoned, comprehensive theory of social morality may be achievable; or, at least, that this ideal may be approached much more closely than is usually assumed. To the extent that this goal is pursued, the scope of intuition and ad hoc rationalization is reduced, and at the same time the debate is focused upon the most basic issues underlying the public debate.

Daniel Wikler

fields than it is for work within one field alone. They are more likely to be characterized by an acceptable process than by a test of outcomes. One must simultaneously try to satisfy different standards, and frequently enough what will satisfy one will not satisfy the other. That is an inescapable tension, but one that will vary with context.

Nonetheless, despite the context-dependent nature of any viable standards for applied humanities, some general norms can be suggested. First, those who attempt to convey the knowledge that the humanities have gained ought to do so in a way that does not compromise the complexity, uncertainty, or nature of the knowledge being conveyed. While it may not always be pertinent or possible to transmit the fullness of disciplinary rigor, it is important that the need for rigor be noted and exposed; that listeners be informed that problems are often more difficult than can be conveyed in brief summaries; and that the findings of the humanities ought to be taken as secure or insecure depending upon the solidity of the evidence and argument available to support them. It is acceptable, indeed necessary on occasion, to find ways of speaking in nontechnical terms, and of adapting the insights and knowledge of the humanities to audiences without professional background in those fields. What is not acceptable is to ignore, or to pass over without notice, the fact that there may be debates and complications within the humanities on those topics, and that in the end there are no simple ways of dealing with many of them.

Second, it will be vital for those in the humanities working with other fields and disciplines to maintain their own critical detachment. While a principal purpose of the applied humanities will be to serve public and social needs, those needs cannot be allowed to manipulate, or alter, the standards of what counts as good work in the humanities. In particular, while a stance of advocacy is by no means always inappropriate, it ought to be made clear that the taking of such a position must not be done in ways that harm good scholarship, or the necessity for integrity in seeking the truth.

Third, there will be occasions when an effort must be made to advance the state of humanistic scholarship in particular areas of public life and public policy. In those cases, the full rigor of a disciplinary approach will be appropriate, and it will not be possible to allow those who are doing such work to evade customary disciplinary standards. In other words, if there is a desire to deal in a strictly historical or philosophical way with a difficult issue of public policy, then that issue must be dealt with in the light of the highest standards of those fields. It will, of course, not always be possible readily to distinguish among efforts to advance a technical argument, to simply perform a bridging function between the humanities and other fields for the sake of clarification, or to provide humanistic knowledge for the general background enlightenment of those working in professional or public life. The categories will often overlap, but the important point is that the appropriate standards for the nature of the work ought to be determined by those in the humanities and then rigorously respected.

There is probably no way that those doing work in applied humanities can avoid encountering or evoking the suspicion and reservations of their more discipline-oriented colleagues. By working with issues that are perhaps not common to those colleagues, or of little interest to them, and doing so in ways that may depart from the standard styles or norms of academic discourse, they will be inviting criticism. The attraction of applied humanities in part is that of breaking stereotypical notions of "good scholarship," of implicitly protesting on occasion at the narrowly scholastic framework of much disciplinary work, and of finding a way to keep alive and vigorous the possibilities of the humanities to illuminate contemporary life and issues. Too rigid an adherence to disciplinary norms will dissipate those possibilities; too lax an adherence runs the risk of trivializing and debasing the humanities.

Particularly in the policy area, an applied humanities must seek to genuinely address a social issue in the terms in which it arises; but it must simultaneously try to respond to the real and perhaps hidden or repressed needs that generate the issue. The very process of bringing humanities perspectives and methods to bear may necessitate a redefinition of the issues, just as it may generate conflict with those from other disciplines. If they are to be helpful, the humanities should on occasion generate debate over appropriate policy interpretations and strategies; their perspectives are likely to be different. At the same time they must struggle with the dual temptation to reduce the issue to one manageable by standard disciplinary means (what might be termed "disciplinary reductionism"), or to limit the humanities' role to adding a faint cultural polish as an afterthought. Those from the humanities, in other words, will have to struggle on occasion as much with themselves as they will with others. Both struggles are equally important.

7. The Humanities: Hopes, Problems, and Needs

A popular belief is that science has the unique task of and capacity for defining and characterizing reality. The "reality" at the heart of that belief is empirical: that which we see, feel, and hear; and that which, with enough investigation, can be codified in elegant theory, verifiable laws, and predictable futures. Properly modified and manipulated, the realities discovered by science can be turned to the improvement of human life. An equally strong belief is that the humanities do not deal with reality at all. Their domain is the imaginative (literature), the speculative (philosophy), the spiritual (religion), the traditional (history), or the evocative (rhetoric or linguistics).

There is enough truth in those popular conceptions to give them a certain credibility, and often enough within the fields themselves. The humanities make no claims about their ability to devise empirical probabilities about the agitations of matter; and the sciences do not pretend to offer interpretations of comedy and tragedy. Yet the unhappy consequence of the dichotomous notion of "reality" underlying the supposed gap between the sciences and the humanities is to relegate the humanities to a lesser, not altogether potent role in our society. Their residual handmaiden task has been to provide palatable meaning and reassuring succor in the face of a world properly (even if sometimes hazardously) changed, manipulated, and modified by the powerful engine of science and technology. On occasion, to be sure, the humanities may be expected to adopt the stance of the prophet, calling a forgetful and wayward people back to their roots and originating values. But even that role is one of response and reaction, not control and initiation. That is not a reassuring or invigorating picture. In response, a powerful motive behind the fresh rise of an applied humanities has been a desire to change the balance of intellectual power and initiative. A wide range of questions have been placed on the agenda of the humanities.

Must the humanities relinquish the future direction of human life to the sciences? Need the allegedly soft insights of the humanities defer to the putatively hard data of the empiricists? And should not the canard that the humanities have staked out the realm of the "soft," and the sciences that of the "hard," itself be laid to rest? Ought not the humanities believe that theirs is the stuff of vigor, potency, energy, and initiative? Do not the humanities have the capacity to offer modes of understanding and analysis that can change our dreams and visions, and thus our history? Do not the humanities tutor our imaginations to dare the belief that meaning can be found and sense made of things? Do they not commend us to continue, whatever the negative odds, the search for moral wisdom, aesthetic sensibility, and political community? Do they not, in brief, forever challenge comfortable notions of just what counts as "reality," endlessly pushing us to those deepest and most ultimate questions that can finally and only be addressed by the humanities?

To each of those questions the applied humanities have responded with an enthusiastic cheer of affirmation. On occasion the enthusiasm no doubt runs away with itself, losing touch with the more enduring traditions and cautionary tales that have undergirded the mainline work of the academic disciplines. On occasion as well, the adulteration brought by ideology, political tendentiousness, self-righteous hectoring, and trendy hypes have induced doubts about the integrity of the interest. The partial justice of such accusations should not, however, obscure the powerful belief in and commitment to the humanities that is at the heart of the effort to find a way to reassert their indispensable value in human affairs.

The task that Congress specified in establishing the National Endowment for the Humanities remains fundamentally valid, that of fostering a constant human movement back and forth among the past, the present, and the future—the traditional, the pragmatic, and the utopian. If the humanities preserve the legacy of humankind in the great texts of the past, they no less provide ways to set the demands of the present against a dead hand from the past; and to help know the difference between the living and the dead. If the humanities provide the makings of a vision of the future, they can also provide the moral constraints that would refuse to sacrifice the rights and dignity of the living for the sake of those to be. Yet the humanities also provide the ingredients to struggle against that radical form of narcissistic individualism that would ignore the lessons of the past or the moral, sometimes self-denying demands of the future.

That complex dialectic of vision and criticism, of enthusiastic hope and sober analysis, of tight logic and bold imagination, allows and invites the fruitful application of the humanities to human affairs. It allows it by a denial that the humanities are irrelevant to either ordinary lives, on the one hand, or to the highest matters of state, on the other. It invites it by an affirmation that without the intervention of the humanities—that is, without the filtered and refined knowledge and wisdom contained in the great texts—neither private lives nor public affairs will have the kind of guidance they urgently require.

To keep that guidance at too great a distance—confined exclusively to the classroom, the professional meeting, or the scholarly journal—risks turning the legacy of the humanities into a too-precious, too-delicate flower, fit to be viewed only under glass. Yet the guidance, to be fully effective, must take care that it not wholly close the distance between the humanities and the flux and flow of daily life, public or private. For if they are to serve well, the engaged detachment that is a mark as well of the humanities must be allowed a full play—engaged because the subject matter of human life in its richness and complexity is too serious for any other stance, but detached in that the aim is depth and understanding, not merely immediate reaction and spontaneous feeling.

The special difficulty and challenge for those who would pursue an application of the humanities will be to preserve a sensible and sensitive balance. They will have to do justice to the humanities in the full rigor of the best possible scholarship. They will have to know when, and how, to adapt that legitimate demand to the need for public intelligibility and literary felicity; and to do so without compromising the scholarship. They will have to discover how to become passionately involved with those social, cultural, and political issues that invite the contribution of the humanities. They will also have to learn how to curb that involvement when necessary, saving it from an uncritical response that would compromise the integrity of the humanities. They must learn how to prod, or nag, or goad, the disciplinary humanities to recollect their animating origins, and their potential bite and impact beyond the academy. They must also be willing to speak sharply against an application of the humanities that is nothing more than a faddish baptism of this or that currently popular cause or value or a thoughtless service of transitory power.

That is a large and difficult set of demands, not at once made instantly compatible or congenial. Its joint achievement requires constant work and self-criticism. No less necessary will be a constant interchange among those in the different branches of the humanities, and between those in the humanities and those in other disciplines; and then with the general public. All the while there must be a constant mindfulness of those human aspirations and needs that have forever fed the humanities: to make sense of things, to find out how life should be led, and to discover that which should be hoped for and how it ought to be pursued. No one should ever be able to say that the goals of an applied humanities are easily attainable. Instead, they call the humanities to a new level of demand, one filled with hazards, but no less filled with high possibility, both for the present and the future.

Notes

1. This report does not directly explore the contributions of the humanities to the life of the individual. Instead, our particular concern is that of their role in the common, public life of society. That emphasis should in no way be construed as a desire to slight the valuable place of the former. The humanities will significantly influence society through their shaping of the character, mind, and imagination of individuals.

2. See Memorandum of December 3, 1980, from Joseph Duffey, former Chairman of the NEH, to "Members of the National Council of the Humanities and Others," which also contains relevant excerpts from the Heritage Foundation Documents.

3. Richard Wasserstrom, " 'Justification' and State Humanities Programs," *Federation Reports* 2 (June 1979): 29–36.

4. While not denying the pertinence of the humanities to public policy issues, William J. Bennett, Chairman of the National Endowment for the Humanities, has been critical of a tendency by some to believe "that the humanities can be applied on a case-by-case basis to resolve political controversies and improve social conditions" (from "The Public Life of the Humanities," paper delivered on January 14, 1983, to American Conference of Academic Deans). See also Robert Hollander, "Serving Two Masters," in VHEPP, Newsletter of the Virginia Foundation for the Humanities and Public Policy, Winter 1981–82; and, by the same author, "State Committees Should Emphasize 'Real Humanities,' " *Humanities Report* 4 (February 1982): 2–3.
For some more general discussions of the nature of the humanities, cf. Walter Kaufmann, *The Future of the Humanities* (New York: Thomas Y. Crowell, 1977); O.B. Hardison, *Toward Freedom and Dignity: The Humanities and the Ideal of Humanity* (Baltimore: Johns Hopkins Press, 1972); Ernst Cassirer, *The Logic of the Humanities* (New Haven: Yale University Press, 1960); "The Future of the

Humanities," *Daedalus* (Summer, 1969) and "Theory in Humanistic Study," *Daedalus* (Spring, 1970); Michael Mooney and Florian Stuber, *Small Comforts for Hard Times: Humanists on Public Policy* (New York: Columbia University Press, 1977); R.S. French and J.D. Moreno, *The Public Humanities* (Washington, D.C.: George Washington University, 1984).

5. A good account of the relationship between the National Endowment for the Humanities and the State Humanities Councils on the subject of the humanities and public policy can be found in Todd S. Phillips, "The Humanities and Public Policy, or: Whatever Happened to a Worthy Idea?" *Federation Reports* (January–February 1983), pp. 20–27. In its 1970 reauthorizing legislation for the NEH, Congress said that the humanities should be studied "with particular attention to the relevance of the humanities to the current conditions of national life." Quoted in Morton Sosna, "National Endowment for the Humanities (NEH)," in Donald R. Witnah, ed., *Government Agencies* (Westport, Conn.: Greenwood Press, 1983), p. 334.

6. Arthur C. Danto, "Toward a Definition of the Humanities," *Proceedings of the General Education Seminar*, Columbia University, 9 (1981): 9–14.

7. Quoted in Robert Hollander, "Serving Two Masters," p. 1.

8. Carleton B. Chapman, "On the Definition and Teaching of the Medical Ethic," *New England Journal of Medicine* 301: 12 (September 20, 1979): 630–34.

9. See, for example, M. Lilla, "Ethos, 'Ethics' and Public Service," *The Public Interest* 63 (Spring 1981): 3–17; P. Drucker, "Ethical Chic," *Forbes*, (Sept. 14, 1981) pp. 159–63; J. Peter Euben, "Philosophy and the Professions," *Democracy* 1 (April 1981): 112–27; and C. Noble, "Ethics and Experts," *Working Papers* 7 (July/August 1980): 57–60.

10. This section is particularly indebted to Martha Nussbaum's paper, "Historical Conceptions of the Humanities and their Relationship to Society," in Daniel Callahan, Arthur L. Caplan, and Bruce Jennings, eds.,

Applying the Humanities (New York: Plenum Press, forthcoming, 1985).

11. For detailed studies of the cultural transformations that took place during the Athenian "enlightenment" of the 5th and 4th centuries B.C. see: Werner Jaeger, *The Ideals of Greek Culture*, 2nd ed. 3 vols. (New York: Oxford University Press, 1945); Arthur W. H. Adkins, *Merit and Responsibility* (Oxford: Oxford University Press, 1960); and Eric A. Havelock, *Preface to Plato* (New York: Grosset & Dunlap, 1967).

12. For a discussion of the complex relationship between the public and the private missions of philosophy in Plato's work see Sheldon S. Wolin, *Politics and Vision* (Boston: Little, Brown, 1960), pp. 28–68.

13. Cf. Wolin, *Politics and Vision*, pp. 69–94.

14. Nussbaum, "Historical Conceptions of the Humanities and Their Relationship to Society."

15. For surveys of renaissance humanism that have guided the very general assessment offered in this report see Nicola Abbagano, "Renaissance Humanism," in Philip P. Weiner, ed., *Dictionary of the History of Ideas*, 4 vols. (New York: Charles Scribner's Sons, 1973), 4: 129–36; and Peter Herde, "Humanism in Italy," in ibid., 2: 515–24. These articles give basic bibliographical references to the vast scholarly literature on this period.

16. J. G. A. Pocock, *The Machiavellian Moment* (Princeton: Princeton University Press, 1975). Cf. also Quentin Skinner, *The Foundations of Modern Political Thought*, 2 vols. (Cambridge: Cambridge University Press, 1978), who, in contrast to Pocock, emphasizes the Stoic rather than the Aristotelian influences on Renaissance humanism.

17. Nannerl O. Keohane, *Philosophy and the State in France* (Princeton: Princeton University Press, 1980).

18. The relationship between Renaissance and Reformation thought is pursued in greater detail in David Little, "Storm Over the Humanities: The Sources of Conflict," in *Applying the Humanities.*

19. The clearest and most extreme formulation of this perspective was developed in the work of Thomas Hobbes. Cf. J. W. N. Watkins, *Hobbes' System of Ideas* (New York: Barnes & Noble, 1968).

20. The general issue of individualism and the humanities is explored more fully in Robert N. Bellah, "The Humanities and Social Vision," in *Applying the Humanities.*

21. See Lionel Trilling, *Sincerity and Authenticity* (Cambridge, Mass.: Harvard University Press, 1972); Isaiah Berlin, *Against the Current* (New York: Viking, 1980), pp. 1–24, 80–110; and Charles Taylor, *Hegel* (Cambridge: Cambridge University Press, 1975), pp. 3–50. For a more complete account of the philosophical sources and implications of romanticism, see M. H. Abrams, *The Mirror and the Lamp* (Oxford: Oxford University Press, 1953) and *Natural Supernaturalism* (New York: Norton, 1971).

22. Cf. Quentin Anderson, *The Imperial Self* (New York: Alfred A. Knopf, 1971).

23. P. O. Kristeller, "Philosophy and Learning," *Minerva* 18 (1980): 313–33.

24. Michael J. Sandel, *Liberalism and the Limits of Justice* (New York: Cambridge University Press), p. 22.

25. This topic is pursued in greater detail in Bruce Kuklick, "The Professionalization of the Humanities," in *Applying the Humanities.*

26. See Carol S. Gruber, *Mars and Minerva: World War I and the Uses of the Higher Learning in America* (Baton Rouge: Louisiana State University Press, 1975).

27. Laurence Veysey, "The Plural Organized Worlds of the Humanities," in Alexander Oleson and John Voss, eds., *The Organization of Knowledge in Modern America* (Baltimore: Johns Hopkins Press, 1979), pp. 51–106.

28. James M. Gustafson, "Basic Ethical

Issues in the Bio-Medical Fields," *Soundings* 52 (1970): 151–80; and L. B. de Graaf, *Survey of the Historical Professions: Public Historians* (Washington: American Historical Association, 1981).

29. Douglas Sloan, "The Teaching of Ethics in the American Undergraduate Curriculum," in Daniel Callahan and Sissela Bok, eds., *Ethics Teaching in Higher Education* (New York: Plenum Press, 1980), pp. 1–57.

30. For some indications of the possibilities for applied ethics growing out of this tradition (broadly defined), see: Frederick A. Olafson, *Principles and Persons: An Ethical Interpretation of Existentialism* (Baltimore: Johns Hopkins University Press, 1967); William F. May, *The Physician's Covenant: Images of the Healer in Medical Ethics* (Philadelphia: The Westminster Press, 1983); and the special issue of *Philosophy and Social Criticism* 9: 3–4 (1983) on "Ethics and Social Theory."

31. Cf. Charles L. Bosk, *Forgive and Remember: Managing Medical Failure* (Chicago: University of Chicago Press, 1979); and Renée Fox and Judith Swazey, *The Courage to Fail* (Chicago: University of Chicago Press, 1974).

32. Richard Rorty, *Consequences of Pragmatism* (Minneapolis: University of Minnesota Press, 1982).

33. See Bruce Kuklick, *The Rise of American Philosophy* (New Haven: Yale University Press, 1977), p. 572: "Like most academics, philosophers spent their time in administration, in committee work, in placing graduate students, in organizing conferences, and in running journals. When narrow professionals turned to their scholarship, they thought of their work as a game. For a few, professional philosophy had become a way, not of confronting the problem of existence, but of avoiding it."

34. Cf. Carl Wellman, "Ethics Since 1950," *Journal of Value Inquiry* 6 (1972): 83–90.

35. Marcus G. Singer, "Recent Trends and Future Prospects in Ethics," *Metaphilosophy* 12 (1981): 207–23.

36. Louis I. Katzner, "Applied Philosophy and the Role of the Philosopher," *Applied Philosophy* (Fall 1982): 31–38; and Daniel Wikler, "Philosophical Perspectives on Access to Health Care: An Introduction," in the President's Commission for the Study of Ethical Problems in Medicine and Biomedical and Behavioral Research, *Securing Access to Health Care*, 2 (Washington, D.C.: Government Printing Office, 1983).

37. Stephen Toulmin, "How Medicine Saved the Life of Ethics," *Perspectives in Biology and Medicine* 25 (Summer 1982): 736–50.

38. See, for example, Norman E. Bowie, "Applied Philosophy: Its Meaning and Justification," *Applied Philosophy* 1 (Spring 1982): 1–18; and Bernard Gert, "Licensing Professionals," *Business and Professional Ethics Journal* 1 (Summer 1982).

39. See Jerome B. Schneewind, "Applied Ethics and the Sociology of the Humanities," in *Applying the Humanities*.

40. Arguments concerning this point can be found in Stanley Hauerwas and Alasdair MacIntyre, eds., *Revisions: Changing Perspectives in Moral Philosophy* (Notre Dame: University of Notre Dame Press, 1983).

41. William F. May, "Professional Ethics: Setting, Terrain, and Teacher," in *Ethics Teaching in Higher Education*, pp. 205–41.

42. This section draws upon the paper by Fred Nicklason, "Applied Humanities Inside and Outside the Academy: A Personal Case of Applied History," in *Applying the Humanities*.

43. Peter N. Stearns, "Applied History: Policy Roles and Standards for Historians," in *Applying the Humanities*.

44. See Ernest May, *Lessons of the Past: The Use and Misuse of History in American Foreign Policy* (New York, 1973); Seymour Mandelbaum, "The Past in Service to the Future," *Journal of Social History* 11 (1977): 193–205; Peter N. Stearns, "History and Policy Analysis: Toward Maturity," *The Public Historian* 4 (1982): 5–29; David F. Trask, "Historians and

Teamwork: The Case of Crisis Management," *American Historical Association Newsletter* 19 (1981): 6–7; Joel A. Tarr, ed., *Retrospective Technology Assessment* (San Francisco: San Francisco Press, 1977); James McCurley, "The Historians' Role in the Making of Public Policy," *Social Science History* 3 (1979): 202–207; Joel A. Tarr, "Changing Fuel Use Behavior and Energy Transitions: The Pittsburgh Smoke Control Movement, a case study in historical analogy," *Journal of Social History* 14 (1981): 561–88.

45. See the journal, *The Public Historian*.

46. Michael C. Robinson, "Retrospective Management Analysis: A Test Case," *Public Works Historical Society*, 1981, pp. 4–6; Thomas W. Riley and John G. Adorjan, "Company History—A By-Product of Good Records Management," *ARMA Quarterly*, October 1981, pp. 5–8; Dan J. Forrestal, "Playing It Straight with Company Histories," *Public Relations Journal*, February 1978, pp. 27–28; Alexander Barrie, "Why Sponsor a Company History?" *Business World*, December 1977, pp. 15–16; G.D. Smith and Laurence E. Steadman, "Present Value of Corporate History," *Harvard Business Review* 6 (November–December 1981): 164–73; Margaret Price, "Corporate Historians: A Rare but Growing Breed," *Industry Week*, March 23, 1981, pp. 87–90.

47. See "Special Issue on Applied History," *Journal of Social History* 14 (1981): 533–738.

48. David J. Rothman and Stanton Wheeler, eds., *Social History and Social Policy* (New York: Academic Press, 1981).

49. On the relationship of applied history to advances in conventional history, see Michael Kammen, ed., *The Past Before Us* (Ithaca: Cornell University Press, 1980).

50. For an informative discussion of the problem of "quick and dirty" research, see Mark H. Moore, "Social Science and Policy Analysis: Some Fundamental Differences," and the response by Kenneth Prewitt, "Subverting Policy Premises," in Daniel Callahan and Bruce Jennings, eds., *Ethics, the Social Sciences, and Policy Analysis* (New York: Plenum Press, 1983).

51. We are particularly indebted to Martha Nussbaum for her contribution to this section.

52. Cf. Robert Gorham Davis, "The New Criticism and the Democratic Tradition," *The American Scholar* 19 (Winter 1949–50); and George H. Nash, *The Conservative Intellectual Movement in America* (New York: Basic Books, 1976), chap. 3.

53. For a provocative discussion, see Gerald Graff, *Literature Against Itself: Literary Ideas in Modern Society* (Chicago: University of Chicago Press, 1979). For a more detailed assessment of the New Criticism and its legacy, see Frank Lentricchia, *After the New Criticism* (Chicago: Univerity of Chicago Press, 1980).

54. Cf. the issue of *Critical Inquiry* (September 1982) devoted to "The Politics of Interpretation."

55. Ronald Dworkin, "Law as Interpretation," *Critical Inquiry* (September 1982), pp. 179–200; and Stanley Fish, "Working on the Chain Gang: Interpretation in the Law and in Literary Criticism," ibid. pp. 201–16. Cf. also Sanford Levinson, "On Dworkin, Kennedy, and Ely: Decoding the Legal Past," *Partisan Review*, Vol. LI, No. 2 (1984), pp. 248–64.

56. This section is particularly indebted to Edwin T. Layton's paper, "Theory and Application in Science and the Humanities," in *Applying the Humanities*.

57. See, for example, Charles E. Lindblom and David Cohen, *Usable Knowledge* (New Haven: Yale University Press, 1979); Carol Weiss, *Using Social Research in Public Policy Making* (Lexington, Mass.: Lexington Books, 1977).

58. James S. Coleman, "Policy Research in the Social Sciences" (Morristown, N.J.: General Learning Press, 1972), p. 22.

59. Robert N. Mayer, "Social Science and Institutional Change" (Rockville, Md.: National Institute of Mental Health, n.d.).

60. Cf. Arthur L. Caplan, "Mechanics on Duty: The Limitations of a Technical Defini-

tion of Moral Expertise for Work in Applied Ethics," *Canadian Journal of Philosophy*, supp. vol. 8 (1982), pp. 1–17.

61. Alvin W. Gouldner, "Theoretical Requirements of the Applied Social Sciences," *American Sociological Review* 22 (February 1957): 92–102.

62. See "Philosophers in Medical Centers," *Hastings Center Report* 11 (April 1981): 12–22.

63. The relationship between the humanities and social vision is developed more fully in Robert N. Bellah, "The Humanities and Social Vision," in *Applying the Humanities*.

64. Lionel Trilling, *Beyond Culture* (New York: Harcourt Brace Jovanovich, 1965), p. 97.

65. See Daniel Yankelovich, *New Rules: Searching for Self-Fulfillment in a World Turned Upside Down* (New York: Random House, 1981).

66. Cf. Daniel Callahan, "Tradition and the Moral Life," in *Hastings Center Report* 12 (December 1982), pp. 23–30; and Bruce Jennings, "Tradition and the Politics of Remembering," *The Georgia Review* 36 (Spring 1982): 167–82.

67. This section is particularly indebted to the paper by Eric Cassell, M.D., "The Humanities and the Biomedical Sciences," in *Applying the Humanities*.

68. See, for example, Joseph Ceccio, ed., *Medicine in Literature* (English and Humanities series) (New York: Longman, 1978); Norman Cousins, ed., *The Physician in Literature* (Philadelphia: W. B. Saunders, 1982); Enid Rhodes Peschel, ed., *Medicine and Literature* (New York: Neale Watson Academic Publications, 1980); Joanne Trautmann, ed., *Healing Arts in Dialogue: Medicine and Literature* (Carbondale, Ill.: Southern Illinois University Press, 1981); G. S. Rousseau, "Literature and Medicine: The State of the Field," *Isis* 72 (September 1981): 406–24.

69. See especially Edmund D. Pellegrino and Thomas K. McElhinney, eds., *Teaching Ethics, the Humanities, and Human Values in Medical School: A Ten-Year Overview* (Washington, D.C.: Society for Health and Human Values, 1982).

70. See, for example, the journals, *Hastings Center Report, Journal of Medical Ethics, Journal of Medicine and Philosophy, Literature and Medicine*; and John Arras, ed., *Ethical Issues in Modern Medicine* (Palo Alto: Mayfield, 1983); Marc D. Basson, ed., *Ethics, Humanism, and Medicine* (New York: Alan R. Liss, 1980); 1st of a series by same title; vol. 4 now published; Tom L. Beauchamp and Terry P. Pinkard, eds., *Ethics and Public Policy* (Englewood Cliffs, N.J.: Prentice-Hall, 1983); Samuel Gorovitz, et al., eds., *Moral Problems in Medicine* (Englewood Cliffs, N.J.: Prentice-Hall, 1976); James M. Humber and Robert F. Almeder, *Biomedical Ethics and the Law* (New York: Plenum Press, 1979); James L. Muyskens, *Moral Problems in Nursing: A Philosophical Investigation* (Totowa: Rowman & Littlefield, 1982); Robert M. Veatch, *A Theory of Medical Ethics* (New York: Basic Books, 1981).

71. Sir William Osler, "On the Need of a Radical Reform in Our Methods of Teaching Medical Students," *Medical News* 82 (1903): 49–53.

72. See Eric J. Cassell, "The Place of the Humanities in Medicine," in *Applying the Humanities*.

73. Cf. Stephen Toulmin, "How Medicine Saved the Life of Philosophy," *Perspectives in Biology and Medicine* 24 (1982): 736–50.

74. E. Haavi Morreim, "The Philosopher in the Clinical Setting," *The Pharos* (Winter 1983): 2–6.

75. A. L. Caplan, "Can Applied Ethics Be Effective in Health Care and Should It Strive To Be?" *Ethics* 93 (January 1983): pp. 311–19.

76. See note 62.

77. See *Summing Up*, published by the President's Commission for the Study of Ethical Problems in Medicine and Biomedical and Behavioral Research (Washington, D.C.: Government Printing Office, 1983).

78. This section is particularly indebted to the paper by Bruce Jennings and Kenneth Prewitt, "The Humanities and the Social Sciences: Reconstructing a Public Philosophy," in *Applying the Humanities.*

79. For a succinct account of the break-off of the social sciences from the humanities, see Donald P. Warwick, *The Teaching of Ethics in the Social Sciences* (Hastings-on-Hudson, N.Y.: The Hastings Center, 1980), pp. 23–36.

80. Cf. Gladys Bryson, *Man and Society: The Scottish Inquiry of the Eighteenth Century* (Princeton: Princeton University Press, 1945); and Anthony Giddens, *Capitalism and Modern Social Theory* (Cambridge: Cambridge University Press, 1971).

81. Cf. Paul Rabinow and William M. Sullivan, eds., *Interpretive Social Science: A Reader* (Berkeley, Calif.: University of California Press, 1979); and Fred R. Dallmayr and Thomas A. McCarthy, eds., *Understanding and Social Inquiry* (Notre Dame, Ind.: University of Notre Dame Press, 1977). For general discussions of this approach and its relationship to positivism, see Richard Bernstein, *The Restructuring of Social and Political Theory* (New York: Harcourt Brace Jovanovich, 1976); J. Donald Moon, "The Logic of Political Inquiry: A Synthesis of Opposed Perspectives," in *Handbook of Political Science*, ed. by Fred I. Greenstein and Nelson W. Polsby, 1 (Reading, Mass.: Addison-Wesley Publishing Co., Inc., 1975): 131–228; Brian Fay, *Social Theory and Political Practice* (London: George Allen & Unwin, 1975); and Norma Haan, et al., eds., *Social Science as Moral Inquiry* (New York: Columbia University Press, 1983).

82. For an account that brings out these underlying affinities between the humanities and the social sciences, see Frederick A. Olafson, *The Dialectic of Action* (Chicago: University of Chicago Press, 1979).

83. A. O. Hirschman, "Morality and the Social Sciences: A Durable Tension," in *Essays in Trespassing* (Cambridge: Cambridge University Press, 1981), pp. 294–306.

84. Clifford Geertz, "Blurred Genres: The Refiguration of Social Thought," *The American Scholar* 49 (Spring 1980): pp. 165–79.

85. Bruce Jennings, "Interpretive Social Science and Policy Analysis," in Daniel Callahan and Bruce Jennings, eds., *Ethics, the Social Sciences and Policy Analysis* (New York: Plenum Press, 1983), pp. 3–36.

86. This section draws upon the papers by Bruce L. Payne, "Policy Analysis and the Humanities," and Daniel Callahan, "The Humanities and Public Policy," in *Applying the Humanities.*

87. See William J. Bennett, "The Public Life of the Humanities."

88. A member of our editorial committee, Otis Graham, Jr., believes that "policymaking" should be understood as the basic category and should thus not be conflated with what was described above as "public policy."

89. Cf. Joel L. Fleishman and Bruce L. Payne, *Ethical Dilemmas and the Education of Policymakers* (Hastings-on-Hudson, N.Y.: The Hastings Center, 1980); David G. Smith, "Policy Analysis and Liberal Arts," in William D. Coplin, ed., *Teaching Policy Studies* (Lexington, Mass.: Lexington Books, 1978), pp. 37–43; Martin H. Krieger, "The Critique of Poor Reason: Using Literature to Teach Analysts," *Policy Analysis* 5 (Fall 1979): 505–20; William C. Havard, "Policy Sciences, the Humanities, and Political Coherence," in Francis Canavan, ed., *The Ethical Dimension of Political Life* (Durham, N.C.: Duke University Press, 1983).

90. Garry D. Brewer and Peter deLeon, *The Foundations of Policy Analysis* (Homewood, Ill.: Dorsey, 1983), p. 6.

91. Gordon Craig, "The Historian and the Study of International Relations," *The American Historical Review* 88 (February 1983): 1–11; see also his "On the Nature of Diplomatic History: The Relevance of Some Old Books," in *Diplomacy: New Approaches in History, Theory, and Policy*, Paul Gordon Lauren, ed. (New York: The Free Press, 1979), pp. 21–42; Ernest R. May, *"Lessons" of the Past: The use and Misuse of History in American Foreign Policy* (New York: Oxford University Press, 1973); Peter N. Stearns, "History and Policy Analysis: Toward Maturity," *The Public Historian* 4 (Summer 1982): 5–29; David J. Roth-

man, *The Discovery of the Asylum: Social Order and Disorder in the New Republic* (Boston: Little, Brown, 1971); David J. Rothman and Stanton Wheeler, eds., *Social History and Social Policy* (New York: Academic Press, 1981), pp. 1–18.

92. See "Ph.D. Employment Shifts Toward Nonacademic Sector," in *Humanities Highlights* 5: 1 (October 21, 1983).

93. See Jerome Schneewind, "Applied Ethics and the Sociology of the Humanities," in *Applying the Humanities*.

94. This section draws upon the papers by Ruth Macklin, "Intellectual Standards in the Humanities: Philosophy"; Peter N. Stearns, "Applied History: Policy Roles and Standards for Historians"; Otis L. Graham, Jr., "Intellectual Standards in the Humanities: A Response"; Katherine Hunter, "Literature and Medicine: Standards for Applied Literature"; and Fred Nicklason, "Applied Humanities Inside and Outside the Academy: A Case of Applied History," in *Applying the Humanities*.

95. R. Delgado and P. McAllen, "The Moralist as Expert Witness," *Boston University Law Review* 62 (July 1982): 869–926.

96. Arnold Eisenberg, "Editor's Introduction" to John Dewey, *Theory of the Moral Life* (New York: Irvington Publishers, 1980), pp. iii–iv.

97. See also A. Altman, "Pragmatism and Applied Ethics," *American Philosophical Quarterly* 20 (April 1983): 227–35.

Citations for Boxed Quotations

Some of the material used in the boxes was taken from the following publications:

Norman Bowie, "Applied Philosophy—Its Meaning and Justification," *Applied Philosophy,* Vol. I, No. 1 (Spring, 1982), pp. 10-11.

Carleton B. Chapman, "Medical Ethics," *New England Journal of Medicine,* September 20, 1979, p. 633.

Richard Delgado and Peter G. McAllen, "Moralist as Expert Witness," *Boston University Law Review,* Vol. 62, 1982, pp. 923, 925.

Charles Frankel, "Why the Humanities?" *Ideas,* Vol. I (Winter, 1979), pp. 2-3; 13.

Otis L. Graham, Jr., Testimony before House Subcommitte on Census and Population, U.S. Congress, House of Representatives Committee on Post Office and Civil Service: Subcommittee on Census and Population. *Hearings.* April 27-28, 1981. Washington: GPO, 1981, pp. 49, 50, 51.

Gilbert Harman. *The Nature of Morality.* New York: Oxford University Press, 1977, pp. viii-ix.

Louis I. Katzner, "Applied Philosophy and the Role of the Philosopher," *Applied Philosophy,* Vol. I, No. 2 (Fall, 1983), pp. 32-33.

Richard Lewis, "Literature and Public Policy," *Federation Reports,* Vol. VII, No. 2 (March/ April, 1984), pp. 3-4.

John Stuart Mill. *Autobiography.* Indianapolis: Bobbs Merrill, 1957, p 55.

E. Haavi Morreim, "The Philosopher in the Clinical Setting," *The Pharos* (Winter, 1983), pp. 2-3.

Hilary Putnam, "Taking Rules Seriously—A Response to Martha Nussbaum," *New Literary History,* Vol. XV, No. 1 (Autumn, 1983), pp. 195-196.

David J. Rothman and Stanton Wheeler. *Social History and Social Policy.* New York: Academic Press, 1981, pp. 7-8.

Fraser Snowden, "Bringing Philosophy into the Hospital: Notes of a Philosopher-in-Residence," *Applied Philosophy,* Vol. 1, No. 3 (Spring, 1983), pp. 73-74.

Stephen Toulmin, "How Medicine Saved the Life of Ethics," *Perspectives in Biology and Medicine,* Vol. 25, No. 4 (Summer, 1982), p. 737.

Daniel Wikler, "Philosophical Perspectives on Access to Health Care: An Introduction," in President's Commission for the Study of Ethical Problems in Medicine and Biomedical and Behavioral Research. *Securing Access to Health Care.* Vol. II Washington: GPO, 1983, pp. 111-113.

History 7–11

Learning history is remembered by many teachers as a passive process involving 'learning dates.' In this book, the emphasis is on 'doing history' – making sense of the past through the process of investigation – as a true historian would. The authors argue that children should be involved in historical investigations, thus developing the skills and processes that underpin historical understanding. Using an action research approach to improving practice, the 'teacher as historian' theme is introduced through a fascinating case-study of Heinrich Schliemann and his discovery of Troy. The authors' own case-study of 'The Vikings' and teachers' accounts are used to illustrate different teaching approaches which fully involve the children as historians in an imaginative and creative way. Each chapter is supported by exercises and activities which demonstrate how to translate theory into practice, together with a specific focus on the problems of planning and resourcing to produce practical teaching strategies.

Jon Nichol is Director of the History Education Centre and Reader in History and Education at the School of Education, University of Exeter where **Jacqui Dean** is Lecturer in History and Humanities.

Curriculum in primary practice series
General editor: Clive Carré

The Curriculum in primary practice series is aimed at students and qualified teachers looking to improve their practice within the context of the National Curriculum. The large format, easy to use texts are interactive, encouraging teachers to engage in professional development as they read. Each contains:

- Summaries of essential research
- Transcripts of classroom interactions for analysis and discussion
- Activities for individual and group use

While all primary teachers will find these books useful, they are designed with the needs of teachers of the 7 to 11 age group particularly in mind.

Other titles include:

Religious Education 7–11
Terence Copley

Science 7–11
Clive Carré and Carrie Ovens

Music 7–11
Sarah Hennessy

Art 7–11
Linda Green and Robin Mitchell

English 7–11
David Wray

Drama 7–11
Neil Kitson and Ian Spiby

History 7–11

Developing primary teaching skills

Jon Nichol with Jacqui Dean

London and New York

First published 1997
by Routledge
11 New Fetter Lane, London EC4P 4EE

Simultaneously published in the USA and Canada
by Routledge
29 West 35th Street, New York, NY 10001

Typeset in Palatino by Solidus (Bristol) Limited
Printed and bound in Great Britain by Bath Press

British Library Cataloguing in Publication Data
A catalogue record for this book is available from the British Library

Library of Congress Cataloging in Publication Data
Nichol, Jon.
   History 7–11: developing primary teaching skills/Jon Nichol with
      Jacqui Dean.
   p. cm. — (Curriculum in primary practice)
   Includes bibliographical references and index.
   1. History—Study and teaching (Elementary)—Great Britain.
   2. Action research in education—Great Britain. 3. History—Study
      and teaching (Elementary)—Great Britain—Case studies. 4. Action
      research in education—Great Britain—Case studies. 5. Education,
      Elementary—Activity programmes—Great Britain—Case studies.
      6. Vikings—Study and teaching (Elementary)—Great Britain.
      I. Dean, Jacqui. II. Title. III. Series.
   LB1582.G7N53   1997
   372.89'0941—dc20   96-36568
                                                                CIP

ISBN 0–415–13281–9

Contents

Figures

Preface

HOW THIS BOOK IS ORGANISED

History 7-11 is divided into an introduction and seven units. The 'Introduction' develops the idea of you, the teacher, improving your practice through systematically researching it yourself using a technique called 'action research'. The concept of action research permeates the rest of the book.

Unit 1, 'Teachers as historians', focuses on what is involved in being an historian, illustrating this through a case-study of Heinrich Schliemann and his discovery of Troy. Unit 1 argues that children should similarly be involved in historical investigations, thus developing the skills and learning the processes that underpin historical understanding.

Unit 2, 'History for the classroom', uses a case-study of 'The Vikings' to suggest how you can turn the findings of academic historians, their histories, into classroom practice.

In Units 3–5, teachers' accounts illustrate how different teaching approaches involve children in their mental reconstruction of the past. Unit 3, 'Investigating the past and the History Curriculum', argues that we can create and present history from numerous perspectives, such as those of the biographer, local historian, detective, artist and film maker. All share the historian's approach to making sense of the past through the process of investigation, a process we call 'doing history'.

Unit 4, 'Bringing the past to life: history as a creative art', demonstrates how we can get children to enter into the spirit of the past through strategies such as pictorial reconstruction, drama, simulation and story telling. In this unit we examine children's logical, inductive, imaginative and creative historical thinking.

Unit 5, 'Teaching and learning concepts', examines the form which conceptual thinking takes in history and how children can develop their understanding of concepts.

Unit 6, 'History in the curriculum: teaching a History Study Unit and whole-class teaching', applies the thinking in Units 1 to 5 to how we taught the Vikings to our class of 7 and 8 year olds. The unit details how we coped with the problems of planning, resourcing, progression and differentiation to produce practical teaching strategies that worked with real, live children. In particular, it shows how you can use whole-class teaching to teach effectively.

Unit 7, 'Assessment', suggests a user-friendly approach to this problem that should square the vicious educational circle of meeting the needs of pupils and satisfying our latter day Spanish Inquisition, otherwise known as OFSTED, Office for Standards in Education.

HOW YOU CAN USE THIS BOOK

For personal study, in-service and professional studies courses

The text and suggested activities together provide the basis for working by yourself, in teams or for more formal in-service, be it on a Baker Day, lunch-time or twilight session. At each group session it would be useful to discuss ideas in relation to examples from your own experience and that of your pupils.

The book was designed to be flexible and user friendly. The following symbols are used throughout the book to denote:

 quotations from published materials

 activities

 transcripts of children and/or teachers talking

 sources

case studies

Jon Nichol
Jacqui Dean

Acknowledgements

We should like to thank all those who have contributed to this book. In particular we are indebted to the children of St Nicholas School, Exeter, and their teacher Mo Shields with whom we went a'Viking. We should also like to say thanks a million to all the teachers who have participated in our in-service courses, especially to the following who have contributed to this volume: Janet Boshier, Frances Doust, Sue Enticott, Karen Foster, Dee Fricker, Jeremy Hodgkinson, Sandra Hosford, Zara Johnson, Janet Jones, Janet Lewis, Carol Merry, Kath Parker, Helen Reese, Alison Robson, Pam Torrington, Jo Tuffney, Irene Wadding and Janet Webb.

Our long suffering secretary, Jennie Vass deserves a special award, as do our spouses, Grant and Rosalind, who kept the home fires burning during our absences running the courses that made this book possible. The series editor, Clive Carré, has been a constant source of support and encouragement, and to him we are deeply grateful.

Introduction: curriculum development, action research and reflective practice

CURRICULUM DEVELOPMENT: PRINCIPLES AND PRACTICE

This book aims to improve the quality of your teaching and, therefore, your pupils' learning of history. Teaching history should be a delight, for all human life is there, triumphs and disasters, love and hate, folly and wisdom. History is the universal soap opera that allows us to 'look through the keyhole' at people in the past, from kings and queens to the poorest slave and peasant. The key to successful history teaching is to bring the past to life in the minds of the children, so that they can imagine themselves there, hear people speak and join in their debates, controversies and adventures, either as voyeur or participant. All this we and our children can do, with one essential rider. Whatever we teach must be honest, in the sense that it must be true to the surviving record of the past, our historical sources.

How can we make history a living pleasure? How can you give yourself and your children, the moment that history is mentioned as the next topic, 'a burning desire that consumes and satisfies him (or her) all his life, that carries him each morning, eager as a lover' (Trevelyan, 1930) to the classroom? A partial answer lies in the incontrovertible fact that the History National Curriculum means that all teachers are curriculum developers. The HNC has forced you to teach a new subject in a new way that is personal to you and your children. Despite the diktats of the School Curriculum and Assessment Authority (SCAA) and its in-house rottweiler, OFSTED, you have almost total freedom to teach history in the way you think best. SCAA and OFSTED's views of history reflect a belief in the subject as a reconstruction and re-enactment of the past. Your continuous programme of history curriculum development should reflect a cycle with five phases:

1. The identification of a philosophical and psychological framework for the teaching of history in schools, i.e. what history is, what children should learn and how they learn it.
2. The translation of these ideas into a history curriculum that covers both curriculum content and the processes of learning history. In concrete terms this means turning the information and sources in history books into classroom teaching materials. Here you creatively develop, adopt or adapt teaching approaches, ideas and strategies to bring the past to life for you and your pupils.
3. The researching of your own and your colleagues' practice so that you can review, improve and extend the quality of your own teaching and learning.
4. The modification of your school's history curriculum based upon a programme of continuous reflection and development.

5.   The transfer of ideas and findings to all teachers of history in the school, who in turn inform your own practice.

Underpinning such a programme are our beliefs about history and how it should be taught. In this we reflect a view of the relationship between academic subject knowledge and teaching subject knowledge that is the connecting theme of the *Teaching Skills 7–11* series.

Classroom history is based upon three elements – substantive, syntactic and pedagogic knowledge (Grossman *et al.*, 1988). Substantive and syntactic knowledge define the history that you teach, both ideas about the subject and a framework of facts, and concepts and the process of enquiry that produces history. Pedagogic knowledge provides a range of strategies and techniques to turn academic history into classroom history for children.

Substantive knowledge

Substantive knowledge consists of beliefs about history, and historical knowledge and understanding.

Your beliefs about the nature of the discipline, i.e. what you think history is, shape your whole approach to teaching the subject. They also frame what you study and how. Thus a Marxist historian, whose interpretation is based upon the idea that historical movements and events are the result of the immutable evolution of economic systems, will have a radically different view of the discipline from a Tory historian, whose interpretation is grounded in the empirical tradition that focuses upon the actions of people functioning both individually and collectively as rational beings. A third belief you might have of history, and one that became central to and played a major part in shaping the English History National Curriculum (referred to throughout this volume as the History National Curriculum, or HNC), is that of nationalistic conservatism. Here the historical body of knowledge is a selection from our culture that helps shape and inform the young citizen. As such, it is based on ideas and information, concepts and conceptions, values and attitudes for pupils to assimilate (Husbands, 1996: 132).

Historical knowledge and understanding, the second substantive element, is the framework of linked facts and concepts. Each draws its meaning from its relationship to other data. Your knowledge framework provides your perception of the historical topics that you teach. Frameworks shape what you teach.

 ACTIVITY I.1 DEFINING HISTORY

•   Produce your own definition of history, based on your beliefs about the nature of the discipline.
•   Then say where historical knowledge and understanding comes from.

Syntactic knowledge

How does the historian go about his work? What are the processes involved, from the inception of an enquiry to its resolution? What discrete skills are needed, how do they interrelate, how are they developed? Processes and skills provide the syntactic framework of the discipline, its procedural knowledge.

Substantive and syntactic knowledge intermesh, and form the basis of Units 1 and 2 of this book. In 1994 we ran a small research project into teachers' perceptions of history, i.e. the nature of their substantive and syntactic knowledge. The teachers were on two separate 20-day in-service courses. From in-depth structured interviews of six teachers chosen at random, three from each course, it became clear that five of them had a view of history that reflected their own experience

of history in school. This presented substantive knowledge as a body of given, immutable facts to be transmitted to children:

Teacher A   *Before, the input was from me, from various textbooks. It was much more teacher-based, giving the information to the children ... actual facts being churned out to them, them receiving these facts.*

Teacher B   *I thought before the course that, something like the Tudors, you had to do it from start to finish.*

Teacher C   *I don't know why history has just got this theme about, it's just learn dates and themes.*

Teacher E   *I think I was probably a bit old-fashioned and a bit textbook based.*

It would be simplistic and crude to say that the teachers had only one view of historical knowledge for teaching the History National Curriculum, but it does seem that memories of their own schooling provided the dominant influences upon their teaching of history:

Teacher C   *Certainly when I was at school it was just learning dates and reading boring textbooks.*

Teacher D   *I did history to A-level and my history was horrendous, based on the approach used by the staff. One master used to enter the room, and on the blackboard went the information, and you spent the lesson copying that out.*

Teacher E   *Because that is the way I had been taught.*

Teacher D   made the link explicit:

Teacher D   *Before, it (his history teaching) was very much teacher directed ... me at the front and them taking it in because you felt you had to. That is really based on my experience of history teaching and how I was taught at school as well.* (authors' emphasis)

Pedagogic teaching knowledge

Teachers' substantive and syntactic views of history seem to play a major role in determining how they teach history, or their pedagogic knowledge (Wilson and Wineburger, 1988). Pedagogic knowledge is the whole range of techniques and strategies that the teacher draws upon in his or her teaching. The repertoire builds up through time, and is deployed according to the teaching circumstances and conditions (Brown and McIntyre, 1993: 111). The form of the repertoire relates directly to syntactic and substantive understanding, and it translates such knowledge into teaching patterns and classroom learning activities. Crucially, the development of the teaching repertoire should be a key focus of both initial and in-service training. Without the repertoire the teacher is unable to translate academic substantive and syntactic knowledge into pedagogic knowledge, i.e. teaching.

One of the teachers we interviewed, Teacher F, felt this strongly. This was because she had no classroom experience or knowledge of history teaching in a form that mirrored her substantive framework and syntactic understanding of history as an academic discipline.

Teacher F   *I've also done a history degree so I think I had the knowledge there. We used primary sources a lot. The Open University course was also geared to using primary sources a lot, and I knew that was how we should be teaching children to do it but I've never actually met anybody in education who says, 'yes, you are right, that's how you do it with children', and he (the in-service course tutor) was the first person I've met that said 'you should be teaching history using sources as evidence rather than just looking at textbooks', and showed us how to do it. Then I thought, at last I've got what I've been looking for in this subject, really. So that's why it (the course) was so good. It pointed me in the right direction in something I knew I should have been doing but wasn't quite sure how I should go about it.*

Everything in this book has taken the approach of providing teachers with a triangle of substantive, syntactic and pedagogic knowledge. All ideas have been tried and tested with children and teachers. We developed the underlying classroom strategies and teaching approaches through teaching the History National Curriculum in a wide variety of schools and localities, keeping a full record of what occurred. Using the findings from this action research we were able to mount our in-service courses. The teaching examples in this book are predominantly based upon lessons which teachers on our courses subsequently taught to their own classes, and on our own experience of teaching a course based on the Vikings during the 1995/96 academic year. The teachers applied what they had learned from the in-service course using an action research approach.

TRANSFERABLE SKILLS: PLANNING LESSONS

A key element of our in-service courses was to develop in participants the skills of the teacher as researcher and reflective practitioner. We believe in the transferability of teaching approaches through the assimilation and adaptation of ideas from one context to another. Our view is that teaching is a performance involving the teacher and pupils. As such, lessons consist of a series of separate, linked episodes. In presenting our teaching strategies our theory is that we can transfer ideas to you through providing a highly detailed description or script of each of these teaching episodes.

Such accounts or scripts are how we store instructions in our mind (Schank, 1985: 229–49). A common example from everyday life is a recipe in a cookery book. It gives you the ingredients, the context, the resources and the precise steps you need to create your own gastronomic masterpiece or, in my case, burnt offering. Similarly, teaching is a performance that draws upon a wide repertoire of skills and knowledge. In teaching our recipes or scripts we explain exactly, step-by-step, how to teach the episodes of a lesson. A teaching script is a blueprint for action, but one that you can change at will and adapt to your circumstances, for all lessons are different.

Teaching depends upon the extent, range and nature of your teaching scripts. These are the detailed pedagogic ideas and strategies that you store in memory, or which are readily available, for you to draw upon and assimilate. In building upon and adapting a teaching idea we consider the following, usually sequential, elements:

1. Think hard about what we are trying to teach – the ideas and concepts, the knowledge and understanding, the skills and processes that we want the pupils to acquire.
2. Sort out the possible resources that we can draw upon, and hunt out new ones.
3. Mentally review the possible approaches that we might use, focusing in on the one we like best both in general terms and in relation to our resources. This means sifting, sorting, discarding and above all using the imagination to try and work out the most effective way of teaching the topic. Thus for the Viking raid (pages 120–2), we used a picture of a Viking landing and an extract from the *Anglo-Saxon Chronicle*. We wanted to give the teaching a personal, dynamic touch. So we adapted an idea from our teaching of the history of the Titanic four years previously. We had a lovely, highly detailed artist's reconstruction of a cross-section of the boat, showing each deck. We asked the pupils to work out where they would hide stolen jewels on their deck. Then other pupils, as 'detectives', had to find where they had hidden the loot. In the case of 'The Vikings' we used an artist's reconstruction of the longboat ready to sail. We asked the children to work out where they would stow away on the boat so that they could take part in the raid.
4. There should be detailed planning and production of the classroom teaching materials. Having a bright idea is one thing, turning it into effective teaching is another. We spend a lot of time planning in detail how we will teach the elements of a lesson, noting down precisely, just like a cooking recipe, what we intend to do at each point.
5. Turn theory into practice. The classroom is a dynamic, changing arena in which there is constant interaction between teacher and children. Consequently what happens to a script can

vary greatly. What is actually taught can differ markedly from the plan, as we adapt to the specific circumstances.

6.   Collect and record evidence about how the lesson went.
7.   Review and modify the original script and supporting resources in the light of experience.

Using this approach means that you have to find out about your own teaching and the effect it has upon your pupils, and then reflect upon this to improve practice. We suggest that you can do this through consciously incorporating action research into your working lives.

THE TEACHER AS ACTION RESEARCHER AND REFLECTIVE PRACTITIONER

Improving your teaching: action research

Buzz-words in education are 'action research' and 'reflective practice'. Both are quite simple ideas, although both are capable of being presented as quasi-mystical experiences shrouded in gobbledegook open only to the priesthood of initiates. As an action researcher you systematically collect evidence about your own teaching, from the planning stage through to assessment of the pupils' work. In our own action research we create our own archive for subsequent investigation. There are many ways of doing this, but our favourite is to keep a full diary of what went on and a collection of teaching materials and pupils' responses and work. Action research may help to improve your teaching through providing a more systematic, planned approach to improving practice. There are six main steps in action research:

1.   Identify the problem;
2.   produce a solution;
3.   implement it and record findings;
4.   reflect upon the findings;
5.   draw up an action plan to implement change, both in terms of the rest of the programme and when you repeat the lesson or lessons you have just taught;
6.   implement the action plan.
Then repeat the process, beginning with Step 1 (see Figure I.1).

Having collected and sorted out your findings, you reflect upon them and draw up an action plan for improvement. The action plan is the result of your reflective, critical and constructive thinking about your practice.

Each step in Figure I.1 can be seen as part of an ongoing, continuous cycle of planning, research and reflection that helps to improve your teaching and the children's learning and satisfy the OFSTED (Office for Standards in Education) inspector.

How do you do action research? Because action research is usually done by 'you on the job' there are a number of approaches you can adopt. A common argument is that you don't have time to do it. The answer is you do have time, if you take a common-sense approach and apply the idea when you feel that it is appropriate. We suggest that you should try the idea for one or two sessions and see if it makes a difference.

Here is a list of approaches you might like to draw upon in your action research. It is impossible to adopt more than one or two at a time.

•   Detailed, reflective diary, written up using lesson notes.
•   Pupil diary – personal, or in the form of a dialogue with you, the teacher.
•   Pupil commentary or review.
•   Tape recording of the lesson.
•   Lesson notes – jotting down things as they happen.
•   Colleague taking notes on all or parts of the lesson, using a detailed plan.
•   Video recording of the teaching.

Steps in undertaking action research: how you might have applied action research to the teaching of your last history topic

1.   What is the problem? and/or
      What do you want to improve?
      What is the context for the teaching?
      What are the constraints?
      What resourcing is available?

2.   What solutions can you dream up?
      What is the best approach?
      Plan out what you will do.
      Resource the plan.

3.   Implement the plan.
      Record what happened.
      Make sure the records are in a usable form.

4.   Reflect upon and evaluate what happened.
      Consider how you could have improved aspects of your practice.

5.   Action plan – use what you have learned to draw up an action plan that:
      •   informs and helps shape your next piece of teaching;
      •   includes a revision of the original plan for your teaching and resourcing to include your improvements.

6.   Implement the action plan.

Repeat the process, starting with Step 1.

Figure I.1 Action research in practice

- Photography.
- Pupil response:
  - collect portfolio of children's annotated work
  - assessment task
  - work you asked them to do as a result of the teaching.
- Interviewing, either you or a colleague:
  - interview can be structured (with a list of questions you stick to), semi-structured (key questions, but with scope for discussion to be free ranging), *or* unstructured (free-ranging discussion).

You can only do so much while teaching a normal workload. Thus you might decide to use action research to review a single lesson. Because of the problem of lack of time, we have developed a simple approach for a lesson. Its headings provide a framework for reflection (Figure I.2).

On the other hand, you might decide to 'blitz' a particular problem, working intensively upon it by employing several of the methods listed above. We suggest that a blitz approach is suitable for from two to four sessions, and no more. It can produce a mountain of information that takes days to sort out. It is far too easy to get snowed under. Alternatively, you can take one approach, like a reflective diary, to continuously review how the programme is going. In a reflective diary you write up what happened and record in full your thoughts and feelings.

What was the point of the teaching? (Attach lesson plan if appropriate.)

How did the teaching go?

What was the response of the pupils?

What have you learned from the lesson?

Action plan – how can you improve your teaching and the children's learning on the basis of the lesson?

Figure I.2 Action research in reflective framework

 ACTIVITY I.2 IMPROVING PRACTICE

- Your husband, wife, partner or close friend is suspicious that you are being 'economical with the truth' concerning your recent movements.
- Empty your pockets, purse/wallet or bag.
- Study the contents.
- Use the contents to create a story that stretches the imagination, is true to the record and which proves your innocence.
- How might you use this idea in your history teaching, using Figures I.1 and I.2 to help you?
- How do you feel about action research as a way of introducing and developing new teaching ideas and approaches?
- How practical do you consider the approach?

Teachers as historians

INTRODUCTION

'Here we go, here we go, here we go' may well be the mindless chant of football supporters, but the same refrain rings in the ears of English, Welsh and Northern Irish teachers when we contemplate yet another round of curriculum reform. The English History National Curriculum emerged from the flames of conflict in 1991 in a battered and bruised form, having been through as many changes in its gestation of three years as a supermodel makes during an evening while strutting her stuff on a Parisian catwalk. Four years later, in 1995, history re-emerged phoenix-like from the Dearing melting pot in a shape that was significantly different from the 1991 model. How can you, as a teacher, make sense of the new post-Dearing History National Curriculum and teach it in a way that interests and informs, intrigues and entrances both you and your pupils?

The History National Curriculum has had a Janus-like existence from its controversial conception. One face is marked content, the other process and skills. Is history a body of knowledge to be acquired or a mode of enquiry? If history is both, what is the relationship between them? And, crucially in our teaching, where does the stress lie? The History National Curriculum is a statutory document, and like all statutes, its meaning depends upon interpretation. Interpretation should be relatively easy, for the post-Dearing curriculum is a slimmed down, even anorexic, version of its predecessor. The key stage 2 History National Curriculum's key elements define what is involved in historical study.

For key elements 1 and 2, history means 'Chronology' and 'Range and depth of historical knowledge and understanding'. So far so good, content is the winner. Key element 3, 'Interpretations of history', muddies the water slightly, for a single interpretation is content, whereas deciding between two or more interpretations involves us in process. Where key element 4, 'Historical enquiry', lies is clear – process, pure and simple. Key element 5, 'Organisation and communication', sways back and forth between content and process. Clearly for the History National Curriculum, content and process are a double helix. Like love and marriage, you can't have one, you can't have none, you can't have one without the other.

DOING HISTORY

Historical knowledge, content, is the outcome of a process of enquiry that we call 'doing history', a phrase Jack Hexter coined in his book on historical study (Hexter, 1971). While there is a fierce and lasting debate on the nature and purpose of history and its educational role, Hexter's view of

historians' mental processes is relatively uncontroversial. Carrying out an historical enquiry from its inception to the presentation of conclusions, the activity of 'doing history' develops the syntactic, procedural knowledge to undertake similar investigations. 'Doing history' results in the personal construction of a history in an appropriate form for communication, such as radio documentary, pictorial recreation or a family history.

The process of 'doing history' depends upon and develops a set of related skills that you, as a teacher, need to acquire. More importantly, pupils must share these in order for them to learn about the past in a genuinely historical way. At all levels history in schools should reflect the thinking involved when historians 'do' history. There should be continuity of thought and practice from children as young historians through to the postgraduate level. If not, what the children are doing cannot be defined as history in terms of how it is learnt.

HISTORY AS A CONSTRUCT

History is something that we construct for ourselves, accepting the simple distinction between what went on in the past and how we make sense of it, i.e. our histories, and those of others, including professional historians. History is created through working on sources, both those that have survived from the period being studied and later interpretations, i.e. the histories of the subject.

The first record

Original sources that have survived from the time of the subject under investigation are the past's 'first record'. Raw data comes in many shapes and forms. In our teaching of the Vikings (see Units 6 and 7), we draw upon literary and written records such as the sagas, poetry, runes and riddles, the *Anglo-Saxon Chronicle*, church charters and letters. We examine artefacts ranging from the Viking ships in the Oslo Viking ship and Roskilde ship museums (Olsen and Crumlin-Pedersen, 1978) to the Lindisfarne gravestone and burnt ashes and fragmentary remains of paint pigment from an archaeological dig on the Isle of Man (Bersu and Wilson, 1966). Other evidence consulted has survived in the form of place names, settlement patterns and the remains of fortifications, such as those at Repton (Batey *et al.*, 1994: 128–9).

The second record

We bring to bear upon the first record of the past our own wealth of experience, our knowledge, our perspectives, what Hexter calls our 'second record'. The second record is individual to each of us, our own mental baggage, as it were. Much of it is wholly personal and private, hidden away until we choose to reveal it. It contains knowledge, expertise, judgements, interests, inference, intuitions and values nurtured through many years. Hexter argues that all historical thinking depends upon the second record, which

is everything he (the historian) can bring to bear on the record of the past in order to elicit from that record the best account he can render of what he believes actually happened in the past. Potentially, therefore, it embraces his skills, the range of his knowledge, the set of his mind, the substance, quality and character of his experience – his total conscious-ness. Since no historian is identical with any other historian, what each historian brings, his second record, differs in some measure from the second record of every other historian...

History, therefore, depends not only on the surviving record of the past but on what historians bring to it. And all any historian brings to the first record lies somewhere in his second record. Every time a historian moves explicitly or implicitly from the record

of the past to a historical assertion about the past he is drawing on his second record, claiming that he has and, if necessary, can produce from his second record grounds for his assertion that the first record means what he says it means.

(Hexter, 1971)

 ACTIVITY 1.1 THE SECOND RECORD AND YOUR HISTORY TEACHING

- Take the last history topic your children studied.
- What were the elements in the second record which you supplied?

Draw up a list as follows:

Second record (e.g. Viking migration, see Unit 6)

1.	Knowledge of the period	Vikings migrated from the west coast of Norway from the late ninth century.
2.	Knowledge of people	King Harald Finehair's policy of conquest played a major part in the migration of the Viking communities.
3.	Circumstances	The Viking communities were faced with a choice of losing their freedom or migrating.
4.	Causes	Threat to survival, alternative place to live (Cumbria).
5.	Significance of events	Explanation of reasons for tenth century Norwegian Vikings' migration and settlement in north-west England.
6.	Materials to refer to	Foote and Wilson (1970), see pages 31–2, 39–40.
7.	Background reading	See pages 31–2.
8.	Other kinds of sources	See pages 110–11.
9.	Learning activities	See pages 110–11.

The second record and whole-class teaching

While children obviously have their own second records, by definition they are as yet underdeveloped. Either directly or indirectly the teacher plays the crucial role in extending the pupils' second records. The teacher can even provide a surrogate second record for the class so that its members can make sense of the first record of the past. As such, the teacher extends each student's historical learning and understanding. Equally important, through pupil discussion in pairs and groups, and teacher-led class discussion, the class can pool all of its members' second records. We deal at length with the controversial issue of whole-class teaching and its role in Unit 6 (see pages 114–16).

Thus when studying the 'space race' and trying to bring to life the sense of excitement at the launch of a rocket, we asked our class of 9 year olds about their thoughts and experience, hoping for at least a few inchoate half-remembered experiences. In response, a bright spark piped up, 'When I was in Florida to see the launch of Atlantis…'. One humbled teacher in the room immediately realised that his own second record was somewhat impoverished. Whole-class teaching thus becomes central at certain times to the process of developing children's understanding.

Frameworks of knowledge: semantic networks (substantive knowledge)

Hexter elaborates further on the difference between the raw data of history and how it is interpreted:

With respect to history the whole record of the past is only a set of points. However closely arrayed they may be, all by themselves they do not make a pattern. The pattern is always the work of a historian or of someone acting in the capacity of a historian. It always involves an inference. The points themselves do not have the dimension of history and cannot alone legitimate the inference. To legitimate it the historian himself must supply something. Without that something there can be no history, and no place else for it to come from. So without resort to the second record there can be no history at all. Let us put the matter in its most radical form. Suppose a French historian in, say, 1700, was writing a history of the English Civil War. In examining the record of the past he finds the following sentences in different documents:

(1) 'Today on January 30, 1648, the murderous rebels dipped their vile hands in the life blood of our martyr king.'
(2) 'January 30, 1648, Today the people of England brought to justice at the hands of the public executioner, that Man of Blood, Charles Stuart.'
(3) 'Execution of King — January 30, 1648.'

If our historian simply quotes those sentences and draws no inference from them he is not writing history at all. To write correct history he will have to continue to write as if he inferred from the documents that King Charles I was executed in January 1648...

There is of course very little likelihood that anyone would challenge what he says. That does not alter the fact that his statement is something other than the record of the past. By making an assertion about the past as he believes it actually was, he moves out of the point sets which are the records of the past and into the line sets which are in the dimension of history...

By seeking out patterns and reconstructing connections among the records of the past, historians attempt and in part achieve accounts of the past as it actually was. In this seeking out of patterns, historians are sometimes bold and imaginative, sometimes rash and fantastical, sometimes cautious and prudent, sometimes timid. In their dealings with the record of the past the very best historians display both imagination and caution, boldness and prudence, each at the right time and in the right place.

(Hexter, 1971: 80–3)

Historical enquiry – syntactic knowledge

'Doing history' thus involves producing a story of the past, an interpretation, weaving a web of understanding that draws upon the 'first record' of the past. How does the historian use the 'first record' to create history? R.G. Collingwood, an eminent academic historian and philosopher whose book *The Idea of History* influenced the shape and form of history for schools from 1970 onwards, argued that the historian works in a similar way to a detective, a point we return to in Unit 2. To illustrate this concept he wrote a short story, *Murder in the Vicarage*, about the death of a vicar, John Doe. The detective solves the murder mystery by making connections between separate pieces of evidence and seeing the pattern that this creates. The network of concepts, ideas and information can be represented diagramatically (see Figure 1.1). Similar networks can be developed for analogous historical investigations, such as into the disappearance of the Princes in the Tower.

Doing history thus involves producing an interpretation of the past, creating a web of understanding from relevant information extracted from historical sources, its past's first and second records. 'Webbing' of facts and concepts has long been common in primary schools, mirroring as it does the creation of concept webs.

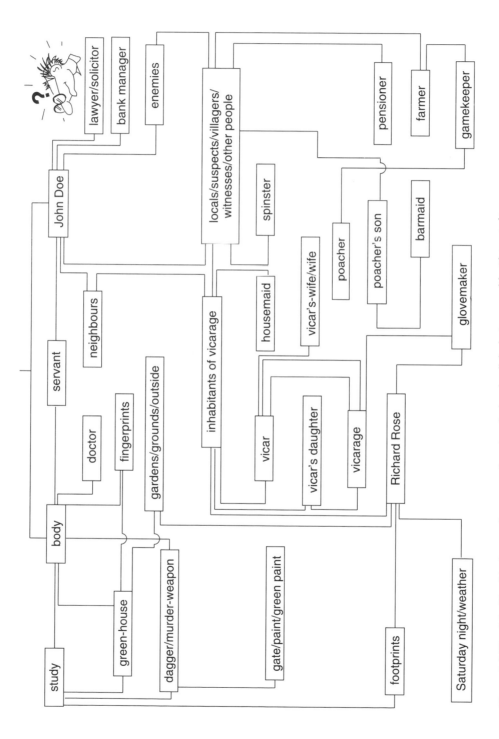

Figure 1.1 The John Doe Mystery: a diagrammatic network showing links between subject keywords

Source: Collingwood, R.G. (1946) *The Idea of History*, Oxford University Press

ACTIVITY 1.2 HISTORICAL NETWORKS OF KNOWLEDGE: CONCEPT WEBS

- Take any current history topic that you are teaching.
- Work out a concept web that shows the links between its different elements.

'KNOW HOW' (PROCEDURAL, OR SYNTACTIC, SKILLS AND PROCESSES), AND 'KNOW THAT' (PROPOSITIONAL, OR SUBSTANTIVE, CONTENT) KNOWLEDGE

To beaver away on the first record the historian relies upon a repertoire of skills or thinking patterns, the procedures of historical enquiry. This 'know how' knowledge (i.e. how we know about the past) enables the historian to conduct and shape an investigation. Each enquiry starts with the asking of a question or questions and moves on to the hunting out of and working on sources, and the development and testing of hypotheses in relation to information gained. Historical 'know how' knowledge results in this 'know that' knowledge (that which we know), i.e. the 'facts' of history. History is thus made up of two intertwined and mutually supporting strands, process and content, neither of which can exist without the other (Rogers, 1979).

The process of doing history or 'know how' (syntactic) knowledge

'Know how' knowledge forms the warp of the fabric of history. The process model draws its strength from the revolution in academic history in the past sixty years. Historians now accept that history is constantly reconstructed from the evidence of the past, according to clearly defined procedures for establishing historical facts, statements and judgements. History, as a body of propositional and conceptual knowledge, is always in ferment. Each age creates its own versions of the past, its history, that reflect current interests and conceptions (Elton, 1969). Even the most widely held and accepted judgements come under the historian's hammer, for example Hitler's responsibility for causing World War II.

The process of enquiry draws upon and develops a range of skills. In 1971, Coltham and Fines analysed the processes and skills required for historical study. Their analysis proved seminal in the debate on historical study, and it still provides a useful checklist of what is involved (see Figure 1.2).

Propositional or 'know that' (substantive) knowledge

If 'know how' knowledge is history's warp, the weft is formed from connected statements (propositions) about what happened in the past.

Propositions link together to form networks of interrelated information and ideas about a topic: our 'know that' knowledge. Such knowledge comes in many shapes and guises, for example the biography of Mary Queen of Scots (see page 29), an account of an archaeological dig and an interpretation of what was found (see pages 34–9) or a textbook account and explanation of a phenomenon such as Viking migration (see pages 39–40).

'Know how' (syntactic) and 'know that' (substantive) knowledge: theory into practice

Extracts below from Marjorie Reeves' *The Medieval Town* (Reeves, 1954) illustrate the distinction between propositional, substantive, (know that) and procedural, syntactic, (know how) knowledge.

A.   ATTITUDES TOWARDS THE STUDY OF HISTORY
      1. Attending
      2. Responding
      3. Imagining

B.   NATURE OF THE DISCIPLINE
      1. Nature of information
      2. Organising procedures
      3. Products

C.   SKILLS AND ABILITIES
      1. Vocabulary acquisition
      2. Reference skills
      3. Memorisation
      4. Comprehension
      5. Translation
      6. Analysis
      7. Extrapolation
      8. Synthesis
      9. Judgment and evaluation
     10. Communication skills

D.   EDUCATIONAL OUTCOMES OF STUDY
      1. Insight
      2. Knowledge of values
      3. Reasoned judgement

Figure 1.2 Processes and skills of historical enquiry
Source: Coltham, J.B. and Fines, J. (1971) *Educational Objectives for the Study of History*, TH 35, The Historical Association

Marjorie Reeves is an eminent medievalist, school teacher and the inspiration behind Longman's 'Then & There' series as both author and editor. First, a propositional ('know that') section from the book, based upon Salisbury:

At Easter in the year 1219 a little temporary wooden chapel was built. In the summer the Bishop and the cathedral priests solemnly moved house from Old Sarum down to the water-meadow at Myrfield. What they moved into we can only imagine. Probably they lived in wooden huts, for to them the most important thing was to begin building the new cathedral. Workmen were gathered and set to work. It was very difficult to build a great cathedral on a bog. So, before they could lay foundations, they had to sink many wattle hurdles into the marsh to form a platform. At last, on April 28 1220, they were ready to lay the foundation stones. There was a grand procession in which the Bishop and clergy wore their richest robes and country people from miles around flocked to see. Three stones were laid by Bishop Poore – one for Pope Honorius, one for the Archbishop of Canterbury, and one for himself. Then the Earl of Salisbury and his wife laid two, and four more were laid by the most important priests.

(Reeves, 1954: 7)

How did Marjorie Reeves use her creative and imaginative gifts to bring the world in the passage above to life? On page 81 of *The Medieval Town* she gives us a glimpse of her historian's craft, her 'know how' or procedural/syntactic knowledge:

HOW CAN WE FIND OUT ABOUT PEOPLE IN THE PAST ?

Perhaps you are suspicious about all I have been telling you. Perhaps you are saying to yourself : 'How does she know? I believe she is making it all up!' I assure you I have not invented anything – only used a little imagination [the second record] on the clues I found. To find out how people lived in the past you have to use every clue [the first record] you can get. Here is a list of all I used for Salisbury.

1.   What I could see with my own eyes:
     The chalk downs, the rivers and the water-meadows (i.e. the geographical position of Salisbury).
     The ramparts of Old Sarum, the cathedral and the churches.
     Old houses in Salisbury.
     The gates and walls, the plan and the names of the streets.
     Furniture and other old things (like the Giant) in the Museum.
2.   What I could see in old pictures, especially pictures which people in the fifteenth century drew themselves.
     Many of the pictures in this book are drawn from these old pictures.
3.   What I could read that the people of the past wrote themselves. For example:
          the letter that the clergy wrote to the Pope;
          the charter which the King gave to Salisbury;
          the books written by the Guilds;
          the rules made by the Town Council;
          the account books kept by the Town Council;
          inscriptions in the churches;
          the wills people made before they died;
          records kept in the King's law courts.

(Reeves, 1954: 81)

She could also have added what she already knew, her 'second record', about medieval history in general and towns in particular, based upon the thousands of books and articles she had read.

Know how knowledge means that we can test if a statement of fact, a proposition, is true. A truth test consists of examining the processes, the procedures, that led to the formulation of the propositions (Bruner, 1960, 1966). Geoffrey Elton gave an insight into what the pursuit of truth entails when analysing a proposition about Thomas Cromwell, Henry VIII's great minister. Elton was the world's leading expert on Thomas Cromwell. The proposition was: Thomas Cromwell blackmailed the priors of monasteries about to be suppressed.

Can we trust the sources on which it was based? How do we check their truth? Elton fires away:

A good example of what should not happen was provided by R.B. Merriman in his edition of Thomas Cromwell's letters. In that collection, nos. 163 and 180 appear to be blackmailing notes from Cromwell to priors of monasteries allegedly saved from suppression by the minister; they have subsequently loomed large in the usual denunciation of him. [Elton provides examples] There is nothing in the edition to raise doubts. But one glance at the originals shows that they were written and signed in a hand quite different from that of Cromwell or any of his clerks; that is to say, they were bits of private enterprise on someone's part who hoped to cash in on the minister's position and reputation, and since they were found among Cromwell's papers we may suppose that the trick was discovered and the minister informed. Read rightly these letters therefore tell in his favour, not against him.

(Elton, 1969: 99–100)

ACTIVITY 1.3 CHECKING THE HISTORICAL TRUTH

1. How would a Martian with an English translator make sense of the know that knowledge presented in Reeves' passage on the founding of the Cathedral – its propositions, concepts and analogies?
    Explain to him, her or it the meaning of the following:

    1219, Easter, new
    Pope, Archbishop of Canterbury, Bishop, clergy, priest
    Earl of Salisbury
    cathedral, chapel
    water-meadow, wattle hurdle, country people

    As you can see, we take so much knowledge for granted, yet its meaning is grounded in context.
2. Compare the kinds of sources you used in teaching your last history topic with those Marjorie Reeves lists for her work on Salisbury. Which are the same and which are different?

 ### ACTIVITY 1.4 CHECKING THE TRUTH TODAY

1. Stage an incident in the classroom, such as a blazing row between a couple of pupils, with lots of shouting and banging of fists on tables. Brief them carefully beforehand!
2. Say that you will have to ask the headteacher to come in to sort out the problem. Ask the children to write down or tell you what they think happened.
3. Hold a class discussion about how we might know what happened. How can we check if the facts are true? What trust can we place on eyewitness reports when there are many different versions of what happened? Can we believe what the two pupils said about the causes – why the quarrel broke out? Do we know what happened – the facts, the events, the overall situation? The consequences – what will be the outcome of the row? How might we check the truth of what happened?
4. Tell the class that the whole thing has been staged!
5. Then give the pupils an historical problem to solve, with evidence that might help them to gain some idea of a version of the truth.

A RELATIONSHIP WITH THE PAST

At the heart of doing history is a relationship with the past. From that relationship understanding, skills and processes develop: understanding of past people and societies, skills and processes that we apply personally and professionally in dealing with problems. History helps us understand past people and their societies, an understanding that provides us with a perspective upon the present. Marjorie Reeves' book *Why History?* (Reeves, 1980) movingly defines the relationship that can make all of us and our pupils historians:

 Learning involves a relationship … But personal knowledge begins with an involvement that is like the developing relationship with another person. It starts with the desire to explore the barely glimpsed unknown 'personality'; it becomes a commitment that engages the imagination as well as the intellect; it develops into a conviction that here is something worth knowing for its own sake. The experience becomes a kind of love affair which is both subjective in origin and objective in intention. You engage in it in order to

enjoy – what? The personification metaphor is almost irresistible in describing this relationship. The historian who wrote in his preface, 'I apologise to my wife for the love affair I have had with my subject' expressed the matter very neatly.

(Reeves, 1980: 1)

VALUES, MORALS AND BELIEFS

Before we move on to trying to 'do' some history you should consider two other elements, the set of values, moral precepts and political beliefs that you bring to bear upon the historical record and the danger of history being the vehicle for political propaganda. By definition history cannot be value-free, yet that should not be an argument for slipping into moral relativism. Because every judgement is a value judgement it is easy to say that we should make no moral statement about anything. Two propositions help us to reconcile the need to understand the past in its own terms with an attempt to retain a moral perspective. While we can explain the behaviour of Genghis Khan, Richard III, Ivan the Terrible, Hitler, Stalin and Pol Pot within their social context and the mentalities of those involved, this is no reason to duck judging their behaviour against our own values and beliefs. Ivan was a cruel and capricious killer, Hitler and Pol Pot responsible for genocide.

ACTIVITY 1.5 MORALS, VALUES AND BELIEFS

1. Take your last history topic.
2. In it, identify the behaviour of an individual or groups that you would condemn using present-day values.
3. Draw up a table showing how you can both explain and condone the behaviour in the context of the time, yet condemn it today.

DOING HISTORY: YOUR TURN

Now we ask you to 'do' your own history, to conduct an investigation by examining sources and coming to a conclusion. This is central to the History National Curriculum as key element 3, 'Interpretations of history' and key element 4, 'Historical enquiry', state. You can work on your own or in groups.

ACTIVITY 1.6 DOING HISTORY

1. The starting point – posing a question or questions:

   Read through the briefing, Source A. What questions would you ask about Schliemann?

2. Investigating the sources:

   (a) Examine Sources 1B to 1O below.
   (b) Weigh up the evidence, and decide what you think of Schliemann and his work. Use your own and these questions to focus your investigation:

   • What historical questions did he ask? How valuable were they?
   • What effect did his character have on his archaeological achievements?
   • How honest was he, either professionally or personally?

- Why did he include his wife in his story of how he found Priam's treasure?
- Did he fraudulently 'prove' his preconceived ideas and beliefs?
- How do you think he found the treasure, and in what form?
- What, if anything, *did* his excavations at Troy show?
- What were the particular difficulties he faced in excavating at Troy? How did he overcome them?
- Was he a great archaeologist, and if so, why?

(c)   Did he perform a service for archaeology?

 ## Source 1A

Schliemann of Troy: briefing

The story starts with Homer, the Greek poet who may or may not have existed. Tradition says he was blind, and lived in the eighth century BC (modern scholars think the seventh century more likely). Homer wrote down part of the story of the Trojan War (in the *Iliad*) and the epic of Odysseus' long journey home afterwards (in the *Odyssey*). Before Homer, the tale had been passed down orally for many generations, for the Trojan War, if it did take place, was fought in the late Bronze Age, *circa* 1250 BC.

Heinrich Schliemann was the wealthy German businessman who in the late nineteenth century excavated the site of Troy, thus winning eternal fame as an archaeologist. In his excavations he found, not one, but seven cities, built one above the other (reclassified by later archaeologists as nine cities). He identified Troy II, the second layer from the bottom, as Homer's Troy, the site of the Trojan War.

Schliemann was a natural and effective self-publicist, who in his books told of his childhood dream of finding Troy, of his excavations in Greece and Turkey and of his magnificent finds, which he claimed proved the truth of the Homeric legends. While the tale of his childhood dream is certainly a later fabrication, he did bring to his excavation of Homeric sites a driven energy and a romantic vision which fired the imagination of his admiring readers.

However, even during his lifetime he was attacked as a cheat and a charlatan. What are the facts? How are we to interpret the sources of evidence about Schliemann? What can we conclude about him and his finds, and about Homer and the Trojan War?

Below we print just a small selection of the many sources about Schliemann and Troy. They centre mainly on his finding of 'the treasure of King Priam', Homer's Trojan king. (Jacqui Dean, 1996)

 ## Source 1B

Homer, the *Iliad* (trs Lattimore, 1951). Descriptions of Troy (Ilium, Ilion) used by Homer (the literary source – Schliemann's inspiration).

strong-walled Ilion;
the well-founded stronghold of Ilion;
great bastion;
the gates and the long walls;
magnificent battlements;
towering ramparts;
the great city of Priam;
sacred Ilion;
windy Ilion.

Extracts from the *Iliad*:

> Such were they who sat on the tower, chief men of the Trojans.
> And these, as they saw Helen along the tower approaching,
> murmuring softly to each other
> uttered their winged words.

> Now he entered the wonderfully built palace of Priam.
> This was fashioned with smooth-stone cloister walks, and within it
> were embodied fifty sleeping chambers of smoothed stone
> built so as to connect with each other; and within these slept
> each beside his own wedded wife, the sons of Priam.

> He [King Priam] spoke, and lifted back the fair covering of his clothes-chest and from inside took out twelve robes surpassingly lovely and twelve mantles to be worn single, as many blankets, as many great white cloaks, also the same number of tunics. He weighed and carried out ten full talents of gold, and brought forth two shining tripods, and four cauldrons, and brought out a goblet of surpassing loveliness that the men of Thrace had given him.

SOURCES 1C–1G: SCHLIEMANN AND HIS CONTEMPORARIES

    ### Source 1C

Heinrich Schliemann, *Ithaque* (1869). His description of the site of Troy (the hill of Hissarlik).

> After having walked more than a half hour over this terrain, we arrived at a hill of some forty metres high, which has an almost perpendicular drop to the plain on the north side and is about 20 metres higher than the mountain-ridge, of which it forms the extremity. If it was possible to entertain doubts over the identity of Hissarlik with Novum Ilium [New Troy], the form of this spur would make them disappear entirely, for it corresponds to the words of Strabo (13.1) 'continuous ridge.'
> The summit of this hill forms a continuous plateau about 233 metres square. By trenches dug in this hill the ingenious Frederick Calvert has determined that it is in great part artificial and that it has been formed by the ruins and the debris of the successive temples and palaces over long centuries. By making a small dig on the east end of the summit he brought to light part of a large building, palace or temple, constructed of large hewn stones superimposed on one another without cement. What little of the building can be seen leaves no doubt that it was of great dimensions and that it was executed with consummate art. After having twice examined all the plain of Troy I fully share the conviction of this scholar, that the high plateau of Hissarlik is the site of ancient Troy and that the afore-mentioned hill is its Pergamon [citadel].

    ### Source 1D

Heinrich Schliemann, *Troy and its Remains* (1875, trs Philip Smith). Schliemann's diary account of his excavations at Hissarlik, in the layer known as Troy II.

> In excavating this wall further and directly by the side of the palace of King Priam, I came upon a large copper article of the most remarkable form, which attracted my attention all the more as I thought I saw gold behind it. On the top of this copper article lay a stratum of red and

calcined ruins, from 4¾ to 5¼ feet thick, as hard as stone, and above this again lay the above-mentioned wall of fortification (6 feet broad and 20 feet high) which was built of large stones and earth, and must have belonged to an early date after the destruction of Troy. In order to withdraw the treasure from the greed of my workmen, and to save it for archaeology, I had to be most expeditious, and although it was not yet time for breakfast, I immediately had 'paidos' [rest time] called... While the men were eating and resting, I cut out the Treasure with a large knife, which it was impossible to do without the very greatest exertion and the most fearful risk of my life, for the great fortification-wall, beneath which I had to dig, threatened every moment to fall down upon me. But the sight of so many objects, every one of which is of inestimable value to archaeology, made me foolhardy, and I never thought of any danger. It would, however, have been impossible for me to have removed the Treasure without the help of my dear wife, who stood by me ready to pack the things which I cut out in her shawl and to carry them away...

As I found all these articles together, forming a rectangular mass, or packed into one another, it seems to be certain that they were placed on the city wall in a wooden chest, such as those mentioned by Homer as being in the palace of King Priam. This appears to be the more certain, as close by the side of these articles I found a copper key above 4 inches long, the head of which (about 2 inches long and broad) greatly resembles a large safe-key of a bank.

 Source 1E

Letter from Schliemann to Charles Newton, Keeper of Greek and Roman Antiquities at the British Museum, quoted in D. Traill, *Schliemann of Troy: Treasure and Deceit* (1995).

On account of her father's sudden death Mrs Schliemann left me in the beginning of May. The treasure was found end of May; but, since I am endeavouring to make an archaeologist of her, I wrote in my book that she had been present and assisted me in taking out the treasure. I merely did so to stimulate and encourage her for she has great capacities.

 Source 1F

31 May 1873, the night Schliemann found 'Priam's treasure'. Schliemann's letter to Frederick Calvert, quoted in D. Traill, *Schliemann of Troy: Treasure and Deceit* (1995).

I am sorry to inform you that I am closely watched and expect that the turkish watchman who is angry at me, I do not know for what reason, will search my house tomorrow. I therefore take the liberty to deposit with you 6 baskets and a bag begging you will kindly *lock* them up and *not* allow by any means the turks to touch them...

The villagers betray me to the turk so that I cannot any more take their horses. So, when I want to remove the baskets, pray, lend me for three hours in the night three horses. I shall gratefully acknowledge this service and pay you for each horse forty piastres; please do not refuse for I am quite in despair; having spent here more than 100,000 franks I cannot take away a little broken pottery.

 Source 1G

W.C. Borlase, 'A Visit to Dr Schliemann's Troy', *Fraser's Magazine*, no. 17, February 1878.

About twenty yards N. W. of the Scaean gate is the point where the so-called treasure of Priam was found, but the details of that discovery, as related by Nicholas Zaphyros, were so utterly different to Herr Schliemann's own account, that I find any attempt to reconcile them out of the question. To take an instance of discrepancy, in which I am able to verify the truth of Nicholas's account, Herr Schliemann states that, upon making the discovery, he sent all his workmen to dinner, and dug out the articles himself, adding, 'It would have been impossible for me to have removed the treasure without the help of my dear wife, who stood by me ready to pack the things which I cut out in her shawl, and carry them away.' Nicholas, on the other hand, told me that he had assisted in digging out the things, and in taking them to the house. On my asking what part Madame Schliemann took, he replied, 'She was not here; she was at Athens at the time'; and on subsequent inquiry this was confirmed at the Dardanelles. I should still have thought there must have been some mistake, were it not that I know on the best authority that Herr Schliemann has himself owned in conversation with a gentleman holding a high and responsible position in European archaeological circles, and who permits me, if necessary, to use his name, that his wife was not really there, but that he brought in her name to give her a zest for archaeology. This little piece of embellishment is in every way unlucky, since Madame Schliemann was held to be a most important witness of the great discovery – in fact, her presence was the only corroboration of it until Nicholas Zaphyros affirmed to me that he was there. He, Nicholas, remembered that there was a large quantity of bronze articles, but his memory was hazy as to the rest of the treasure. He persisted in stating that it lay not 'on', as stated by Herr Schliemann, but close to the outer side of the wall; that there were no signs whatever of its having been compacted into a chest, but, on the contrary, that it was contained in a little place built round with stones, and having flat stones to cover it; and lastly, that the key, reported as found 'close by the side of the articles,' came from the stratum of the time of Lysimachus (to which it much more properly belongs), at a distance of some 200 yards from the spot. The man's statements on these points were direct and graphic, and I think it is right to record them.

(N.B. Lysimachus was one of Alexander the Great's generals in the fourth century BC.)

PICTORIAL AND DIAGRAMMATIC SOURCES

 Source 1H

Looking west from the Scaean Gate after demolition of Schliemann's wooden house.

See Figure 1.3. From Traill, 1995: 17.

 Source 1I

Schliemann's wife Sophie wearing 'the jewels of Helen'.

See Figure 1.4. From Wood, 1985: 59.

 Source 1J

The archaeological view of Troy today: Schematic section through the hill of Hissarlik.

See Figure 1.5. From Wood, 1985: 90–1.

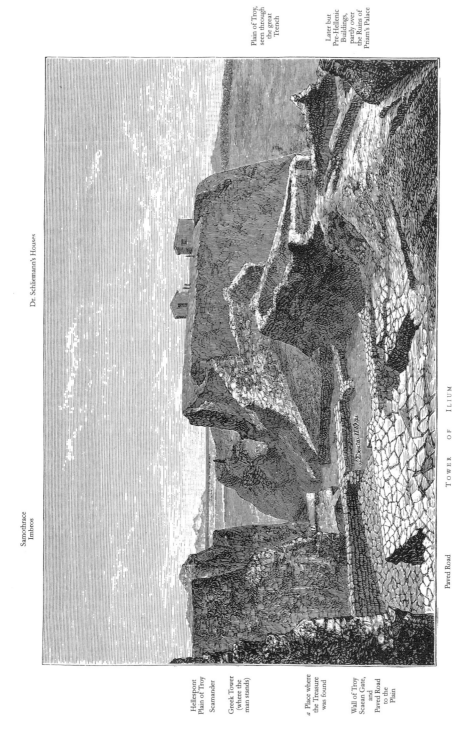

Samothrace
Imbros

Dr. Schleimann's Houses

Plain of Troy,
seen through
the great
Trench

Later but
Pre-Hellenic
Buildings,
partly over
the Ruins of
Priam's Palace

Hellespont
Plain of Troy
Scamander

Greek Tower
(where the
man stands)

a Place where
the Treasure
was found

Wall of Troy
Scaean Gate,
and
Paved Road
to the
Plain

Paved Road   TOWER   OF   ILIUM

Figure 1.3 Source 1H: Looking west from the Scaean Gate after demolition of Schleimann's wooden house
Source: D.A. Traill (1995) *Schliemann of Troy: Treasure and Deceit*, John Murray

Figure 1.4 Source 1I: Sophie Schliemann wearing the 'jewels of Helen'
Source: M. Wood (1985) *In Search of the Trojan War*, BBC Books

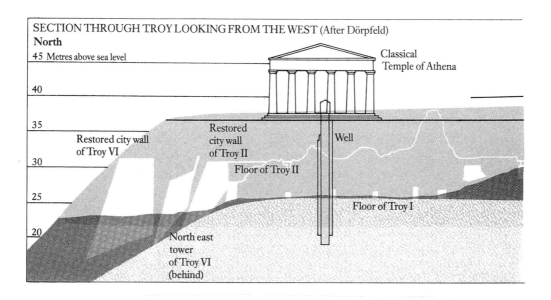

Figure 1.5 Source 1J: Cross-section through the mound of Troy
Source: M. Wood (1985) *In Search of the Trojan War*, BBC Books

Figure 1.6 Source 1K: How Troy might have looked
Source: M. Wood (1985) *In Search of the Trojan War*, BBC Books

    Source 1K

Artist's reconstruction of Troy as it may have looked at the time of the Trojan War, in the late Bronze Age *circa* 1260 BC.

THE VIEWS OF TWENTIETH-CENTURY HISTORIANS

    Source 1L

M.I. Finley, *The World of Odysseus* (1977).

> He [Schliemann] may, as has been said, have dug a site as if he were digging potatoes, but he was also the first man in this field, and virtually in any field of archaeology, to stress stratigraphy and the primacy of pottery for relative chronology. He also appreciated – the significance of which is not often acknowledged – that the highest aim of archaeology is to answer questions... (p. 168)

The stratification of Troy, the architecture and the pottery, and so on, are as settled in all essentials as they are ever likely to be. But these were not what Schliemann set out to discover. He was after something far greater, the truth about an ancient and famous historical question. And that is still the central question, one hundred years later... (p. 167)

And now I return to the central question. In his struggle to obtain official Turkish permission to launch his first excavation in 1871, Schliemann wrote repeatedly, in one form of words or another, that he had 'the purely scientific aim of showing that the Trojan War was not a fable, that Troy and the Pergamos of Priam existed in reality'. Did he succeed? Do the ruins of Troy confirm the historicity of the war which Homer recalled and in part recounted? (p. 169)

Normally, material evidence without documents cannot answer the question Schliemann first posed. The most that can legitimately be said one hundred years after Schliemann is that, if there was a Trojan War at all like the Homeric one, Hissarlik is the sole fortress in that part of Asia Minor which could have been under siege... (p. 170)

Neither the war nor Troy itself is mentioned in any contemporary document in any language, from any excavation, so far as I know. (p. 175)

Source 1M

W.M. Calder, 'Schliemann on Schliemann: A Study in the Use of Sources', in *Greek, Roman and Byzantine Studies*, 13, 335–53 (1972).

He would not hesitate a moment to deceive a colleague. He was an eager war profiteer, whether from the Crimean War or the American Civil War. A dream on 17 March 1855 inspired him to corner the saltpetre market and win a fortune from the Crimean War. This same lack of conscience made him a successful archaeologist. The Turkish government forbade him to excavate Hissarlik. He excavated Hissarlik. The owners of the property forbade him to excavate their hill. He excavated it. The Turkish government forbade him to export his finds. He smuggled them to Athens.

Source 1N

D. Traill, *Schliemann of Troy: Treasure and Deceit* (1995).

Is there any hard evidence that Priam's Treasure has been assembled from earlier finds? The answer, rather surprisingly, is an unqualified 'Yes'. Plates 193 and 194 of the Atlas illustrate a total of twenty-seven objects attributed by Schliemann to Priam's Treasure, no less than eleven of which were found prior to 31 May 1873 (p. 120)

The gold jewellery is not mentioned in the earliest accounts of the discovery. Should we accept Schliemann's account as essentially true with a few honest mistakes, or was Priam's Treasure actually a more modest find of bronze and silver pieces enhanced by the season's unreported gold pieces and even some earlier finds? The building just within the Scaean Gate, which he identified as Priam's Palace, was not very impressive. Was the treasure a dramatic attempt to authenticate it? (p. 305)

Source 1O

M. Wood, *In Search of the Trojan War* (1985).

Recently some scholars have even argued that the treasure itself was fabricated and planted, but it was certainly of the right date for its context, which recent research suggests was possibly a cist grave dug into Troy II layers from Troy III, though Schliemann's account is too imprecise to be sure. We also now know that gold had been found sporadically at this level earlier in the year, including a major find of similar jewellery in illicit digging by his workmen. Also, when the Americans re-excavated this area in the 1930s they found scattered gold in almost every room, as if the inhabitants of Troy II had fled in panic before the onslaught which engulfed their city. (pp. 59–60)

If your appetite for the world of Homer's tales has been whetted, these three books are highly recommended:

M.I. Finley (1977) *The World of Odysseus*
D. Traill (1995) *Schliemann of Troy: Treasure and Deceit*
M. Wood (1985) *In Search of the Trojan War*

Investigating the Schliemann story should help you to understand how, through posing questions, we can test our ideas against surviving evidence. How can we translate these ideas into classroom action? A simple way is to take a well-known fact and test it against the available evidence. Let us take an old favourite, the Bayeux Tapestry (Figure 1.7, Source 1P).

ACTIVITY 1.7 DOING HISTORY WITH CHILDREN

- Study Figure 1.7.
- The question we ask is, *Was Harold shot in the eye?*
- Cover up the points below with a sheet of paper.
- Move the sheet down the page, uncovering one point at a time.
- After each point say whether you think Harold was shot in the eye or not, or whether you cannot say.

1. Is Harold the man clutching the arrow poking out of his eye?
2. The writing is in Latin. Is Harold the man below Harold or the person under *Interfectus Est* [Killed is]?
3. The picture is from the Bayeux tapestry. English needlewomen made it some twenty years after the Battle of Hastings for Odo of Bayeux, one of the noblemen who fought with William the Conqueror at Hastings. There is no account from the time of the battle that Harold was shot in the eye.
4. The man with the arrow in his eye is standing in a line of Saxon soldiers. These footsoldiers were King Harold's housecarls (his bodyguard). They fought on foot in a line. Are they standing in front of the king? Is the knight on horseback striking Harold down?
5. The arrow was added to the tapestry later – it is not from the time when the tapestry was made.
6. Restorers have, however, found needle holes in the tapestry that show there was a thread in the original that would have represented an arrow poking out of the eye of the figure in the tapestry.

Figure 1.7 Source 1P: The death of King Harold
Source: The Bayeux Tapestry

CONCLUSION

The relationship between history as a process (procedural, syntactic or know how knowledge), and as a body of substantive, or propositional, (know that) knowledge should now be clear. There are as many histories as historians. We create our histories from the sources available to us. Academic historians work in the same way, with the proviso that they are working on the frontiers of knowledge. As such, they are engaged in a dialogue and debate between different and competing versions of the past. The debate can break out into open warfare, with competing parties justifying their positions by citing interpretations and evidence from the 'first record' that supports their stance.

History, as a creative activity, is essentially subjective. The networks of concepts and propositions that result reflect the beliefs of the historian about the nature of the subject and how conclusions are reached. These beliefs provide the historian's orientation, and influence the form and shape of his or her endeavours. Likewise, the teacher of history has to be a historian, no matter how unwittingly, in the creation of the corpus of knowledge that he or she teaches to children. The relationship between history as academic knowledge in both its substantive and syntactic forms, and how it is taught (pedagogic or teaching subject knowledge), is the focus of Unit 2.

History for the classroom

PRINCIPLES AND PRACTICE: SUBSTANTIVE AND SYNTACTIC KNOWLEDGE

The unrecorded writing of the first history textbook for schools is lost in the mists of time. Since then a major concern for history curriculum developers has been the relationship between history as an academic discipline and how it should be taught to children. From the early 1970s the focus in history teaching shifted from coverage and the mastery of content, and conceptual understanding, substantive knowledge, towards the acquisition of the skills and the procedural knowledge of the historian, syntactic understanding. A fierce and continuing debate has developed as to the form the history curriculum should take to accommodate syntactic skills and processes (Aldrich, 1991; Bourdillon, 1994; Brooks *et al.*, 1993; Chaffer and Taylor, 1975; Cooper, 1992; Farmer and Knight, 1995; Husbands, 1996).

In the mid-1980s academic educationalists woke up to the problem in terms of the whole curriculum. They noted the importance of the relationship between teachers' academic subject knowledge and what and how they teach children (Anderson, 1991; Grossman *et al.*, 1988; Kennedy, 1991; Schwab, 1978; Shulman, 1986; Shulman, 1987). Significantly, research in America and Britain has suggested that there is a close correlation between teachers' academic training and perceptions of a discipline, and how they teach the subject. The question of the bridge between academic history and the history you teach your pupils becomes central when we pose these questions:

1. What do we mean by academic history?
2. What do we mean by history for schools?
3. What, in relation to both of these, do teachers possess?
4. What is the nature of the gap between academic history and the history that you teach?
5. If you do not have the academic subject knowledge needed to teach a topic, how do you acquire it?
6. How do you translate academic history into classroom teaching strategies that engage pupils in the processes of academic historical study and equip them with its historical knowledge and understanding?
7. If you do not have these strategies, how do you acquire them?

WHAT DO WE MEAN BY ACADEMIC SUBJECT KNOWLEDGE?

As Unit 1 explained, there are as many histories as there are historians. The history that we read in academic monographs and articles, although the product of individual academics, also reflects a continuing debate between them. Among the factors that influence historians' beliefs about the discipline are:

1.   Their personal interests and predilections.
2.   The prevailing intellectual climate.
3.   Shared academic interests and concerns.
4.   The current body of academic historical knowledge in relation to a topic.
5.   Their intellectual training and education – the procedural, syntactic knowledge that they use in pursuing an historical enquiry.

Personal interests and predilections

Personal interest provides the focus for academic study, the 'insatiable curiosity' that marks out the historian in pursuit of his or her quarry. Lady Antonia Fraser's biography of Mary Queen of Scots reflects this:

I had two principal aims when I began to write this biography. First, being possessed since childhood by a passion for the subject of Mary Queen of Scots, I wished to test for myself the truth or falsehood of the many legends which surround her name. In order to tear away these cobwebs – or in certain cases reverently replace them – I delved into as many published and unpublished sources as I could discover, taking as my starting-point Mary's own letters and the calendars of state papers (although of course there may well be some sources of which I was unhappily ignorant). Secondly, for the sake of the general reader, I hoped to set Mary anew in the context of the age in which she lived. [Lady Antonia found there was no modern life of Mary taking into account academic scholarship on the period.] So in the end my two aims converged, and I found myself with the single objective of showing, with as much accuracy as is possible in the light of modern research, what Mary Queen of Scots might have been like as a person... The task of writing such a book – covering ground well-trodden by scholars of the present, as of previous generations – would not have been possible without the benefit of their works, which are listed in the bibliography, and whose assistance I gratefully acknowledge.

(Fraser, 1970: 11–12)

The prevailing intellectual climate

This shapes how the historian tackles a topic. Thus from the 1920s onwards, in general terms, Marxist theory played a major role in how all Western historians approached their work. Within the Soviet Union Marxism, or the Soviet State's interpretation of it, determined the history that was written there. In 1931 Stalin intervened in what had become a polemical dispute between Russian academic historians on the nature and purpose of the study and teaching of history in Russia at all levels. Stalin violently attacked the dominant group of academic historians as Trotskyites, and reinstated a view of history that intertwined nationalist achievements with Marxist dialectic:

Stalin's intervention in 1931 tied the historical profession to the party. The intellect was now utterly subservient to the state and the Terror ensured it. The history text books were brimful with names, dates and statistics, absent were the pogroms, slave labour camps and forcible national repatriation. In its place all school children could now read of

Russia's powerful heroes, past and present. They could read about their dear 'grandfather' Lenin, and 'father' Stalin, and the struggle to make their country mighty.

(Glasfurd, 1993)

Shared academic interests and concerns

The community of academic historians reflects changing perceptions of the past and approaches to its study, such as the history of women, local and social history and the use of information technology for analysing masses of raw data. Do we, in our teaching, place sufficient stress upon 'history from below', upon the questions of culture, class, gender, ethnicity, and the role of women, upon regional diversity and interests? Or is the history we teach still confined to the top ten thousand white, Anglo-Saxon, Protestant and predominantly male figures who had one of their homes within a mile of the palace of Westminster and who were members of the court circle or Parliament? The school history curriculum should evolve to reflect the interests of the academic history community. Indeed, the History National Curriculum's key stage 2 (KS2) Programme of Study stipulates the study of men and women at different levels of society and its key element 2 reflects the immense change that has taken place in academic history of the past thirty years:

 Pupils should be taught:

about characteristic features of particular periods and societies, including the ideas, beliefs and attitudes of people in the past, and the experiences of men and women; and about the social, cultural, religious and ethnic diversity of the societies studied.

(HNC, 1995: 5)

The current body of academic knowledge in relation to a topic

In the classroom we should present to children information that reflects the current state of academic understanding of the subject, i.e. the network of facts, the conceptual framework, the interpretations and perceptions of the past. By definition there will always be a gap between the knowledge of academic historians working on the frontiers of the subject and the classroom teacher. The problem is at its starkest where the gap between school history and academic history is so great that we are in fact telling children a set of myths, presenting them with a distorted view of the past. These may reflect academic concerns and interests of the past century, or more likely a corpus of taught knowledge that has built up excrescentially through time. Is history in schools merely a vehicle for peddling values and messages, mythical in origin? Is the history you teach a form of political indoctrination, perhaps more insidious for not being recognised as such?

The intellectual training and education of historians – 'doing history'

The final element is how we undertake historical investigations, an issue addressed in Unit 1.

 ACTIVITY 2.1 FACTORS INFLUENCING LADY ANTONIA FRASER

Take each of the five statements:

1. The personal interests and predilections of the historian.
2. The prevailing intellectual climate.

3. The current interests and concerns of the academic community.
4. The current body of academic historical knowledge in relation to a topic.
5. The intellectual training and education of academic historians – their procedural knowledge.

What evidence is there of each one's influence upon Antonia Fraser (see p. 29)?

TRANSFORMING ACADEMIC HISTORY INTO PEDAGOGIC KNOWLEDGE

History for the classroom: two case studies on teaching the Vikings

When teaching history, how do you turn academic history into classroom history, both in terms of the skills and process and of the knowledge and understanding of the content? In our teaching we handle process and content through *investigations*, i.e. the process of finding out about the past with its attendant skills, and content through study of *interpretations*, i.e. the body of knowledge, the findings of historians, that we study. We will examine the relationship of academic history to the history we teach children through two case studies. Case Study 1 is a report of the teaching of an archaeological investigation into a burial mound (an investigation). Case Study 2 concerns Viking migration from west Norway in the late ninth century (an interpretation). What steps are involved in turning academic history into classroom history?

Step 1 General questions

The first step is to ask general questions of the area of study to be taught – where? when? what? who? why? how? and how do we know?

Step 2 Finding out: researching the topic – teaching materials and academic writings

School topic and textbooks and academic books provide both a framework of information and a collection of sources you need for your teaching. On the Vikings, a popular topic, there is a wide range of highly illustrated and resourced teaching materials. These present academic interpretations of the subject, artists' reconstructions, photographs, dioramas and numerous pictures of Viking remains that reflect current professional historians' findings. In particular, the Usborne Time Traveller books make academic knowledge accessible through artists' recreations of Viking life based upon academics' findings (Civardi and Graham-Campbell, 1977). The text and the artistic illustrations are based upon the findings of leading academics. Teaching materials also include a plethora of ideas on how to teach, ideas that you can adopt, adapt and modify in your own teaching.

Contemporary written sources provide a wealth of first-hand materials that can bring children face to face with the past. For the Vikings we have the *Sagas*, a wonderfully rich and varied source, and the *Anglo-Saxon Chronicle*.

Modern fiction, in the form of children's literature, novels, short stories and poems is also valuable. In particular, novels such as those of Henry Treece are marvellous for presenting historical situations in a way that can vividly bring the world of the Vikings to life (Treece, 1955/1969). Equally useful are video and audio materials, and information technology in the form of CD-Roms and computer programs.

Academic writings are another source of information. You will find both the latest findings of historians and how they view the subject in a single academic book written for a mass audience, for example, for the Vikings, Wilson (1970) and Batey (Batey, 1994). When we teach a new topic we head for the local bookshop or the town library and hunt eagerly along the shelves for a readable academic book with lots of illustrations. Remember that using the laser printer you can turn such illustrations into source material for your children to investigate. For Case Study 2 (below) we used an interpretation of Viking migration by Foote and Wilson (1970: 41)

as the basis for our teaching. It gave us a clear focus in terms of time, place and human interest. In 890 AD King Harald Finehair, founding father of modern Norway, was on the rampage, facing independent Viking communities on Norway's fjord coastline with an agonising choice of whether to capitulate, flee or fight.

Academic articles can also be turned into teaching material. For instance, we spotted an account of the excavation of a Viking burial mound on the Isle of Man in *The Vikings and their Origins*, a book that Professor Wilson, an academic historian, had written for the general market (Wilson, 1970: 113–14). All human life seemed there, including sex and violence, for the grave seems to have contained a sacrificial female slave and the remains of a Viking warrior/farmer and his personal goods. Using Professor Wilson's bibliography we followed up the original archaeological report by Bersu and Wilson (1966).

Step 3 Framing questions: focusing learning

Throughout your reading you will think of questions that can provide a stimulus to excite and inform. Such questions enable children to study in depth, the kind of study that is essential for developing historical understanding. When, where, what questions provide the cross bearings for a study in depth. Thus for our case study of Viking migration:

Focusing questions for study in depth	*Viking Migration*
Where – a particular place	Sunnfjord, a valley in west Norway
When – a specific point in time	980, March
What – a specific historical situation	A Viking community under threat from King Harald Finehair

Similarly, the focus for our case study of the burial mound came from questions where, when and what:

Where was the burial?
When was it?
What was buried in the mound?
What kind of people were they?
What happened to them?
What does the evidence tell us about them?
What does the evidence tell us about their society?

The development and refinement of questions is a continuous process that involves both you and your pupils. Study in depth enables the pupils to answer general questions about the topic, such as what was a Viking? and what was Viking society like?

Step 4 Creating a teaching and learning archive: pedagogic knowledge

Having decided upon your topics you can then hunt through your source books and published collections of source materials to extract the sources that you want to use with the children. These you can copy to build up a resource bank/collection for children to investigate. Most towns and cities have a copyshop that can copy any picture or source that you consider relevant, to a high level of quality.

Equally relevant is the collecting of a set of teaching strategies and ideas to use in the teaching of the children. These strategies provide a bridge between academic history and the history that your pupils learn.

ACTIVITY 2.2 COLLECTING THE SOURCES AND TEACHING IDEAS

1. Take the next history topic that you are teaching, listing possible areas to cover as the History National Curriculum requires.
2. Work out the general questions.
3. Using your local libraries and resource centres, and your school collection of materials:
    - decide upon a particular focus for the teaching
    - identify resources that you might use with the children
    - develop and refine questions
    - identify possible teaching ideas and approaches.

Step 5 Curricular constraints, pedagogic knowledge

The questions you develop provide a clear idea of what the children should learn. Your information, sources and repertoire of teaching ideas and approaches suggest particular strategies you might adopt. These you have to relate to the constraints within which you work, such as:

- the amount of time available
- the ability level of the pupils
- the pitch and pace at which they work best
- the classroom 'culture' *vis-à-vis* teaching and learning patterns and styles
- the requirements of the History National Curriculum
- the school's overall programme of study
- the school's general ethos

Whilst teaching the Vikings, for example, we were working with a mixed gender and ability class of thirty 7 and 8 year old children. The topic of the Vikings lasted a term of twelve weeks, with a morning per week allocated to the subject. The morning was split into two sessions, one of an hour, the other of an hour and a half.

Step 6 Pedagogic knowledge: teaching strategies and learning activities – planning and resourcing

The final element in transforming academic history into classroom history is to adopt a teaching approach that enables the transfer to the pupils of the academic history. Your knowledge and understanding of the history you are teaching, and the procedural knowledge upon which it is based, provides a framework upon which your teaching approach is built (Carré and Ovens, 1994: 5). Within the framework there may be many such teaching approaches but they all have in common the fact that they reflect the academic knowledge that you teach.

The selected teaching approach has both a strategic and a tactical dimension. In choosing a strategy you have to review and select from your existing repertoire, or one that the review of the literature suggests (see Activity 2.3, below and Figure 3.1, page 50). Having decided upon the strategy, tactics are then used to determine how we present information, translating it into a form that pupils can understand. These issues are addressed more fully in Units 3, 4 and 5.

What strategies did we ourselves adopt for our two case studies of teaching an investigation and an historical explanation? For our investigation we asked the class in our first three sessions to work as archaeologists excavating a burial mound. We built the teaching of the explanation of Viking migration in sessions six and seven around a decision-making simulation, casting the pupils as a community of Vikings under threat from Harald Finehair.

Step 7 The selection and reorganisation of relevant academic subject knowledge

Our next task was to select, reorganise and present the relevant academic subject knowledge in a form that was accessible to our pupils.

 ACTIVITY 2.3 ORGANISING YOUR TEACHING

1.   Having completed Activity 2.2 and chosen a specific topic, consider Steps 5 to 7 and how you will implement them.
2.   Keep Steps 1 to 7 above in mind as you read through the two case studies below.

CASE STUDY: A HISTORICAL INVESTIGATION – THE VIKINGS

How, in practice, do we turn academic knowledge into teaching knowledge? To bring Viking society to life we wanted our pupils actively to study sources in a similar way to academics. Bersu and Wilson's academic account (Bersu and Wilson, 1966: 45–62) of the excavation of a Viking burial mound at Ballateare on the Isle of Man was perfect. The excavation report was extremely detailed, and fully illustrated with plans and photographs of the burial mound during excavation and the main finds. The site was particularly appropriate, as the Isle of Man during the Viking period was a microcosm of Viking society.

What kind of information did the academic account present? What elements would we want our children to study? We reorganised the material in the article relevant to teaching under five headings:

1.   The context of the excavation.
2.   Its conduct.
3.   What was found.
4.   Typological interpretation of the remains. A typological interpretation involves recognising similarities between a discovered piece of evidence and another piece or pieces of evidence that you know about, and applying to the new piece of evidence attributes already known.
5.   The academic explanation of the burial.

The context of the investigation

The archaeologists decided to excavate a mound that stood in a farmyard:

 To the north and east the ground is flat. From the site there is a wide view over the sea, the distant mountains to the south and the plain to the north. In this district the light, sandy soils, alternating with more clayey soils, form rich agricultural land. In the farmyard a quite substantial mound (known as Cronk Keeilleig) had survived centuries of agricultural activity, protected by the belief that anyone digging in an old burial mound – and it was always regarded as such – would suffer a terrible punishment...

(Bersu and Wilson, 1966)

At this point in the article there was no evidence that this was a Viking burial mound, although the mound was similar to other Viking mounds on the island.

The conduct of the excavation

How did the archaeologists excavate the mound?

> The rugged outline of the mound demonstrated that its surface had been disturbed by farmyard activities, but, surprisingly enough, such disturbance had not affected the essential features of the burial. The ground plan of the mound, as we found it, is shown ... Originally it was presumably circular and had a diameter of about 12m. The highest point of the mound was 3m above the surface of the yard which inclines slightly to the south-east... The mound was removed to the old ground-surface in four quadrants, as shown in the plan ... , and when it had been completely removed the old ground-surface was carefully cleared... In the middle of the mound, however, a rectangular area of somewhat greyish, rather fine, sand, measuring 2.1 m × 0.7 m was uncovered. This was a burial pit of the Viking period and was oriented east to west.
>
> Each quadrant of the mound was excavated in horizontal layers of 20cm.
>
> (Bersu and Wilson, 1966)

The remains – evidence

What did the archaeologists find?

> Towards the top of the mound, immediately below the modern humus and under a thin layer of the soil of which the mound was constructed ... was a thin layer of cremated animal bones, extending from the centre eastwards. The extent of this layer is shown in the projected plan ... The same material also provided the filling of a post-hole (Figure 2.2), 70cm in diameter, in the centre of the mound. The edge and walls of this roughly circular post-hole were lined with packing stones. It was pointed at the bottom and about 40cm deep.
>
> This layer covered, and partly included to the south of the post-hole, the very much decayed bones of a skeleton, which lay outstretched horizontally; it was oriented north to south, the head being towards the north. The smaller bones had completely disappeared and the fact that the strongest ones had survived at all may have been due to the fact that the calcined bones of the covering layer countered the acidity of the soil. The arms of the skeleton were raised upwards, the upper parts of the arms at right angles to the body. The forearms were also possibly raised in the same direction and would then have protruded quite high above the layer of cremated bones, but they were so badly preserved that this cannot be stated with any certainty ... Examination of the skull revealed that it belonged to a young female (between 20 and 30 years old). At the top of the skull there is a large hole made by the slashing blow of a heavy implement.
>
> (Bersu and Wilson, 1966)

The rest of the mound consisted of turves brought from a distance. The mound builders did not use the earth in the mound's vicinity.

The remainder of the report dealt in detail with the excavation of the burial pit (Figure 2.4). The body had been laid in a wooden coffin. Remains were found of:

1. an iron sword, broken into three parts, in its scabbard
2. a scabbard mount
3. a bronze strap end, to hold scabbard sling
4. a strap holder
5. an iron spear-head
6. second iron spear-head
7. third iron spear-head

Figure 2.1 The Ballateare mound
Source: D.M. Wilson (1970) *The Vikings and their Origins*, reproduced courtesy of the Manx Museum

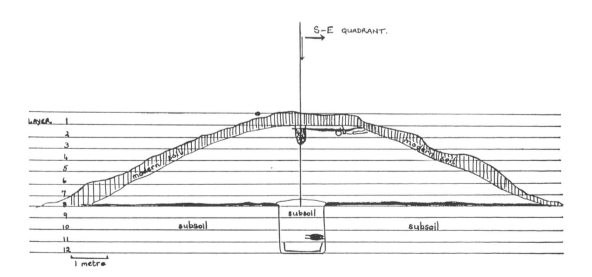

Figure 2.2 Cross-section of the Ballateare mound

Figure 2.3 The woman's skull
Source: D.M. Wilson (1970) *The Vikings and their Origins*, reproduced courtesy of the Manx Museum

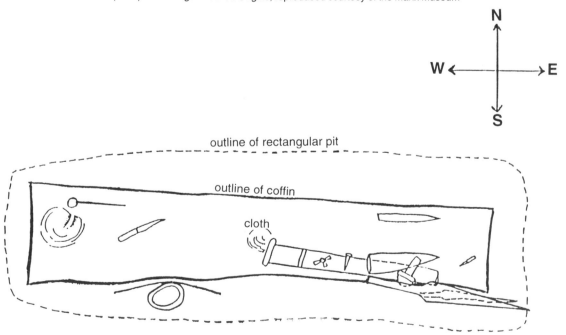

Figure 2.4 Plan of the coffin and grave goods

8.   a shield boss and decayed remains of shield, and white and red paint remains; the shield boss had two deep indentations, caused by heavy blows from an axe or sword
9.   an iron knife with wooden handle and leather sheath
10. a ring-headed bronze pin
11. a skull, decayed, only teeth enamel survived

The typological information – comparing these remains with similar ones from other sites that the archaeologists knew about

Within their Viking context, what was the significance of the remains? The authors give a detailed explanation about each of the artefacts, drawing upon a wealth of research into similar Viking remains elsewhere. In the Ballateare grave was the body of a slave girl, apparently sacrificed. A highly detailed description of a similar Viking sacrifice in Russia survives from the same period, an account of which we found in another academic book on the Vikings (Jones, 1984). We decided to use this account with our pupils (see page 43).

The explanation

Bersu and Wilson used their historical imaginations, based on their depth of knowledge and interpretations of the evidence in the mound, to provide an explanation of the burial that, through inference, recreated what had happened:

We can now visualize the sequence of events involved in the interment and the ritual connected with it. First, the rectangular pit was dug and the coffin placed in it. When found, the grave-goods were presumably in their original positions in the coffin. The man's body was dressed in a woollen cloak, which was fastened by the ring-headed pin, while the knife was laid on his chest. His sword was broken into at least two pieces, and the pieces laid on top of each other. The scabbard and sling, with its mounts and strap-distributor, were also placed in the grave. The spear was put into the coffin with its head towards the man's feet; there would be room for it if the wooden shaft was not longer than 1.50 m. If it was longer, the shaft would have had to be broken to enable it to fit into the coffin.

Two further spears, pointing in the same direction, were placed on top of the coffin ... The shield was outside the S. (south) side of the coffin. We cannot say whether the shield-boss received its two heavy blows at the time of the burial ceremonies; but, as the sword was deliberately 'killed' before burial, it would be reasonable to suppose that the shield had been similarly treated, just as it is possible that the spears had also been broken. The arms and armour of the dead man may have been destroyed either to prevent grave robbery, or in the belief that a man's weapons had to be made useless to prevent his haunting the living.

(The grave was filled with white sand)

A circular mound, 1.20 m high, was then built up with the pit as its centre, with turves brought from different places not in the immediate neighbourhood of the mound. I feel inclined to suggest that this also had a symbolic meaning. It would have been much easier to dig earth for the mound from the fine, white sand of the immediate neighbourhood. The sods may represent the fields of the dead man, so that more of his property, in addition to the grave-goods in the coffin, might be represented in his burial...

When the mound had reached a height of 1.20 m the dead woman was laid on the southern part of the platform so formed, as a sacrifice. The woman may not have been killed where she lay, for rigor mortis had already set in, as is indicated by the raised arms of the skeleton.

In the centre of the platform, just above the middle of the burial pit, a hole had been

left for the insertion of a substantial post, which must have been kept in a vertical position by packing stones.

The woman sacrificed to the dead man, together with the whole platform around the post, was then covered with a solid layer of cremated bones, bones of animals mixed with black earth and with charcoal. This layer was up to 3 in thick and had been collected from a pyre which had consumed the animals. Ox, horse, sheep and dog could be identified among the animal bones. They apparently represent an offering of the livestock of the dead man and suggest that he was a farmer.

(Bersu and Wilson, 1966)

ACTIVITY 2.4 TEACHING THE VIKING BURIAL

• Brainstorm how you would teach the Viking burial at Ballateare to your pupils?
• Compare your ideas with those on pages 41–3.

CASE-STUDY: A HISTORICAL EXPLANATION – LATE NINTH- AND TENTH-CENTURY MIGRATION FROM WEST NORWAY

Using the table of contents and the indexes of our academic books, we found that interpretations of Viking migration focused on the role of King Harald Finehair (*circa* 860–930 AD), which gave the perfect opportunity for children to study this topic in detail.

On the west coast (of Norway) there was a population who farmed and fished, but among them were also a comparatively large number of seaborne warrior chieftains. They were not in a good position to maintain themselves by trade, because they had nothing much to sell (no demand for Norway's fish existed at this time), but they were in a position to take a toll of other people's commerce and able by foreign raiding both to enrich themselves with plunder and to take a share in international trafficking, especially perhaps in slaves. They applied themselves to piracy and sometimes to conquest in the British Isles, particularly in Scotland and Ireland, but also held a commanding position in Norway because they sat on the coastal waters through which the traffic to and from Trondelag and Halogaland passed. The need to solve the problems posed by these gentlemen partly explains the enforced unification of Norway, against the geographical odds, at an early stage in the period we are considering.

Towards 900 AD the young king of Vestfold, encouraged by his advisers, took it into his head to become sole ruler of Norway. His name was Harald, son of Halfdan, generally called Harald Finehair. Community of commercial interest dictated alliance with the earls of Lade, and when this combination was effected, the allies moved steadily southward from Trondheimsfjord against the chieftains of the west coast. Some of these joined them, others fought or fled, but Harald's success was constant and he finally won a decisive victory sometime in the 890s, in a naval battle fought in Hafrsfjord, just by Stavanager. Henceforward it was accepted in principle that there should be a king over all the Norwegians, and Harald Finehair's right to rule was so firmly established that the same right was freely accorded to men of his blood for centuries thereafter.

(Foote and Wilson, 1970: 41)

Two other pieces of academic knowledge informed our teaching preparations: the nature of the communities that lived at the head of the fjords and how they regulated their affairs. Viking society consisted of independent farming families under a local chieftain. The Vikings were freemen who ran their affairs through local and regional assemblies, *Things*. The *Thing* took decisions, settled disputes between freemen and made and interpreted the laws that governed

affairs. Iceland, settled in *circa* 900 AD by Vikings from West Norway, was also governed by local *Things*:

 The early settlers had soon established their own district assemblies (*Things*) to create local laws and settle local disputes, on the old Norwegian model. The *Thing* was where political power was evolved: an assembly of free-born farmers meeting under the presidency of the local priest-chieftain (godi) who had both secular and religious duties. These chieftains (godar) were the dominant political force in Iceland.

(Magnusson, 1980: 199)

Combined, the ideas of the valley community and the *Thing* gave us a focal point for children to relate to the threat that Harald Finehair posed to west coast Viking communities after 890 AD. Accordingly, we organised the academic knowledge we had found under four headings – the situation, the problems, solutions and outcomes.

The situation

1. Vikings lived on the west coast of Norway at the heads of valleys/fjords.
2. These Vikings were ruled by sea-going warrior chieftains.
3. Each community took decisions at a local assembly, the *Thing*.
4. The society was made up from independent freemen who farmed the land, fished, traded and engaged in piracy.
5. As pirates, they preyed on shipping that passed up and down the coast of Norway.
6. Harald Finehair was the king of Vestfold in the north of Norway.
7. Harald Finehair wanted to stop the piracy.
8. Harald wanted to extend his kingdom.

The problems

1. *For Harald*: how could the Viking chieftains be stopped from disrupting trade?
2. How could Harald extend his kingdom?
3. *For the west coast Viking communities*: how could the Viking chieftains and their communities respond to Harald Finehair's threat?

The solution

1. *For Harald*: Harald Finehair, with allies, pushed south on a policy of conquering the chieftains.
2. At a major sea battle in about 890 Harald defeated the Viking chieftains.
3. *For the west coast Viking communities*: they could surrender, flee or fight.

Outcomes

1. End of piracy.
2. Assimilation of Viking communities into Harald's kingdom.
3. Migration of west coast Vikings to Iceland, Ireland, west coast of Scotland and England (Cumbria), and the Isle of Man.
4. Harald became the first King of Norway.

ACTIVITY 2.5 TEACHING VIKING MIGRATION

- Brainstorm how you would teach about Viking emigration to your pupils.
- Compare your ideas with those on pages 41–3.

TEACHING AN INVESTIGATION: SYNTACTIC KNOWLEDGE – THE BURIAL MOUND

We introduced our children to the investigation of the burial mound through the medium of a modern-day mystery. A standard approach is to take something which is here and now, immediate and real to children as a way into the past. Here we work analogically, moving from the known, familiar and masterable to a situation in the past which is similar, where the children can transfer their skills to the unknown, the unfamiliar and the challenging. So, we got the class to investigate a suitcase that mysteriously appeared in the classroom. I made up a suitcase from my daughter Rose's possessions. It is a good idea to try and use a child's possessions who is the same age as the pupils you teach. Our suitcase contained:

Letter, party invite, school report, French sheet, French club, postcard, 'I am 6' sticker, Isle of Scillies brochure, drawing, drawing of house, worksheet, language sheet, drawing book, coloured stickers, flowery dress, school uniform, coat, shoe, hair bands, bangle, hair clip, photo album, *Cinderella* book, *Little Witch's Night Book*, maths book, maths work, recorder, music, skipping games book, skipping rope, Barbie doll, doll's dress, snap cards, tape.

The teaching involved the pupils investigating the contents of the suitcase, weighing up the evidence, and reaching conclusions about the owner. Now we were ready to introduce the excavation of an historical 'suitcase', a burial mound.

The children were to be archaeologists excavating the burial mound and the pit at its base. The lesson's aims and objectives were to:

- involve the children in an historical mystery in the form of an investigation
- enable them to use the clues to build up a picture of Viking life.

On the basis of our academic subject knowledge we selected our key questions:

What was buried in the mound?
What kind of person was he or she?
How did they live?
What happened when he or she was buried?

For the children to excavate the mound we had prepared blank templates for them to fill in, of both the mound and the grave (Figures 2.5 and 2.6). We had also prepared a set of photographs of remains from the Viking period, artists' reconstructions of scenes from Viking life and a collection of KS2 text and topic books on the period, and a tape recording of the story of the Viking sacrifice in Russia (Foote and Wilson, 1970: 408–11). How did the teaching go?

The teaching

1. Introducing the dig
    - Start by saying that we are going to investigate something similar to Rose's suitcase but from a long time ago.

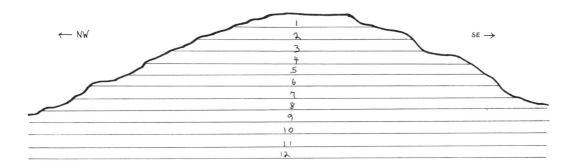

Figure 2.5 Blank cross-section of the Ballateare mound for pupils to fill in

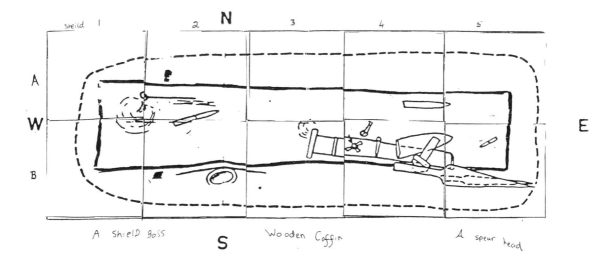

Figure 2.6 Completed dig of the grave. The grave has been divided into 8 rectangles. The class 'dug' these up and stuck them on their outline

- We are going to be a team of investigators.
- We are going to find out about a burial mound.
- Ask questions about who would do this and how they would do it.
- Move on to the idea of the burial mound. We asked the class what questions they would ask; Figure 2.7 illustrates their response.

2. The dig
    - Split the class into pairs.
    - Hand out the templates for the dig, i.e. the cross-section through the mound, one per pair.
    - Read out the levels in order or get a child to do it. For each one the children draw in and note down what is found.
    - As appropriate hand out the pictorial clues, plus any additional information.
    - Do likewise for the excavation of the coffin.

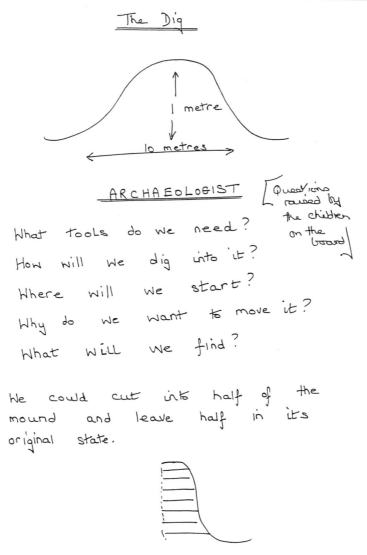

Figure 2.7 Pupils' questions about the mound

3. Discussion/investigation
    *   Put out the source books and resource sheets with examples of the kinds of objects excavated in the mound. Ask the pupils to find out more about the remains they have excavated.
    *   Play a tape recording of the account of the Viking funeral in Russia.
    *   Discuss what the clues tell us about the person who was buried there.
    *   Build up a picture of what they were like, and who they were.
    *   Get the children to recreate what might have happened at Ballateare.

The lesson went according to plan, with full engagement of the pupils throughout, discovering, researching, discussing, arguing and explaining as more and more finds unfolded. We followed the same pattern for excavating the coffin.

TEACHING AN EXPLANATION: SUBSTANTIVE KNOWLEDGE – VIKING MIGRATION

To understand history we must be able to explain what our judgements are based upon. Explanation also requires insight into the motives and actions of people in the past. In dealing with interpretation we try to involve pupils with the historical situation and the issues that influenced behaviour. Through thinking about the possibilities that faced people in their historical context, the pupil can grasp the complexity of the thinking and the factors involved in change, and their relative importance. Consequently, as the two highest levels (7 and 8) of the English History National Curriculum for 5–14 year olds states, students can 'analyse relationships between features of a particular period or society, and ... analyse reasons for, and results of, events and changes' (HNC, 1995: 16, level 7) and give 'explanations and analyses of, reasons for, and results of, events and changes [which] are set in their wider historical context' (HNC, 1995: 16, level 8). The development of appropriate teaching strategies to achieve this means turning academic history into teaching and learning materials that reflect as fully as possible the findings of historians.

How did we attempt to ensure the quality of learning to develop such thinking in our teaching of the Vikings to our 7 and 8 year olds? The first step was to choose an appropriate teaching strategy from our repertoire. In this case we knew that the Vikings of the west coast of Norway had a problem that threatened their existence, that they had to take decisions about how to deal with it and act upon them. They would do this through the democratic medium of the *Thing*. So we decided to use a dramatic simulation in which the class would represent the *Thing*, deciding what to do in the face of Harald Finehair's threat. Here we turned academic history, as given in Foote and Wilson's explanation of the Viking migration, into an active dramatic experience for the 7 and 8 year old pupils.

The simulation structure we adopted was quite simple:

1   The class of 30 is divided into ten families, three pupils to a family.
2   A 'newsflash' informs the families what is happening and how the situation is developing.
3   Each family then has to discuss what it should do in the face of Harald's threat.
4   The *Thing* meets. A spokesman from each family presents its case.
5   The *Thing* then votes on what to do.
6   The next 'newsflash' is received.

Having decided upon the teaching strategy and how to implement it we now planned the lesson in detail. We took the academic knowledge and decided upon our aims and the key question that the children would tackle.

Aims

•   To develop an understanding of why and how the Vikings left home and settled abroad.
•   To understand the nature of Viking settlement and society.

Key question

Why did the Vikings leave their homes to settle abroad?

The teaching

The first step was to present the historical situation that the pupils would react to as Viking families. To do this we needed a map of Norway and an explanation of what life was like at the heads of the fjords, and how each Viking community farmed, fished, traded, pirated and took

decisions through the *Thing*. Having briefed the children, we were now able to commence with the drama. We split them into their ten families. Each family and its members would be able to say at the *Thing* what it wanted to do, and would have a vote. We decided to begin the drama in March 890, a time of year favourable for migration. The next step was to hand out the briefing sheet (Figure 2.8).

In order to make the meeting of the *Thing* dynamic, the pupils cleared their tables to the side of the room. They sat on their chairs in groups of threes to discuss their family reactions, and then formed a large circle to represent the *Thing*. One pupil, Ellie, was chosen to be the chieftain or law giver. She controlled the meeting with a rod of iron, being a natural leader.

The pupil-families discussed animatedly what they were to do, either fight, migrate or surrender. The *Thing* argued back and forth about what the community as a whole should do. Finally the decision of whether to fight, capitulate or migrate was put to the vote:

Fight	14
Surrender	8
Migrate	8

Interestingly, this reflected the academic findings; Vikings did respond to Harald Finehair's threat in these three ways. As we were looking at migration in the light of an increasing threat from Harald Finehair, we announced a second 'newsflash' in the form of a message from a neighbouring

---

The King's messenger arrives: 1 March 890 AD
You live in Sunn Fjord on the west coast of Norway.

A messenger has just arrived from the king of Norway, Harald Finehair.

The jarl or chief of the village calls a meeting of its people – its *Thing*. The chief speaks:

> Harald Finehair has ordered me to go to court with all fighting men to serve in the King's army. Harald says that we must stop our raids on trading ships.

> The King also says that from now on he will rule our village.

> One of the king's jarls says that he owns our land.

What shall the *Thing* decide to do?

> Surrender?
> Fight?
> Flee abroad with all your families and animals, tools, household goods?

How might you flee?

> You have just come back from a raid on Britain.
> You sailed to the port of Dublin and raided some farms on a rich island, the Isle of Man.
> From there you sailed to West Cumbria and looted a monastery in a rich valley full of fish and timber.
> Tied up in the harbour is your raiding boat, ready to sail.
> There are also three trading boats.
> You can take all of the village's ten families with you.

Figure 2.8 Briefing sheet – the king's message

valley that Harald had just attacked. The message contained dire warnings about what would happen if the community decided to fight Harald Finehair and was defeated. We said that as the community did not have a majority in favour of fighting on the first vote we would have to reconsider its decision.

As the discussion proceeded we fed in additional information about how Harald Finehair had treated valleys that had fought him – the men were killed, the women and children enslaved, the lands handed over to Harald's followers.

Again in turn each of the *Thing's* families said what it would do. There were loud protests, fatalistic comments and even an argument that it would be better to die fighting and go to the Viking heaven than stay under Harald's rule. We finally voted:

Surrender   6
Migrate   24

CONCLUSION

The teaching of the excavation of the burial mound and Viking migration illustrates the process of transforming history into classroom history. The lessons were highly active, every pupil being fully involved.

Investigating the past and the history curriculum

INTRODUCTION

History as a construct: syntactic knowledge

History in the classroom involves you and the children working together to make sense of the past from the sources you provide. Children, with teacher support, can work in the same ways as historians. Historical enquiry is based upon asking questions, hypothesising and investigating sources. As historical investigators pupils enter into the spirit of the past, consider causes, situations and consequences and produce and present conclusions. An historical investigation develops a set of intermeshed skills that draw upon and reinforce each other, skills such as comprehension, analysis, synthesis, extrapolation, deduction and inference. The process involves the pupils in planning, organising, producing and presenting a piece of history. Children acquire the skills that 'doing history' requires through a continuous, incremental programme of training and practice. Central to the process is the ability to imagine what it was like to be present at a particular place at a specific point in time (see Bersu and Wilson's account of the Viking burial on pages 38–9). In coming to grips with the past, the historian also draws upon and develops a network of conceptual understanding (expanded upon in Unit 5, Teaching and learning concepts).

What, in reality, do these different aspects of historical learning involve? In 1995 we ran numerous five-, ten- and twenty-day in-service courses for primary school teachers of history. On these courses, members learnt how their pupils could undertake historical investigations and understand historical explanations (see pages 34–46). This was done through placing the teachers in the role of child historians, making them engage in the same processes of learning as their pupils. Through active participation, our aim was that the teachers would assimilate the teaching strategies, adding them to their own repertoire. They then tried out the ideas through action research, reinforcing the process of assimilation. The teachers' action research occurred within the context that the English History National Curriculum had laid down. In this and subsequent units we draw upon examples drawn from the 1995 cohort of teachers' reports from Avon, Leeds and West Sussex of their action research.

HISTORY IN THE NATIONAL CURRICULUM

There are five linked factors that affect the shape and form of your taught history syllabus, factors that are reflected in the key elements of the History National Curriculum (HNC, 1995):

1. The school's *curriculum* requirements and constraints.
2. Pupil exposure to and experience of different *types of history,* such as archaeology, biography, local history and artistic reconstructions.
3. The *process* of investigation and *working with sources.*
4. *Experience of historians' interpretations* that children can engage in to develop and show historical understanding. Such experiences can take the form of story telling, drama, gaming and simulation and expressive movement.
5. *A network of conceptual understanding* that pupils need to make sense of the past, acquired from historical study.

This unit looks at factors 1 to 3. Unit 4 deals with factor 4, while Unit 5 concentrates on conceptual understanding (factor 5). Unit 6 draws together all factors in a case study of teaching 'The Vikings'. Throughout this and subsequent units we use examples of the action research of teachers with whom we have worked closely on our in-service courses.

FACTORS THAT INFLUENCE THE CREATION OF YOUR HISTORY SYLLABUS

How can we begin to construct a history syllabus around these five factors? A central element is education for citizenship, as this provides an overall goal and gives the teaching a focus. We recommend that you consider citizenship, and nine other factors, in creating your syllabus. Factors that influence the creation of your syllabus include:

1. *Citizenship*   History should aim to develop a set of values, ethics, morals and beliefs and the thinking skills to exercise the judgement that being a citizen involves.
2. *'Doing history'*   Learning arises from pupil involvement in the syntactic process of under-taking and resolving historical enquiries.
3. *Skills*   Historical enquiry develops related skills such as ordering, cataloguing, analysing, and synthesising.
4. *Social learning*   History fosters pupils' ability to work co-operatively.
5. *Depth*   Historical knowledge and understanding arise from study in depth.
6. *Sources*   Sources are central to developing historical understanding:
       authenticity   sources should be authentic
       construction   pupils create their own understanding under teacher guidance
       economy   teachers select the minimum number of sources needed.
7. *Imaginative reconstruction*   The imagination plays a crucial part in historical reconstruction.
8. *Communication*   The outcome of historical learning should be communicated.
9. *Assessment*   Assessment should be integrated into the teaching.
10. *Progress*   The programme should promote pupil development.

   ACTIVITY 3.1 PRINCIPLES AND PREMISES FOR TEACHING HISTORY AT KS2

1. Take each of the ten factors in turn.
2. Mark yourself on a five-point scale as to how well you think you implemented them before reading this book.
3. Repeat the process after studying the book.

Curricular constraints

You can consider those ten factors above in relation to your curricular requirements and constraints:

1. The length of the programme.
2. The age of the children.
3. The amount of time for history.
4. The teaching environment.
5. Planning procedures and patterns.
6. Progression.
7. Differentiation.
8. Processes and skills – the History National Curriculum's requirements in the key elements and attainment target – the development of procedural knowledge and understanding, and related skills.
9. Content – factors influencing the selection of content
   - conceptual knowledge and understanding
   - chronology/time
   - knowledge and understanding of historical situations
   - knowledge and understanding of period
   - cultural constraints.
10. Assessment and evaluation of pupils' learning.
11. Evaluation of the teaching.
12. Teacher development – the teacher as a reflective practitioner.

Elements 1 to 5 above are peculiar to each school. The criteria that underpin progression are laid down in the History National Curriculum's key elements and developed in the levels of its attainment target. Three dimensions to pupil thinking indicate the progress that they are making within the HNC's attainment target: depth of knowledge, sophistication of the learning and coherence of argument (see page 130). Points 8 and 9 also operate within the mould of the History National Curriculum. Your taught history curriculum depends upon your interpretation of the skeletal History National Curriculum (Department for Education, 1995). In two pages it lays down guidelines for use when constructing your own course of study. One page lists the prescribed content, the study units, the other lists the required skills, processes and concepts of historical enquiry, knowledge and understanding as encompassed in the key elements. From the discrete building blocks of the HNC you can construct a programme of study and schemes of work that reflect your own requirements and map neatly on to your existing patterns of teaching. Through not prescribing detailed content, the new History National Curriculum provides a framework curriculum that gives you freedom to choose your own topics to study.

 ACTIVITY 3.2 WHAT KIND OF HISTORY SHOULD WE TEACH?

You have just applied for a post as history co-ordinator in a primary school. You attend an interview with the new chair and vice-chair of governors.

The chair of the governors is a member of an extreme left-wing revolutionary party. She believes that children should learn history that tells of the struggles of the working class against oppression and of the fight against imperialism, racism and sexism.

The vice-chair belongs to the National Front. He believes children should be taught British history from a nationalistic viewpoint that stresses Britain's military, political and imperial triumphs, and how Britain has developed as a parliamentary democracy since the Middle Ages.

Your predecessor has left you with a history curriculum based upon the first eight factors listed above under 'curricular constraints' and the key elements of the History National Curriculum.

- Decide which of the factors the chair and vice-chair of governors might object to.
- What arguments would you advance to get them to agree to the propositions they might oppose?
- Explain to the chair and vice-chair what each of the key elements means in relation to the history curriculum you support.

TYPES OF HISTORY: PUPILS' OWN SUBSTANTIVE REPRESENTATIONS

Pupils can construct their own histories, what they believe to be true, from many different perspectives, using a common set of historical skills and processes. What are these types of history? And, having identified them, how can we use them to shape and form what children do? Figure 3.1 outlines the different types of history that can be employed in the classroom.

Each perspective produces a unique way of representing historical knowledge. How can we translate the idea of children constructing the past from particular perspectives into practical teaching approaches? In our in-service course we illustrate an approach and engage the teachers in undertaking it. Thus in 'historians as detectives' our teachers first investigate a murder in a vicarage and then, as history detectives, they excavate and work on the remains found in a Saxon burial mound at Sutton Hoo, Suffolk. In each case they examine the evidence for clues and study other sources to produce a plausible, defensible explanation.

 ACTIVITY 3.3 TYPES OF HISTORY IN THE CLASSROOM

- In your own teaching, how often do you get your children to produce history from any of the perspectives in Figure 3.1? Make a list, using the following headings:

  Type of history   Examples from own teaching

- Consider the next history topic that you are going to teach. How might your class be able to work in the ways suggested in the list above?

Types of history	Types of people	Examples
1. History as detective work	The detective	Rose Nichol, page 41
2. Family history	The family historian	
3. Local history:		
the school	The school historian	
locality	The local historian	
4. Biography	The biographer	
5. Archaeology	The archaeologist	The Viking burial mound, pages 41–3
6. Narrative	The story-teller	Alcibiades and the invasion of Sicily, pages 88–93
7. History and fiction	The novelist	
	The dramatist	
	The story-teller	
8. Poetry	The poet	
9. Visual representation	The painter	
	The cartoonist	
	The engraver	
	The illuminator	
10. Physical representation	The potter	
	The weaver	
	The tapissier	
	The sculptor	
11. The moving image	The film maker	
12. Music	The composer	

Figure 3.1 Different types of history in the classroom

INVESTIGATION: MOUNTING AN ENQUIRY, PUPILS' SYNTACTIC KNOWLEDGE

Pupils can produce their own histories from many perspectives, including all those in Figure 3.1. Thus when learning about the Anglo-Saxons, for example, pupils acted as detectives to investigate a body found in a Danish bog. During the study unit 'Britain since 1930', they behaved as family historians and produced personal timelines. When working on the Victorians, as local historians they enquired into the history of their school. Similarly, for other topics they produced models, pictures, radio scripts and plays, becoming in the process modeller, artist, script-writer and author. In every case they worked as historical investigators to develop a knowledge and understanding that enabled them to present an interpretation of the past, their substantive knowledge, from a chosen perspective.

 ACTIVITY 3.4   INVESTIGATING THE PAST

- For each example note down the particular teaching strategy and how you might apply it in your own teaching.
- Also note the skills you think the children needed and developed during their investigations.

PERSPECTIVES ON THE PAST

At any point of a History Study Unit pupils may be working in one or several of the modes outlined in Figure 3.1. Children can work in different ways during a single investigation. In the example below a class of 10 and 11 year olds are primarily operating as local historians. Within that context they are, at different times, historical detectives, artists and craftsmen, as the pupils of Kath Parker, the first of our in-service teachers, demonstrated:

 CASE STUDY 1: CHILDREN WORKING HISTORICALLY IN DIFFERENT WAYS

INTRODUCTION

This was a local history study, that drew upon the children's own memories, the oral evidence of local people, documentary sources and the evidence of the buildings and the school environment.

The teaching

1. Family/personal history:

I decided to start with the present – looking back at the changes the children themselves remembered, during their years at school. We discussed/wrote and drew sketches of anything that had changed.

2. Oral history:

My next resource was to invite a retired former teacher to the school, to tell us about her memories. She brought photograph albums for the children to look at. This covered the period of the 1970s to the 1980s.

Our next visitor was Mrs Riddle (a dinner-lady), who spoke about being a child at the school during the war – air raids over Bristol, sirens, gas masks, evacuees from Harwich, etc., were all

discussed. She also talked about her head teacher, changes to the building, and school routine. An added bonus was the fact that Mrs Riddle's mother had taught at the school during the 1920s. Mrs Riddle brought in many old photographs of herself, and of her mother.

3. Documentary sources:

We had also been using the school log-books, and the children were able to find many references to events and people we had already heard mentioned – including Miss Young, as Mrs. Riddle's mother was then called. For example, there was a reference to Miss Young's leaving present, when she left the school to get married.

4. Children as detectives:

Many changes to the building had been mentioned, so the next step was for the children to become 'history detectives', walking around the school, inside and outside, noting any signs of alteration. We took photographs, noted changes on sketch maps, then made scale plans. Again we referred to the log-books to try and work out when the changes had occurred.

Many royal and historical events were mentioned in the log-books, so we tried to find pictures of these in books on old Bristol, borrowed from the library.

5. Children as newspaper reporters:

The children then chose an event that interested them and researched and wrote about it in the form of a newspaper item.

We found pictures of old Victorian classrooms, and discussed and wrote about how they compared with schools in the present day. Several other types of school were mentioned in the log-book (such as Dame Schools) so we searched out information about them.

6. Children as artists:

We discovered that truancy was a common occurrence in earlier times. The children drew a picture story to show which 'reason' occurred most frequently – for example, hay making, bird scaring, apple/potato picking and driving cattle to the local market were among the most common in this farming area, but helping mum at home, or sneaking off to watch the hounds also came high on the list!

7. Children as story-tellers and artists:

Annual events were also recorded – Thornbury Christmas Market and Thornbury Mop Fair, for instance. One highlight was the annual arrival of the circus – so the children wrote a story about the circus arriving in Thornbury in 1870, and completed some paintings on the same theme.

8. Children as craftsmen:

Finally, we looked at the type of lessons children in the past had. A sewing mistress was employed, and we decided to make samplers. These turned out very well, and some of the children had their sampler framed.

QUESTIONS AND QUESTIONING

The asking of questions drives forward the process of historical investigation. In history teaching there are two important sources of questions, the teacher and the pupils. They coexist happily;

1887.

March. 9th. George Till having broken or forced the staple in coal house was punished with Herbert + Nicholas Grove by being locked up from 9 a.m to 12p.m in the coal house.

March. 11th. The Dictation of the 1st class was very fairly spelt but the writing with a few exceptions was poor and must be sharply looked after. The same remarks apply to Standard III. The Reading has improved during the month also the Arithmetic of all Standards.

March. 14th. One family Jones away with the measles. Several absentees returned to school to day.

March. 15th. Snowed all day. In some places it was eighteen inches deep: roads impassable. Master came to school with two boys who returned.

March - 16th. No school: roads still impassable.

17. Examined Registers & Summary & found them correct: Grove for managers.
No school as only a few came —

18th. School kept to day. 37 absent morning + aft.n Sent monthly return to School attendance Committee.
Average for the week: 83. 5.

Figure 3.2a Extracts from the school log-book

1936

Jan. 21st The King is dead. The human [flack] was hoisted at half-mast at 9.am to mourn for the death of King George V.

21st. A load of coal (1¼ cwt) delivered this morning by Mr Watts. "The Knapp", Thornbury.

28th. To-day is the funeral of his late Majesty, King George V. In accordance with the wishes of the Revd R. Thackwell, the Chairman, and the Managers, the children will assemble at School at 9.45 am, and at 10.10 am will proceed in an orderly manner to Church for the Memorial Service.

After the service is ended they will return to school for their milk, and will then dismiss for the rest of the day.

The registers will not be marked.

Feb. 10th The fires in the two big rooms are smoking very badly, so that the rooms are filled with smoke. The cause of this is, it seems, the N.E. gale that is blowing.

The pump that has recently been attended to by Mr Curtis is still faulty; there is no water in the pump to-day.

Figure 3.2b Extracts from the school log-book

teacher questioning can lead to pupil questioning, and vice versa.

Questions kick-start the process (see 31–2). The framing, selection and refinement of questions give a historical enquiry its shape and form. Questions are of many kinds, falling within a framework of who, what, when, why, how, where and if. In terms of difficulty and complexity questions range from simple observation to the purely speculative, *counter-factual questions*, for example, 'what if Cleopatra had been ugly?' and 'what if Queen Elizabeth had been a man?'

The second of our teachers, Sue Enticott, built a local history study around her questions. She made a preliminary visit to the local church to plan out the field-work. Her revised lesson plan and comments were as follows.

 CASE STUDY 2: QUESTIONS AND QUESTIONING – LOCAL HISTORY

INTRODUCTION

The following lesson can be used both to introduce a local study and for work on festivals in religious education.

Aim

To develop an understanding of the local church.

Resources

1.   A collection of wedding photographs taken outside a church or in the church grounds. Make sure that some part of the background is visible and that there are enough for one photo for two children.
2.   Clipboards, pencils, sketchbook or paper.

The teaching

1. Questions:

Ask the pupils questions:

> Are there any places in our village we have all visited?
> Are there any public buildings you've never been to?
> Are there any you would like to find out more about?
> Which do you think are the important buildings?
> Has it always been like that, do you think?

Let us look at the church:

> What happens inside a church?
> What kinds of services have you been to?

Look at the photographs of the weddings:

> What can you see in the background?

Sue commented that the pupils generated their own questions, 'Back at school each child had at least one question he or she wanted to know the answer to – questions which will keep us going for some time.'

Another of our teachers, Dee Fricker, took the detective metaphor and used it with her class of thirty-two 7 and 8 year olds. The first session of forty minutes involved the children investigating

objects in the local museum service's Victorian house, using questions to drive the process on. Dee's account of the teaching was as follows.

  CASE STUDY 3: QUESTIONING AND VICTORIAN ARTEFACTS

INTRODUCTION

The visit included a session handling Victorian household artefacts, a session in a Victorian schoolroom and a visit to exhibits around the house. In the handling room the class was divided into groups of three to five.

The teaching

1. Questions:

Each group was given one object and asked to consider the following questions:

> What is it made from?
> How does it work?
> What does it do?
> Where does it come from?
> Does it remind you of anything we use today?

2. Children as detectives:

The children were not asked to say what they thought the object was, as this could shut down avenues of thought and investigations. They were asked instead to act as history detectives, and at the end of ten minutes to report back to the class what they had found out.

3. Discussion:

During the discussion time the children came up with sensible answers to the questions. The artefacts they were looking at were foot warmers, candle holder, candle snuffer, an invalid feeding cup and a moustache cup.

The group investigating the silver candle snuffer had come up with the idea that it could be used for squeezing or crushing objects and thought that it might be used for nuts. However, once it was established that there was a link between their object and the, by now correctly identified, candleholder, several children immediately made that connection, that it was to 'switch out the light' – great detective work!

HYPOTHESIS, SPECULATION AND IMAGINATION

From the start to the end of a historical enquiry, hypothesis, speculation and imagination run riot, feeding off questions and questioning. There is a constant interplay between questions–evidence––hypothesis–speculation–imagination. Janet Boshier highlighted the role of speculation in fuelling an enquiry into the age of photographs.

CASE STUDY 4: HYPOTHESIS, SPECULATION AND IMAGINATION: PHOTOGRAPHS

The pupils were asked for explanations about age, they were worried by a man's beard that was to be seen in a photograph of a wedding but was missing in a later photograph of the same person with children. (This is an issue in dating Henry VIII's portraits!) The same idea applied to hair – the lighter/greyer it got, the older the person. The children were thinking logically, applying logical patterns.

The next idea tied into looking at how old things were. Janet said that she had bumped into an old man, who had given her a magic carpet that could fly into the past. She was borrowing it to try it out. How old did they think it was?

WORKING ON SOURCES: SKILLS DEVELOPMENT

Any historical investigation takes the form of an interaction between the pupils and available sources. All sources are grist to our mill. Jeremy Hodgkinson describes the process at work in bringing an 1851 census to life, focusing on two families.

CASE STUDY 5: PROCESSING SOURCES: THE 1851 CENSUS

Divide the class into small groups (ideally two per group, preferably a boy and a girl, to give the children a broader perspective). Explain that they are going to try to recreate the lifestyles of the individuals whose names are recorded on the census sheet they have all been examining. Each group will be concerned with a different person on the sheet. To avoid unfairness, they draw the name of their person out of a hat. They may get a man or a woman, a boy or a girl.

Next, discuss with the class what sort of information they will need to find out and where they might obtain it. Make a check-list of their suggestions on a blackboard or overhead projector. Remind them that each person is a member of a household and that there will need to be some agreement between the individuals making up a household as to information that is common to all of them, such as:

What sort of house do they live in?
Can any hidden information be deduced from the census sheet?
If children go to school, where do they go?
If adults are employed, where?

Explain that they will need to find out all they can about their person from the census sheet.

POSSIBLE SOURCES

Books

These provide a plethora of information, in the form of both text and visual sources. We use boxes of topic books, sets of textbooks and information books. We colour code book pages using stick-on note labels, directing pupils to the relevant section, thus making the books accessible to all children. A common use of books is for reference, for pupils to be able to use them to find out more about a particular source or sources we have investigated. Thus in our Viking Study Unit (see Unit 6), we 'dug up' a Viking burial mound, containing the possessions of a Viking farmer/warrior and the body of a slave girl. The pupils had worked as archaeologists, and recorded the finds in the

burial mound. Using reference books they were then able to find examples of the different kinds of goods and animals buried in the mound. One of the excavated objects was a Viking sword, deliberately broken into four pieces.

The pupils searched through their reference books, looking for examples of similar swords and how Vikings would have fought with them. This kind of analogical thinking, the matching of remains and objects with information in source books, is central to the development of understanding, for it enables the children to build up an increasingly clear picture of what the past was like.

Objects

Objects come in many shapes and sizes. Groups of objects are powerful in allowing an association of ideas to develop. You can present pupils with a collection of mystery objects in a variety of ways. One of the most striking was the visit of a 'Tudor pedlar' to Pam Torrington's school.

 CASE STUDY 6: PROCESSING SOURCES: OBJECTS AND IMAGINATIVE RECONSTRUCTION

The lesson focused on the children coming to grips with everyday life in Elizabethan England in the 1590s. The main stimulus was a dramatic re-enactment, with an Elizabethan pedlar visiting the school. He wore Tudor costume, and had prepared a pedlar's basket of genuine Tudor goods. He used them in an interactive way, passing them round for discussion.

The visiting pedlar showed the children a very wide range of Tudor artefacts, from spices to horn cups and spoons, from a longbow to a musket. He had made ink from oak galls, and had woven and dyed his own cloth. He had some gunpowder too! They then had a lot of fun making ink from oak galls, gunpowder, tallow rush lights, weaving and dyeing cloth and making a tin musket ball by smelting the tin.

Once the pupils had investigated the pack, they looked through their books, to try and find the things that he had brought in. They found some pictures of ordinary people. The Tudor portrayal of the poor was significantly lacking in detail. However, the class was able to find ten or twelve of the things that he had brought with him, such as the tall, beaver hat. The children found lots of pictures. They were able to distinguish between different kinds of pictures, such as engravings and paintings. They were also able to work from evidence from excavations – archaeological objects. The rush light was a problem, as they could find no pictures of it (apart from those in the Weald Museum). Also, his tankard could not be found in a picture. Pupils raised the problem of the textbooks and evidence – although objects appear in the books, there is no indication of where the objects are from. They are not real sources.

Objects can stimulate interest and enquiry in many ways. We often use a single object to bring the society it came from to life. A series of well-directed questions can focus thinking:

Who made it?
What was it made from?
Who produced these materials and how?
What tools were needed to make the object?
How was it made?
Who owned it?
How was the object used?
What was it used for?
(Either describe it in use or draw a picture of it being used.)

1595

Figure 3.3 The Tudor pedlar visits the school

Who used it?
What did it look like new?
What other things that have since rotted away might have been with the object when being used?
What has happened to the object since it was made?

Pictures: paintings, illuminations and prints

All these provide a graphic insight into the past at a particular point in time. They allow children to think about the picture from various points of view: such as the artist, illuminator or engraver; the person commissioning it; an observer at the time it was being made; or the person buying or receiving it. Pupils can also enter into a picture, telling the story of what is going on from the point of view of a person it shows or explaining what it might have been like to have taken a role in the scene portrayed. Typically we cut up detailed pictures and then ask the children to tell us about what is going on. We provide a perspective for them, for example, in the form of a story, interview or spy's account or allow them to choose their own genre.

With a detailed, complex picture we often split the class into two teams and play the game 'I spy with my little eye'. Out pours detail in great profusion, everything is exposed through the enthusiasm of the game. Because a picture is in a real sense a 'time frame' we frequently use it to work out what went on before and after, or outside, the frame.

Learning comes from going below the surface of a picture and examining its significance. With portraits we look at the messages the elements give – the face, body language, clothes, props and background, and, where a group is involved, the dynamics of the group of people and their relationships. Zara Johnson, a teacher on one of our in-service courses, had been on a course on portraits at Montacute House. Lecturers from the National Portrait gallery had taught her a great deal about imagery. Analysis of portraits of Henry VIII had been a vehicle for developing an understanding of the King, how his portrayal changed through time and how this reflected his relationship to his courtiers.

Zara attempted to do the same for her class, using portraits of Queen Elizabeth I:

CASE STUDY 7: PROCESSING SOURCES – PORTRAITS: BRINGING QUEEN ELIZABETH TO LIFE

To make the connection between themselves and Elizabeth's portraits, the pupils were asked to say what they would want a photograph of themselves to show. They then related these ideas to the Tudor pictures, noting that she 'couldn't take a joke', having been told that she destroyed any portrait she did not like.

The class looked at different portraits of Elizabeth I, trying to work out what messages the pictures conveyed through the face, clothes, symbols of office (crown, orb, sceptre), body language, props. They worked on how things could be added to the picture to build up the image, and how the picture was created. To help them understand these pictures they looked at other sources. The class then pooled their ideas.

The children were introduced to the idea of 'pouncing' to produce a template for copying portraits. Using pictures from magazines, they were able to work on outlines of faces, picking out the jaw lines, hair, jewellery.

The class was set the task of creating a portrait of Queen Elizabeth. The task was split up between them – the result was a large picture.

Photographs

Photographs are of particular value. The same principles apply to using a photograph or photographs as a picture or pictures. Jo Tuffney was teaching her pupils the topic 'food and shops', using photographs as her main source. The teaching lasted for four hours. Jo issued the children with magnifying glasses, asking them to be 'detectives' and find answers to the questions.

    CASE STUDY 8: PROCESSING SOURCES: PHOTOGRAPHS

Objectives

- To develop the skills necessary to 'read' information from pictures, including communicating their findings orally, pictorially or in a written form.
- To start to make generalisations based on evidence.
- Being curious and interested in the past.

Opening session: discussion

The teaching focused upon change, with a comparison between food and shops today and those in the past. The class was asked to volunteer what might have been different between shops in the past and those today. Replies ranged from there being rats and no freezers, to no 'Frosties'! The critical point here was the way in which the picture was introduced.

Observation skills: pictures

The class had to extract information from pictures, starting with the *Let's Find Wally* books. Then they moved on to other pictures, starting with simple questions and tasks, such as how many people are there in the picture, how old do you think the scene is? The observation then became more focused, moving on to looking at clothes which are not the same. The questions were structured, starting easy and progressing to more complex, to help the children access the information. They hypothesised conversations as well as making more general comments about the scene they were studying.

Imagination

Having analysed the picture, the next step was to ask the children to imagine they were the photographer who took a bigger photograph, who was able to look into places that were concealed. What would they see? Under the floorboards there was hidden money, and a token rat!

Using a photograph

Jo gave the children a photograph of a Victorian shop, rolled up into a tube. They started by looking down the tube to say what the picture was. With the photograph unrolled they had to say what the picture showed. The class pooled ideas, such as a shop, food and drink. They had to come up with descriptive word and phrases, to deduce, pick things out and to focus. The class was able to move from noticing that it was old, 'We don't have chairs like that', to discussing differences in lighting – whether they had electric light or used candles. The question arose of when lightbulbs were first introduced.

Comparisons – pair work

In pairs, they had to do a comparison between a modern shop and a Victorian one. In reaching conclusions they were able to support their arguments with evidence drawn from the photograph.

The children used 'evidence' from the photo to make deductions, although these were not always correct. For example, 'The man must be a manager because he has glasses, a jacket and looks cross.'

The children naturally slipped into role-play when discussing what the shop sold and people's jobs.

The class also discussed the fact that photos do not necessarily give the whole story – the men appear to have no legs (they are standing behind a counter), but it is reasonably safe to assume they do!

The next step would be to encourage the listing of observations under given headings, to help slow them down. Role-play could also be used to develop understanding.

What Jo learnt

- The starting point, hiding the picture, giving the children magnifying glasses to be history 'detectives', and scrolling the picture is critical in gaining children's interest.
- It is important to structure questions.

What the children learnt

- Improved observation skills which can be used in other curriculum areas (art, geography, science).
- Confidence to express their opinions and use evidence to support them.
- History can be fun (the most gratifying part was when one child said, 'Can we do some more looking at pictures?').

Jo's commentary highlights the need to regard a photograph as a living testimony about a point in the past. The photograph mirrors a reality – it shows what the photographer's eye saw at that place, from a particular point of view, at a specific point in time.

Reading documents

Working on authentic documents is central to historical learning. A document brings a pupil immediately into contact with the past. Yet there is a problem when children are limited in both their reading skills and their knowledge of the topic. How do we deal with these two issues?

A starting point is that the children can all read *something* in a document. Through the use of highlighter pens and underlining, the pupils can begin to decode the messages that the document contains. The second factor is the crucial role of the teacher in directing the learning and pooling pupil responses so that they can all share in the information. A teacher of a combined class of 6 to 8 year olds adopted this approach in getting her class to make sense of a document on workhouse diets. The class had already interpreted a workhouse plan.

 CASE STUDY 9: PROCESSING SOURCES: READING DOCUMENTS – THE WORKHOUSE DIET

The next activity involved the highlighter pens (instant excitement!). Each child was given one section of the document and asked to highlight the words they could read. Eventually the children began to look at the more difficult words and realised that the document was about food in the workhouse. The children reported back to the group with great pride, and with help on the more difficult words and language, the children gained their own picture of the nutrition provided in a workhouse.

In working with a class of 8 and 9 year olds, Karen Foster followed the same technique, breaking down the document into manageable parts. Here she describes in detail the process of working with the whole class on a document.

 CASE STUDY 10: PROCESSING SOURCES: READING DOCUMENTS – A LOG-BOOK

We began by looking at the Crew's Hold school log-book. As a class we listed:

1. Words I know   Words I don't know
2. Phrases
3. Whole sentences

Some of the best readers took turns to read the whole document aloud. They could read most of it. Then I read the whole thing several times.
    The children worked in groups of four, answering these questions:

1. How is the school's lighting in 1892 different from ours? Which words tell you?
    Draw a picture and explain (we used reference books here).
2. What did children in 1892 do in the afternoon and why?
3. Write what you think it was like to go to school then. Say if you would have liked it. Give a reason.

Investigating buildings and surrounding area

In a local study, buildings play a key part, providing opportunities for questioning, investigation and recording. School buildings are an accessible historical source. Janet Webb took her school as a starting point for a local study.

 CASE STUDY 11: PROCESSING SOURCES: BUILDINGS AND THE LOCALITY – LOCAL HISTORY AND THE SCHOOL'S BUILDINGS

Setting

Local history study, using the school buildings and site and immediate area.
    The school buildings consist of three large Victorian houses (two detached and one semi-detached), and a new block built eight years ago. The school is situated in an old established residential area, one mile from the centre of Bristol.
    Using concepts of change:

1. Look at buildings and site, and make plans noting the differences in building age and style.
2. Consider any changes that have occurred in the seven years the children have been at the school.
3. Look at photographs of school events over the last twenty years and note changes that have taken place to the school.
4. Walk around the school site and find evidence of some of the changes discovered from the above sources, and more. Evidence included the names of the houses, evidence that they were all once private residential houses (post boxes, bell pulls, boot scrapers, front doors, back doors), interior decorations (ceiling rose, curtain rails, ornate banisters, etc.).

Questions

All the above evidence generated lots of questions:

When did the houses become a school?
Did they all become a school at the same time?
Why did they become a school?
Who lived in the houses?
What were the people like?
Did just one family live in each house?
When were the houses built?

The investigation: group work

The questions were investigated by the children, working in five groups, each focusing on different sources. These consisted of:

The school log-book
The school admission registers
Kelly Street directories
Census data
Old maps

Maps and Plans

How did Janet continue with the work, using local maps and plans? A map or a plan is a 'model' or representation of a reality at a point in time. The form of the representation depends upon the producer of the map and the audience for which it is intended. Children have to use their skills to unpack the knowledge that the map contains. Janet used maps of the area from 1837, 1854 and 1878, plus a present-day aerial photograph.

    CASE STUDY 12: PROCESSING SOURCES: MAPS AND PLANS – LOCAL MAPS

The children investigated where the school houses were built and what the surrounding area was like before they were built. They explored what on the map is present today on the photograph.

Discoveries were made from the 1854 and 1878 maps of the area. The children initially found locating the area where the school houses were to be built difficult. However, once they had looked at the aerial photograph and deduced that the only thing that might be older than the buildings was a line of old trees, they then had no difficulty in finding on the map where the houses were to be built.

Considering what the area would have been like also caused problems until they discovered that the lines and small buildings could have been fields and a few houses, and a few hints on the nearness to the city centre did eventually spark off the idea that food was grown for the people living in the city.

Lists and statistics

Our final category of source work is handling lists and statistics. These come in many shapes and sizes, from the Domesday Book through to the Yellow Pages. Probably the most common and

widely used statistical sources are school admission registers, street directories and census returns. Such records are complex. Making their information available to children is a challenge that draws upon the teacher's own teaching skills. In her local study, Janet Webb tackled all three types of source, revealing how to adapt successful strategies to her needs. The focal points of the investigations were the school admissions registers, a street directory and census returns.

 CASE STUDY 13: PROCESSING SOURCES: LISTS AND STATISTICS – SCHOOL ADMISSION REGISTERS, KELLY'S STREET DIRECTORY, THE CENSUS

School admission registers

1. To discover when the school started and which buildings were used.
2. To compare two similar terms' entries twenty years apart – consider the similarities and differences in not only the recording but also the content.
3. To discover a change that takes place in the registers, such as increasing numbers in terms of:
    more girls than boys
    areas pupils come from
    schools pupils go on to.
Record information in graph, table or diagram form.

Kelly's street directories

Appropriate pages at ten-yearly intervals, except during the war when three-yearly intervals were chosen.

1. Who lived in each of the houses, and how long did they live in the houses?
2. When did the houses change use to a school?

Record information for each house as a time line/chart.

1895 Census data

This was photocopied from the microfiche located at the town's library. It was used to discover who lived in each house in 1895, what they did, and where they came from. The children then made their own charts for each house, using headings similar to the original.

The pupils studied each source in detail, working from the known and familiar to the unknown and difficult. The tasks were broken down into manageable steps matched to the children's abilities. The handling of the 1895 census shows the process at work.

1895 census data initially caused problems because of the difficulty in reading the photocopies of the micro-fiche, but using hand magnifiers and tracing paper most children had a good attempt at deciphering the names. It helped having an old map of the area to locate where people had originated from.

Fascinating information was discovered. For instance, one house at this time housed a Baptist minister and his wife and family. One of the daughters was a missionary. Using an 1865 map of the area the Baptist church was located near by. In another house was a widowed ship merchant who lived with his father, who in turn lived on his own means, with his own nurse, servant, caretaker and carter.

This group took their information further by looking at the house the particular family resided in and deciding which room they would have used for different activities. They made a plan and drew pictures of the way they thought it would have looked.

CONCLUSION

History is a living subject, whose vitality initially comes from bringing pupils face to face with the past through mounting an investigation and presenting their findings. During their investigations children can vicariously gain insights into the past through transforming the information from their sources into a form that they can understand. The process of transformation serves as the focus of the next unit.

Bringing the past to life: history as a creative art

INTRODUCTION

How can we transfer into the classroom the endless fascination that history topics such as the Romans, Anglo-Saxons and Vikings have for children on films and videos (*Spartacus, A Man for All Seasons*), in television series (*Blackadder, Robin Hood*) or in comics (*Asterix*), but which too often evaporates at the classroom door? Central to the teaching and learning of history is the teacher's ability to bring the past to life in the pupils' minds, involving them in real issues of life and death. They can do this from the perspective of both the historian and historical characters. When children 'do history' we stress imaginative reconstruction, a topic G.M. Trevelyan, the eminent Cambridge historian, was positively lyrical about:

The appeal of history to us all is in the last analysis poetic. But the poetry of history does not consist of imagination roaming at large, but of imagination pursuing the fact and fastening upon it. That which compels the historian to 'scorn delights and live laborious days' is the ardour of his own curiosity to know what really happened long ago in that land of mystery which we call the past. To peer into that magic mirror and see fresh figures there every day is a burning desire that consumes and satisfies him all his life, that carries him each morning, eager as a lover to the library and the muniment-room.

(Trevelyan, 1930)

What kind of imaginative children's thinking was involved when one of the teachers on our in-service course, Francesca Doust, got her pupils to investigate some remains and involve themselves in stories from the past? Francesca asked the pupils to work as archaeologists.

 CASE STUDY 14: ARCHAEOLOGISTS INVESTIGATING BURIED REMAINS

I had broken up some old plates and buried them. The pupils dug them up and pieced them together as archaeologists.

Using wax crayons, the pupils drew and decorated Greek vases. Then the children cut up their drawings of vases (or photocopies) and chose a partner to swap vases with.

Each child had to piece together the vase and then present their vase to the class, telling the

story of the vase based on the evidence and any knowledge they have. For example, they could try to establish when it was made, who made it, what it was used for, what it shows.

There are many facets to the imaginative thinking of Francesca's children. We stress five: imaging, sensing, inferring, association and empathy. All of these elements can combine in the development of historical understanding and explanation.

Imaging literally means the ability to picture and present what the past was like, a quality that artistic reconstructions such as that of one of the Viking Skuldev ships exemplify (see Figure 4.1).

Sensing is related to imaging, but it involves the smells, tastes, sounds and feeling of people in the past. It can range from cooking and eating food to the playing of music, and this idea is well demonstrated at the Yorvik Viking Centre at York, which has recreated Viking daily life.

Inferring involves filling in gaps in the historical record through suggesting what might have been, and checking this against the existing evidence. Thus, for example, a fragment of a Viking cross-slab at Andreas in the Isle of Man is placed in a reconstruction of the whole block (see Figure 4.2).

Such inferences are often tentative, based upon incomplete and often contradictory evidence. In reconstructing the past using inference, interpretations can change. Thus Alan Sorrell's pictorial reconstruction of Totnes Castle's bailey (courtyard) as being relatively empty of buildings over twenty years ago has been replaced with a current drawing that reflects archaeological research that has found that baileys were packed with a wide range of buildings.

Associative thinking requires the pupils to make links between different, separate pieces of evidence so as to build up a plausible explanation. Bersu and Wilson show this skill in interpreting the remains of the Viking burial mound they excavated on the Isle of Man (Bersu and Wilson, 1966 – given in this volume on pages 38–9). Again, such interpretations are tentative; they are one historian's attempt to make sense of a plethora of evidence that another historian might interpret in a completely different way.

A final, central aspect of the historical imagination is to try and understand, no matter how inadequately, what people in the past were thinking and feeling: empathy. We try to get our children to enter into people's minds and take on their roles, their thoughts and feelings through story-telling and role-play in the form of drama, expressive movement and simulation.

  ACTIVITY 4.1 USING THE IMAGINATION?

- Think of a history topic that you and your children have enjoyed least.
- Consider each of the elements of imagination in history.
- When might you have used one or more of these in your least successful teaching, to cheer it up? Make a list:

Topic; Imaging; Sensing; Inferring; Associating; Empathy

THE HISTORICAL IMAGINATION AND HISTORICAL SOURCES

The historical imagination must work off the historian's sources, such as film, cartoon, novel, academic monograph, biography, school textbook, artistic reconstruction, wall painting, poem, letter, chronicle or street directory. If imaginative recreation is not based upon our sources we enter into a world of unbridled whimsy and fantasy (Vikings with horned helmets, and so on). R.G. Collingwood suggested how we should use sources to recreate imaginatively the spirit of the past. Collingwood was a philosopher and academic historian, whose thinking shaped changes in school history teaching from 1970 onward:

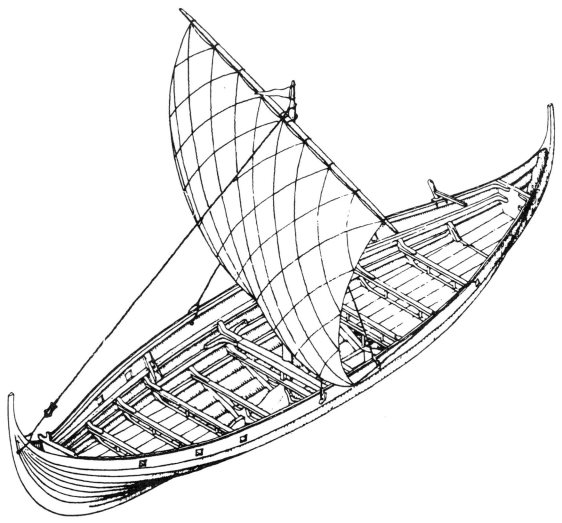

Figure 4.1 Reconstruction of a small Viking trading ship
Source: O. Olsen and O. Crumlin-Pedersen (1978) *Five Viking Ships from Roskilde Fjord*, The National Museum of Copenhagen

When a man thinks historically, he has before him certain documents or relics of the past. His business is to discover what the past was which has left these relics behind it. For example, the relics are certain written words and in that case he has to discover what the person who wrote those words meant by them. This means discovering the thought (in the wider sense of that word) ... To discover what this thought was, the historian must think it again for himself.

Suppose, for example, he is reading the Theodosian Code, and has before him a certain edict of an emperor. [The Theodosian Code regulated relationships between the Roman Catholic Church and the Roman Empire.] Merely reading the words and being able to translate them does not amount to knowing their historical significance. In order to do that he must envisage the situation with which the emperor was trying to deal, and he

Figure 4.2 A fragmentary cross-slab
Source: Batey, C. (1994) *Cultural Atlas of the Viking World*, copyright Manx National Heritage, Isle of Man

must envisage it as that emperor envisaged it. Then he must see for himself, just as if the emperor's own situation were his own, possible alternatives, and the reasons for choosing one rather than another; and thus he must go through the process which the emperor went through in deciding on this particular course. Thus he is re-enacting in his own mind the experience of the emperor; and only in so far as he does this has he any historical knowledge ... of the meaning of the edict.

(Collingwood, 1946: 283)

ACTIVITY 4.2 USING A SOURCE TO BRING THE PAST TO LIFE

* What might involvement in the thought processes of the producer of a source entail for children?
* Why is re-enactment important?

In getting children to use their informed imaginations we have to make a bridge between the past and present. Bridging involves the transformation of knowledge and information into a medium that is immediate, real and attractive for children. Children deepen and widen understanding both through translating information from a medium they find hard to understand into one that is more immediate and accessible, and through encountering the same ideas in different forms (Bruner 1966; Rogers, 1979).

To achieve this, your role is to provide, through a surrogate second record, the knowledge and experience that the children lack. With your help the pupils can then develop their understanding through experiencing the same thing in four different ways – the iconic (visual), enactive (dramatic/physical enactment), symbolic (linguistic/speech, written signs and symbols), and aural (non-linguistic sound). The teacher's role is to *translate* information from one mode into another, for example, transforming a written account into a picture of the scene or discussing in depth the meaning of a picture.

Because of the integrated nature of our lessons, with strategies encompassing a number of approaches, at different times pupils may be working in two or more modes. Thus in recreating Greek pots and making them from clay the pupils can be working both *iconically*, drawing their pot designs and decorations, and *enactively*, taking on the role of the Greek potter in making the pot, transforming a visual image into a physical reality through the process of creating the pot.

The Iconic medium

The visual medium is a most powerful tool in developing understanding. A picture is literally worth a thousand words. Most important, all sighted children can relate and react to pictures at their own level and transform the pictures' visual messages into their own images. Pictures make imaging a reality, the ability to form a picture in the mind of what the past was physically like. Iconic representation means both working from images and transforming information from the symbolic or enactive modes into pictures. In presenting this idea to teachers we ask them to reconstruct visually a situation from a document. The will of a Saxon Bishop, Aelfwold of Crediton, is perfect (see Figure 4.3).

In bringing the will to life we work in groups of two and three, using reference books and other sources to find out what the will's entries might mean visually. Soon, on sheets of cartridge paper a Saxon bishop and his household emerges, many of the men armed to the teeth.

THE WILL OF BISHOP AELFWOLD

This is Bishop Aelfwold's will, that is, that he grants the estate at Sandford to the minster at Crediton as payment for his soul, with supplies and with men just as it stands, except for the penally enslaved men.

And   he grants one hide of it to Godric, and a plough-team of oxen.

And   he grants to his lord four horses, two saddled and two unsaddled, and four shield and four spears

and   two helmets and two mail-coats, and fifty mancuses of gold which Aelfnoth of Woodleigh owes him, and a sixty-four oared ship – it is all ready except for the rowlocks; he would like to prepare it completely in a manner suitable for his lord, if God allows him.

And   to Ordwulf two books: Hrabanus and the Martyrology;

and   to the aetheling forty mancuses of gold and the wild cattle on the Ashburn estate, and two tents;

and   to the monk Aelfwold twenty mancuses of gold and a horse and a tent;

and   to the priest Brihtmer twenty mancuses of gold and a horse;

and   to his three kinsmen, Eadwold, Aethenoth and Grimketel, to each of them twenty mancuses of gold and to each of them a horse;

and   to his kinsman Wulfgar two wall-hangings and two seat-covering and three mails-coats;

and   to his brother-in-law Godric two mail-coats;

and   to the priest Edwin five mancuses of gold and his cope;

and   to his priest Leofsige the man whom he released to him earlier called Wunstan;

and   to Cenwold a helmet and mail-coat;

and   to Boia a horse; and to Maelpatrik five mancuses of gold;

and   to Leofwine Polga five mancuses of gold;

and   to the scribe Aelfgar a pound of pennies he lent to Tun and his sisters – they are to pay him;

and   to his sister Eadgifu a 'rubbing-cloth', and a dorsal and a set covering;

and   to the nurse Aelfflaed five mancuses of pennies;

and   to Leofwine Polga and Maelpatrik and Brihtsige, to each of the three of them a horse;

and   to each man of his household his mount which he had lent him; and to all his household servants five pounds to divide, to each according to his rank.

And   to Crediton, three service-books: a missal, and a benedictional and an epistle-book, and a set of mass-vestments.

And   on every episcopal estate freedom to every man who was penally enslaved, or who he had bought with his money.

And   to Wilton a chalice and paten of a hundred and twenty-mancuses of gold – all but three mancuses.

And   to the chamberlain his bed-clothes.

And   as witness to this are: Aelfgar's son Wulfgar, and Godric of Crediton, and the priest Edwin, and the monk Aelfwold and the priest Brihtmaer.

Figure 4.3 The will of Bishop Aelfwold of Crediton, Devon

ACTIVITY 4.3 PICTURING BISHOP AELFWOLD

- You will need a collection of books, pamphlets and visual sources on Anglo-Saxon England.
- Create a spider diagram showing the bishop, family, members of the household and possessions of Bishop Aelfwold.
- Base the diagram on information that you can find in your source books.

Children expressing their understanding through art is a consistent theme in the action research the teachers on our courses undertake. Five examples illustrate the transfer of ideas at work, two from 'Ancient Greece', two from 'Life in Tudor Times' and one from 'Victorian Britain'. In the first of these, Case Study 15, Francesca Doust continues the work she had introduced through the children working as archaeologists. Francesca's two one-hour lessons on the Ancient Greeks cast the 8 and 9 year old children as artists and potters.

 CASE STUDY 15: GREEK POTTERS AND ARTISTS

INTRODUCTION

An introductory activity to Ancient Greeks.

OBJECTIVES

1. For children to look closely at primary/secondary evidence and make deductions about life in Ancient Greece.

RESOURCES

Greek pots and vases
Pictures of the above (plentiful in books/on cards)
Pot/vase outlines
Black and orange wax crayons, paper, etc.

The teaching

Assume that the children already have an idea of why we need to look at evidence/be a detective and have access to a timeline.

1. Introduce the idea that Ancient Greeks made and decorated vases and pots, and that we can find out a lot about them by examining vases and pots found by archaeologists.
2. Ask the children to look at pictures of pots and to list as many things as possible that they can deduce about Greek life from the pictures on the pot (this can bring in the question of whether the pictures represent fact or the artist's opinion/point of view).
3. The children then design their own pots using the pictures/pots that they have studied as an example.

(In using the visual medium, Francesca noted the importance of the teacher in forcing the children to work from their sources. Less able children tend to copy the designs in the pictures.)
   The children's designs must depict Greek as opposed to modern ways of life.
   It is probably best if the children do a draft design first, although mine mostly managed to create a sucessful design at the first attempt. I gave them a choice of three outline Greek vase shapes, as it is quite hard to draw the shape well, and the design was the main objective.

They then filled in the vase using thick orange wax crayon, covered this over with black and then scratched their design in with a sharp pencil. (A word of warning - the wax crayon flakes magically attach themselves to any nearby books - a good reason for draft designs on paper.) The children then cut out their vases for display - perhaps grouped by features, e.g. gods, warriors, leisure activities.

Picture work can be highly flexible and adaptable. Sandra Hosford was teaching the Tudors. She told the class the story of the *Mary Rose*. The children worked in groups on different aspects of the story and its background, translating ideas into a visual form in four ways.

 ## CASE STUDY 16: TUDOR PORTRAITS

- Copies of Holbein's portrait of Henry VIII – paint pastel miniatures of Henry VIII, with embossed gold frames.
- Paint pastel miniatures of the *Mary Rose*.
- Create stained glass windows of the Tudor rose from cellophane.
- Paint a Tudor house.

The next example is also from 'Life in Tudor times'. Zara Johnson, whose introductory work on Tudor portraits is on page 60, concluded her children's investigations by asking them to create their own Tudor portraits and a collage of Queen Elizabeth I.

 ## CASE STUDY 17: THE PORTRAIT OF QUEEN ELIZABETH I

The class was set the task of creating a portrait of Queen Elizabeth I. The task was split up between them – the result was the picture displayed at the in-service day.

In translating a document or story into visual form we often get our children to draw the story as it unfolds. On our in-service courses we play a tape of the story of Robinson Crusoe and ask the teachers to draw the scenes described on A4 plain paper folded into four. Similarly Janet Jones, in working with her combined class of 6 to 8 year olds on 'The Trojan Horse', told them the story and then linked this to other activities.

 ## CASE STUDY 18: A STORY IN CARTOON FORM: THE TROJAN HORSE

Drawing a story in sequence

Having listened to the story, the pupils in pairs or threes had to plan it into sequence, dividing it into eight parts. (This is a technique covered during the in-service course. Divide a sheet of A4/A3 into six or eight, with a space for a caption or comment under each of the six or eight spaces. See Figure 4.4.)

The pupils started by drawing the beginning and the end, and they then filled in the other six sections. The planning was done as a group, though the actual language used and pictures drawn were individually produced. One such plan ran:

1. Helen stolen.
2. Menelaus cross.
3. Got soldiers.

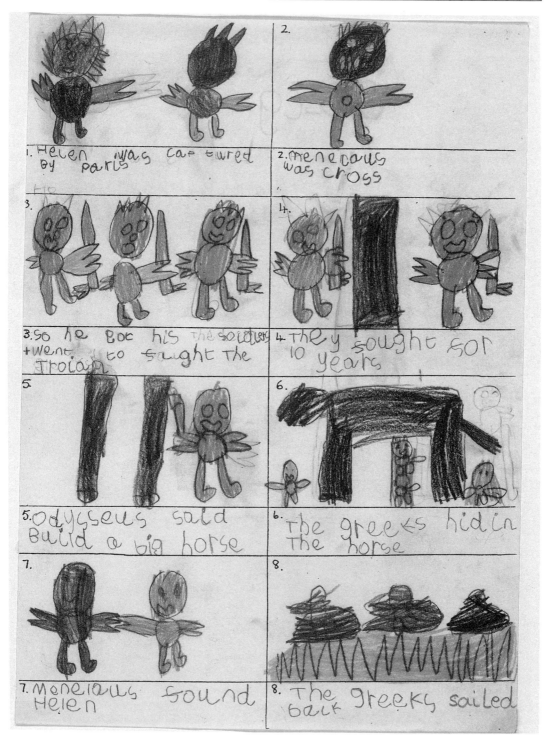

Figure 4.4 Drawing a story in pictures

4. 10 years fighting.
5. Odysseus' plan.
6. Horse taken in.
7. Find Helen.
8. Back to Greece.

Art

The story linked beautifully into art. The children were shown pictures of Greek vases in books and then they discussed briefly the types of things portrayed. One group was given an outline of a vase on A4 with a template of a horse (really just to get the horse the 'right' size!). They could choose one of the Greek border designs shown on the sheet (Figure 4.5) to decorate the vase, or they could use their own design, but it had to be a repeat pattern. They embellished the picture in their own way, using felt tip pen.

The children were also given a paper plate and horse template. The plate had grooves around the outside which made it easier for the younger children to create a pattern, as they chose two colours to alternate in the grooves (Figure 4.6).

Half of Karen Foster's class of 8 and 9 year olds, after she had told them the story of Tiny Tim, decided to tell the tale themselves via illustrations:

 CASE STUDY 19: DRAWING THE STORY OF TINY TIM

They had illustrations of children in different positions up chimneys and pictures of children being pulled out of walls feet first to look at.

Creating pictures and modelling provides a medium in which all children have a chance to succeed. Vitally, creating pictures and models are genres in which children who find writing difficult can represent what they know and understand.

 ACTIVITY 4.4. CHILDREN CREATING PICTURES

*   Take each of the examples above, extract the teaching strategy and then consider when you would use it in your own teaching

Case study	Example of iconic teaching	When it might be used in own teaching
13 15		
14 16		
15 17		
16 18		
17 19		

*   Select a document that you would ask the children to turn into a picture.
*   Work out how you would teach that particular element of the lesson.

Figure 4.5 The Greek vase

Figure 4.6 The Troy plate

The enactive medium

A major element in bringing the classroom to life is role-play. Role-play takes many shapes and forms, from spontaneous drama through to carefully planned and organised simulations. There are three critical elements in role-play:

- a detailed description of the characters and the roles that the pupils will play
- the placing of the characters in the historical situation
- the presentation to the pupils in role of a problem or problems to solve.

Role-play can last from a few minutes to a whole academic year, providing the backbone for a course in which the class is faced with an unfolding historical scenario. We followed this approach in teaching 'The Vikings' to our class of 7 and 8 year olds. After, as a village, deciding whether to flee from Norway, they then had to decide what to take with them and how to load their ship.

Following their voyage to England they faced a new set of problems, the settling of a valley.

Role-play can play a part in history teaching at any point. After the telling of the Tiny Tim story Karen Foster's class decided to dramatically re-enact the story of little Tim.

 CASE STUDY 20: CHILDREN CREATING A PLAY ABOUT TINY TIM

Fifteen of my children wanted to role-play 'Little Tim' and divided themselves into two groups. The more successful of the two had its own 'director'. I took a back seat. The remainder of the class wrote and illustrated the story.

A standard role-play technique is pupils taking the roles of different characters with different needs who barter both goods and services. Formally this can take the form of activities as contrasting as organising the farming of a Saxon village and Viking trading between the towns of the Viking commercial world, stretching from Dublin to Novgorod. Helen Reese used the approach with her class of 7 to 9 year olds in learning about a Roman market (Figure 4.7). The crucial point is that in deciding what to make, the class has to work from available sources and extract from them the goods to be made and sold.

 CASE STUDY 21: THE ROMAN MARKET

The whole class made the items to sell in all of the shops. The class was split up into five groups; each group had to decide what it would sell, choosing shop names as appropriate. Alfredo's Olive Oil sold olive oil and wine (Ribena!), Juicy Fruits was a fruit and vegetable shop (sold real fruit plus paper maché vegetable models). Karl's Butchers sold meat made of foam, paper, etc. The Pottery Shop sold pots that they had made and designed. Hadrian's Bread made bread.

After deciding on their shop they had to design it and produce a model of what it was like. The model was based upon their investigation of the sources, including lots of books. What would they need? As well as togas and money, they designed and made produce as diverse as pots, meat, vegetables and bottles. The bakers even made bread. When the market was set up, they spent the morning putting the finishing touches to their shop fronts. The class wore their togas. They used money, as the course suggested. The market was videoed.

The class spent four weeks in working on their stalls. The activities involved a lot of technology. How did the children respond to participating in the market? The bakers and potters tell us.

Our Roman market: the bakers

'To make our Roman market we had to design it so that people knew we were the bakers. We all designed a shop front and then we got another piece of paper and did another design which had a bit from all our designs. Then we made a little model of what it would look like – it had an arch with the title on and two pillars and two shelves and a table but the problem was we could not make the table stand up; in the end we slotted it on to the pillars. Then we made things to sell. We made pots. My pot was brown with black lines and red dots. Then I made another one which was blue with black and green spots, then we made bread and cooked it. Then we made paper maché fruit. I did a pear which was green and had a brown bruise. Then we made the big shop front. I painted shelves and painted the arch. It was fun. Then we had to make Roman money, we made denarius and sestertii and asses.

'After that we decided on a price list, which was 3d for big, 255a for medium and 37a for small. Our title was Hadrian's Bakers, because of Hadrian's Wall.

'I wore my sailor's dress and a sheet like a cloak. On my feet I wore black sandals.'

Figure 4.7 The Roman market place: an artist's reconstruction
Source: *The Romans – Activity Book* (1986) British Museum. Drawing by William Webb, copyright Trustees of the British Museum

Our market day

'First we set up our shops. Then we got dressed up. Then we got all the bread. First me and Holly were selling, then Jamie and Karl. I bought two pots, five pieces of fruit, three drinks of Ribena, two pieces of bread and meat.'

Our Roman market: the potters

'In our Roman market we had to make some pots for the pottery shop and make some bread for the bakers. We all brought some Roman clothes to wear as well. The name of our shop was the Pottery Shop. Making the shop was very fun. I hope we do something like it again. Also we made a price list to tell people the price of the pots. The most expensive our shop could go up to was 5 denarius. It was very fun for me because I really like building. All the names of the money was denarius, sestertii and asses. We also had to make a model first before we made the real thing. I like our topic about Invaders and Settlers. I hope we could make a big model of a Viking Longship.'

Our Roman market

'First we designed a shop front (together) and we made it, well we tried to make the model. Then we all made pots and designed them and mine was just brown with some patterns. After that we made bread, fruits then meat for the orange table [the butcher's]. Then we made money to buy things. We made 32 Asses, 12 Sestertii and some Denariuses. Denarius is the most, then Sestertii, then Asses. After money we made a price list so we know how much the object is if someone wanted to buy it, and then they would pay for it. At home we had to find something like a Roman toga to wear, then we would bring it to school.'

Roman market day

'On the day we settled everything out and got changed, then we play, and Miss C. was video recording us and we had to not notice her. And me and Karl were in the shop first (for the Butcher) and then we changed over. When I was in the shop for the butcher's I ate a sausage roll, so did Karl. When I went out I bought a roll, a plum, my pot and Hannah's pear and red wine and then I bought two sausages, I mean sausage roll. After we watched our Roman market and we all enjoyed it.'

The enactive approach can involve children with firsthand experiences of life in the past. Thus we have involved our children in grinding grain using a Roman quern. Likewise Janet Lewis got local experts to work with her class.

 CASE STUDY 22: BUTTER-MAKING

Being a village school, the local community also contribute a great deal. One of the children's granny volunteered to show the children butter-making. It was lovely that she let each one in the class make their own pat of butter using the butter pats. This was followed up with bread making.

Another element of children working enactively is the making of a model. Here the children recreate in a three-dimensional form an object from the past. Modelling is infinite in its variety, from producing Roman clay lamps to building Tudor houses. Modelling shares a common process:

Research	Using both visual and written sources, they find out about what they are modelling. The model should be based as closely as possible upon the sources.
Planning and design	They have to plan out and design the model, relating it to the features in the sources.
Resourcing	To create the model they need to collect the raw materials.
Creating	The process of producing the model.
Presenting/display	The models are presented.

 ACTIVITY 4.5 DRAMA AND SIMULATION

- Take the example of the teaching of the Roman Market.
- How might you adapt it to teaching about trade in either:
  a Viking town like York
  the Tudor town?

- How might you use:
  making things
  modelling
  in your history teaching?

The symbolic medium: language

All history teachers are language teachers. The main ways of developing historical understanding are through speaking, reading and writing. History is a supremely literary subject, and the main source of historical information is the written word. History is built around story telling, often in the form of a historical narrative, be it story, poem, novel or textbook account. The ability to tell children stories is a much-neglected aspect of the teacher's craft. While all primary school teachers read stories to their classes, few work as story tellers. Learning to tell stories is relatively simple. As a teacher you can create and present stories to your class. Story telling involves the children. As the audience the pupils become wrapped up in the tale and can participate in it. Story telling is a supreme way of presenting a historical interpretation to the children. It then provides a springboard for subsequent learning.

Story telling

How are stories created? Central to story telling is posing a problem, be it how Alfred can defeat the Vikings, or whether Tiny Tim can be rescued from the chimney sweep. Once a problem is found, the story teller builds up the story through describing characters and scenes and bringing them to life through voice, gesture and movement.

   Karen Foster took these ideas and adopted them in her telling of a story about the Victorians. The class had been doing some work on Victorian schools in Bristol. She worked with the children on a document and a photograph of rather ragged children in Crew's Hold, Bristol. Karen chose one of the children in the picture and used him as the basis for the following activity.

   CASE STUDY 23: A STORY ABOUT RAGGED CHILDREN AND TINY TIM

My gran told me a tale of long ago which is true as true can be...

Background

Little Tim has been sold as a climbing boy to Bad Harry, the sweep master, unbeknown to his mother who is working away.

Problem

How will little Tim, in dire straits, be rescued?

Resolution

Sweet Annie, Tim's impoverished mother, throws herself in despair at the feet of kindly Solicitor Sam and begs for help. He represents her before the Magistrate and orders Tim's return. Bad Harry is fined five pounds.

Situation

- Tim's dad dies and mother (Sweet Annie) goes to work in a rich Victorian house.

- She leaves Tim with greedy cousin George, who sells him for three guineas to bad Harry Holland the master sweep.
- Bad Harry mistreats Tim terribly - beats him, gives him a dirty, cold place to sleep in.
- Tim is sent to work with little Peter and John, both of whom die in horrible accidents. Tim himself gets stuck up a chimney, is pulled down and beaten by Bad Harry, and despite the fact that he has been working since 3.00 a.m. is made to walk five miles in deep snow and cold so terrible 'you wouldn't put a dog out in it'.
- He trudges back to Bad Harry's hovel half dead and Mum, who has returned and learned that cousin George has sold him, eventually finds Tim.
- Bad Harry demands his three guineas. Mum can't pay. In despair she begs Solicitor Sam to help her, which he does. Mum and Tim are reunited in tears.

Janet Jones applied the same approach to story telling to tell the story of the Trojan Horse.

 CASE STUDY 24: THE TROJAN HORSE

Introduction

The class was well into a half-term topic of 'Boxes' when the course occurred. We had completed two lessons on the history of packaging. This involved a brief history of trading, shops and shopping, and the transport of goods from further abroad leading to need for more packaging/boxes. How could I fit history into this topic? The Trojan Horse, of course!

Teaching Strategies

The focus was on story telling. The diagram (Figure 4.8) shows how the Trojan Horse fitted into the topic and naturally expanded into the whole of the English area, i.e. talking, listening, drama and improvisation, and writing. The children loved the story and had no trouble with the unfamiliar names.

The outline of the story as told to the children

Background Introduction of Helen, the very beautiful wife of Menelaus, the King of Sparta. She is seen by Paris, a prince from a city called Troy quite a long way away. Bewitched by her beauty he steals her away. Menelaus is angry, very angry, furious, etc. [Build up the tension]. He called all the warriors and other kings in Greece together and they set off, overland, overseas. Odysseus, a Greek ruler, leads his men to Troy.

Time factor Many battles and fights for ten years – longer than you all have been alive. [Emphasise missed family life, hardships away from home.] Greeks decide to call it a day and leave. Odysseus comes up with an amazing plan - it will not cost any more lives and only take about twelve men to get into the city. He is ridiculed by others but he eventually gets twelve men to support him.

Building the horse Without saying what is being built, Odysseus gets men building a base of four legs, and a large, hollowed-out box shape. [Children do not know at this point that it is a horse.] The build-up of disbelief amongst the soldiers reaches its climax when the order goes out to make a horse's head and tail.

The plan Odysseus now tells the men the plan - twelve soldiers in the horse, all others to strike camp and sail out of sight. One volunteer to be tied up and left for the Trojans to find and be told that the Greeks have left, disillusioned, leaving behind an offering for the Goddess Athena. What sort of man was the volunteer – brave, heroic?

Trojans bring in the horse Build up the tension felt among the Trojans, and their indecision as to

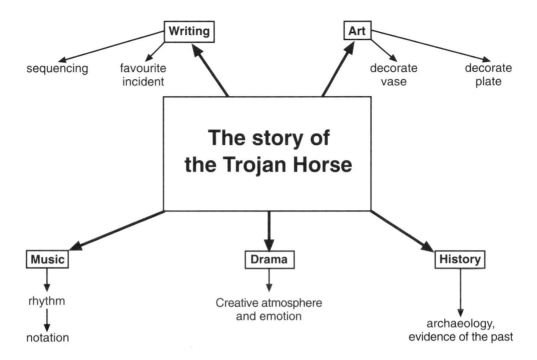

Figure 4.8 The story of the Trojan horse

whether it is a trick or not. They are helped by the 'volunteer' to make the decisions to bring the horse into the city. All quiet, men inside the horse are keen to be released, more tension here. Finally the Greeks inside the horse silently climb out and open gates to let the returning Greeks in and attack the Trojans, who are sleeping and taken by surprise.

Happy ending Helen is found and reunited with Menelaus, and the Greeks sail away.

Follow-up work from this story involved art, archaeology and music.

 ACTIVITY 4.6 STORY TELLING

- Take a major situation in the next history topic that you are due to teach.
- Work out how you can tell a story about it.
- Tell the story to the children involved.
- What work developed out of it?
- Record how the story went.
- If successful, plan out how you will tell a story in your next topic.

The symbolic can take both a spoken and a written form. Children's writing is a powerful medium for showing what they understand. Four factors are involved:

1. The informed imagination that the pupil brings to bear upon the subject.
2. The point of view from which the pupil is writing.
3. The voice, or voices, in which the writing takes place. Language has thousands of registers, and the voice chosen reflects the writer's view of what is the right voice to use at that point in the writing.
4. The intended audience. It is vital that the pupil trusts the teacher as an audience who will be sympathetic, responsive and understanding of efforts made at the boundary of the pupil's performance, and build upon the efforts made constructively.

Below we present two pieces of children's writing, John's (page 86) and Huseyin's (page 88–93). Both relate to one of those most dramatic incidents in Greek history, the imprisonment in a quarry of the captured Athenian army that had failed in its attack on Syracuse in Sicily. What role did the teacher play in the creation of these pieces of work?

Sensitivity	You need to be sensitive to the point at which the pupil is willing to undertake a piece of writing.
Time	You need to make time for it to happen. Time, not only in the sense of a set period, but time to give the child the opportunity to explore the topic, to expand ideas, to draft, to stop and return as the spirit moves. Huseyin's work took two days to complete. Other subjects were cleared away from the timetable.
Support	Support at all stages is essential. The teacher must be able to lock into the child's mind, so as to stimulate and push the work on.
Encouragement	Encouragement when things are not going well is essential. Praise is a major part in support.
Expansiveness	The pupil should have the chance to expand and elaborate on ideas and visions throughout, and use language to its optimum.
Vision	The pupil must have a clear vision of what s/he is trying to do. There must be a goal in mind of where the writing will end.
Ownership	The pupil must own the writing, it must be a projection of his or her own personality, something created and in which pride can be taken.

Writing goes through a series of stages, from initial inchoate thoughts to the finished piece. The teacher's role is vital in carrying on a dialogue that gives the pupil the support at each stage needed to realise the original conception in its evolved form. The stages are: planning; drafting; organising; researching; selecting; framing passages in terms of their structures. We deal with the final factor separately (pages 86–87).

 ACTIVITY 4.7 THINKING ABOUT WRITING

How do the ideas outlined above fit in with your current policy on children writing?

An example of the writing process comes from our work on Ancient Greece. We studied in depth the Athenian invasion of Syracuse. The Greek attack was a disaster, and ended with the Syracusans imprisoning the captured expeditionary force in a quarry. The 10 and 11 year old pupils studied the subject in depth, through working intensively upon documents, story telling and drama. One pupil, John, aged 10, wrote vividly about the fate of the Athenians. John's imagination was fired up, and he brings the past to life.

CASE STUDY 25: THE STORY OF THE ATHENIAN ARMY IMPRISONED IN A SYRACUSE QUARRY

The Athenians were lapping up the water like dogs. The Syracusans were crouching behind the peaks of the mountains on either sides of the river ready to attack. Then all of a sudden they all ran down the mountain like rolling rocks with swords and spears held high. And then there were heads being chopped off and people being stabbed. Weeping, the few survivors were led to a pit where they were left to die. Then one of the guards persuaded the head guard to give them the chance to get free. Then the head guard said in a bold voice if anyone big or small can recite one line of Euripides, and this bit is very important, that I haven't heard before, you can go free.

At the end of this unit is Huseyin's account of Alcibiades. Huseyin's story is more like a young novel; occasionally one comes across a pupil like this who becomes captivated by a story and in his own time writes, and writes, and writes. Here we see the young historian at work, entering into the spirit of the times and recreating it with all the limitations of knowledge and understanding of a ten year old. Huseyin's previous written work was negligible.

ACTIVITY 4.8 CHILDREN WRITING

* Read through 'Alcibiades and the Invasion of Syracuse', page 88.
* As you read it, note down evidence for:
* Well informed imagination

What is his story based on?
How much detail does it include?
How sophisticated is the writing?

* Point of view from which the piece was written (Huseyin's)

What is the point of view of the writer?

* The voice, or voices, in which the writing takes place

What different voices can you detect in the writing?

* The intended audience

Who was the piece written for?

* Time

How might time have been provided for Huseyin to complete the essay?

* Support at times of difficulty

What signs are there of the teacher providing support?

* Encouragement

Indications that the teacher had encouraged Huseyin.

* Vision

Evidence that Huseyin had a clear idea in his mind of what he was doing and where he was going.

* Ownership/pride

Indications that this was Huseyin's own work, in which he took pride.

Writing frames

An important new development in helping children to write is the use of linked prompt phrases in writing frames to focus, structure and support children's written work (Lewis and Wray, 1996). Lewis and Wray have devised such writing prompt frames to help children write in six different genres, from reports to persuasive arguments. Teachers can develop, in conjunction with the children, their own history frames. These help children express more fully their understanding in a written form. Such frames can mirror the multiplicity of genres (Figure 4.9) that written work

can take. You and your pupils can develop frames for all involved in extended writing. Lewis and Wray's writing frame for a museum visit ran:

Although I already knew that…
I was surprised that…
I have learnt some new facts. I learnt…
I also learnt that…
Another fact I learnt…
However, the most interesting thing I learnt…

Using this frame, the account below of a museum visit, by a Year 5 girl, contrasts starkly with conventional descriptive narratives (e.g. 'We walked around the Roman walls and then a lady showed us some pots and then…').

A Trip to Plymouth Museum (spelling corrected)
Although I already knew that they buried their dead in mummy cases *I was surprised that* the paint stayed on for all these years.
I have learnt some new facts. I learnt that the river Nile had a god called Hapi. He was in charge of the river Nile and he brought the flood.
I also learnt that sometimes people carried a little charm. So if you tell a lie and you rubbed the charm's tummy it would be o.k. again.
Another fact I learnt was they put pretend scarab beetles on their hair for decoration.
However, the most interesting thing I learnt was they mummified cats and sometimes mice as well.

(Lewis and Wray, 1996: 17)

 ACTIVITY 4.9

How might you develop the use of writing frames in your teaching of history?

The aural medium: music

Music is a form of symbolic knowledge and understanding relatively under-used in history teaching. Should we not consider how best to use rhythm and song, both in presenting this aspect of the past to children and engaging them in it as musicians? Janet Jones used rhythm work to help the children make sense of Greek names.

 CASE STUDY 26: RHYTHM WORK AND GREEK NAMES

Much to my surprise the children had no difficulty with the Greek names. As we had been doing rhythm work clapping the rhythms of their own names, I thought I would try the same with the Greek/Trojan names. This was taken a step further when we added notation. Eventually they could guess the name/word from the notation alone. I had eight words. Two examples are:

Men e la us
!   ! – !   (short, short, long, short)

O dyss e us
– !   – !   (long, short, long, short)

acknowledgement	gloss	poster
advertisement	graffiti	prayer
affidavit	greetings card	précis
announcement	guide	proclamation
article	headline	prospectus
autobiography	horoscope	questionnaire
ballad	instruction	recipe
biography	invitation	record
blurb	journal	reference
brief (legal)	label	report
broadsheet	letter (various types)	résumé
brochure	libel	review
caption	list	rule
cartoon	log	schedule
catalogue	lyric	script
certificate	magazine	sermon
charter	manifesto	sketch
confession	manual	slogan
constitution	memo	song
critique	menu	sonnet
crossword	minutes	specification (job)
curriculum	monologue	spell
curriculum vitae	news	statement
definition	notes	story
dialogue	notice	summary
diary	novel	syllabus
directory	obituary	synopsis
edict	pamphlet	telex
editorial	paraphrase	testimonial
epitaph	parody	travelogue
essay	petition	voice bubble
eulogy	placard	weather forecast
feature	play	will
forecast	poem	
form	postcard	

Figure 4.9 Types of writing

Source: Husbands, C. (1996) *What is History Teaching?*, Open University Press

Alcibiades and the Invasion of Syracuse by Huseyin

Socrates sat in his front room listening to his wife.

She wouldn't stop nagging at him, he'd heard it all before. 'Do this, do that, don't do this, don't do that.' It just goes on and on. His wife wasn't very pretty. She had fuzzy black hair and a big wart on her nose. Her clothes were very tatty and she wore a very plain head dress.

Socrates wasn't very handsome at all either. Actually he was very ugly, he had white hair, oily and plastered to his skull with sweat. He had a hunched back and a lot of warts on his face, his teeth are rotten completely away. His clothes were soaked in sweat and food. He had a thumb on his left hand missing. Also Socrates had a terrible limp. So he wasn't very good looking. Even with his gross looks he had a very posh voice. He had very, very, very badly bitten finger nails and he stunk of sweat and rotten fish.

Socrates decided to leave right now. He grabbed his sandals and staggered out the door, followed by his screaming wife who was throwing things at him. He walked towards a very big

stone hut with a very BIG door. He opened the door and was greeted with shouts of anger and frustration. Socrates cocked his eyebrow and sat down on the nearest seat and just listened to the screaming. They were voting.

Voting had become a thing in Athens. If they couldn't decide, they'd vote. Sometimes it took ages, other times it took one day, other times they just gave up. Socrates was getting bored and angry. At once he stood up and cried, 'Why are you voting? Why, it's stupid you should just find a man who can just boss you around and tell you what to do instead of all this pathetic voting.' Then there was silence. Then an old man said, 'Who have you got in mind ... eh.' Socrates answered instantly 'One of my students, Alcibiades.' Silence.

'He is the one your looking for, the big guy, the powerful man, please choose him.' The same man stood up and said 'Why?'

Socrates was very quickly losing his patience. 'Because he has many children and is very strict and I think that the way he treats his children is fantastic ... so I thought that he could treat you the same way.'

The same man spoke to him again. 'We are not children. We are sensible adults.' Socrates was beginning to lose his temper. 'Sensible adults, hah hah, you are just pathetic big children.' A different man whispered to his neighbour and cried, 'When can we meet him?' Then the doors flew open and a huge man came in, followed by short thin men. The man was huge with a black beard and huge muscles plastered his body. He wore huge garments made of silk. He wore black sandals. He had a clean face complexion, his skin looked oily. Socrates greeted him, 'Everyone meet ALCIBIADES.'

He stomped towards a small shrimp of a person and picked him up by his throat and threw him as far as he could, the man collided into the wall and was knocked unconscious. 'Can I borrow your chair?' Alcibiades rumbled. 'I'm having your chair,' he added. He sat down on the chair and listened to the debate very carefully, eyeing Socrates.

'My dear Socrates what are you doing debating, tut-tut.' Socrates stepped off the stage. 'I was just talking about you,' he said in a shaky voice.

'And what were you talking about,' said Alcibiades in a very sinister voice. Socrates grinned, showing his rotten teeth. 'That you Alcibiades should be the leader of Athens.' Alcibiades raised his eyebrows 'Uh-huh and why me?' yelled he. Socrates was backing away from his student, 'B.b.ecause you s.s.should b.be a leader,' said Socrates very shakily.

Alcibiades rolled his eyes, 'Very interesting, but why did you choose me, because of my ravishing good looks? Yes, I know I am the most good looking person on this whole world.' There was sniggering behind him. Alcibiades shot his head around the room looking for the person who had laughed at him. Then he found who it was, it was the same old man who had been very cheeky to Socrates.

'You!' Alcibiades hissed. The man looked puzzled. 'You' 'Yes,' he said 'come hither.' Two guards seized the man and dragged him towards Alcibiades. 'You laughed at me just now didn't you.' 'No,' the man said. Alcibiades narrowed his eyes, 'Come on, tell me the truth.' The man burst into tears.

'Say it,' Alcibiades said in a very friendly way. 'Yes I did' the man said in tears. 'Oh you made a boob-boo.' The man nodded. 'Yes the Boob-Boo box yeah.' 'NOT THAT NO NO NO PLEASE.' They threw him in a treasure chest. 'BOO! BOOO BOO!', cried his henchman as they dropped fat tailed Scorpions in the small air holes. Then the screaming stopped.

Socrates buried his face in his hands. 'Help,' he wept. Alcibiades stepped towards Socrates 'Now I am the right person to be the leader, yes.' Socrates nodded. 'Of course, what do you want to start with?'

Alcibiades gave an evil smile showing his pearl white teeth. 'You out of the picture.' Socrates frowned. 'What do you mean?' 'I'm going to kill you tee-hee.' He dug into his pockets and showed a bottle saying:

HEMLOCK
Poison! Don't drink!
(It kills)

Two men grabbed (the same men who grabbed the old man) Socrates and threw him in the cellar below.

Alcibiades stood up on the stage and cried, 'I am the big boss now OK, so if you make a Boo-Boo you go to the Boo-Boo box, and if you want kick it with some one you kick it with me. Comprendo.' Everyone nodded. 'I can't hear you,' he cried indicating his ear. 'Yes Alcibiades' everyone chanted.

'Good, now have a nice day,' and he disappeared towards the cellar.

Socrates was finding it very uncomfortable in this very small cellar, there were rats nibbling at his toes which were wiggling crazily. The guards were watching him carefully. The doors flew open and Alcibiades stormed in. 'Hello Socrates old pal,' he said loudly. 'Alci come on let old Socy out of this hole,' Socrates said.

'NO'

He took out the Hemlock and placed it on the floor. 'You may drink it with your own free-will, but, if after the sun rises and you haven't had any, I'll force it down your throat ...' And he walked out, slamming the doors behind him.

That night Alcibiades held a huge party, he had two HUGE pots of wine. 'Drink my friends, drink then by the time we're sober Socrates will be RIP. Huh drink.' They drunk until they were crazy but Alcibiades only had three cups and was still sober. 'My friends, we need more wine ...' He snapped his fingers and a huge Korian brought five in 'Let's have a hoot of a time ladies and gentlemen ... Let's use this city as our own personal play ground.' Then they drank all night.

Socrates stared at the hemlock, he'd better take it. No, yes, No! Oh no he thought, I don't want to, but I have to or that Greek Mobster will force it down me. Help. He reached towards the Hemlock but drew his hands back. 'No,' then he heard a door open, then he heard a voice, HIS voice. 'Has he had the "stuff" yet?', asked Alcibiades. 'No' the guard said. 'Oh righty then,' Alcibiades hissed.

Socrates lunged towards the hemlock so fast he still thought he was shuffling on the floor.

Alcibiades flew open the jail door. 'Good evening Mr Socrates,' he said grinning. Socrates tumbled open the lid of the hemlock and forced the acrid tasting liquid down his throat. Alcibiades sneered, 'You silly fool, now that you are lost and gone forever, looks like I'll have to be the big bad I said NO around here heeeeeee teeee.'

Socrates, who was feeling a bit light-headed, started to jog around the room. Alcibiades, puzzled at first, suddenly caught on. 'Very sensible ... I'm glad I thought of it,' he snarled. Socrates was still jogging when Alcibiades left the room. 'Well at least I'll go to Mount Olympus and be a god with big ol' Zeus, fingers crossed,' he mumbled.

It was twelve noon when Socrates died and Alcibiades took over. 'Right you stupid idiots, firstly I just want to say something. You are red Indian warriors and me big chief right, so that means you have to do what I say,' he roared. 'Now I've heard that you and Syracuse haven't got on very well have you.' Every one shook their heads. 'Good, so lets say ... have they attacked your country or Athens rather?' Alcibiades asked.

'Yes.'

'Good so that means that we have every god given right to invade there little bit,' he said.

'Hold on,' said a small voice.

'WHO DARES TO SPEAK WHILE MOI IS SPEAKING,' he screamed.

'Me,' the voice said again.

'WHO?' he boomed.

'Nicias,' said the voice. Alcibiades frowned.

'Nicias, who's Nicias?' he cried.

'Me,' said the voice then he stood up.

He was a small titchy very small little shrimp of a man with snowy coloured hair and a greyish white sharp angle moustache. His face looked like a date and he was as skinny as a stick insect. 'I'm Nicias,' (the reason he speaks like a mouse is because he's so small) he said. Alcibiades started laughing, 'You little prawn, ha ha ha ha ha.'

'What do you want, and make it quick,' he said through the laughter.

'I don't think that invading Syracuse is a very wise idea,' Nicias squeaked. 'WHO'S ASKING FOR YOUR DUMB OPINION?' Alcibiades snapped. Nicias frowned and then he squeaked 'No

one but someone might get hurt … like the um … Syracusians.'

'YOU TRAITOR, YOU FOOL. IF THEY ATTACKED ATHENS AND TRIED TO CONQUER, WHY CAN'T WE DO THE SAME AND CONQUER?'

'No,' Nicias squeaked as loud as he could. Alcibiades was fuming, 'What the heck would you know about the army and the navy?'

'I am a retired soldier,' he squeaked.

'Huh, huh you a retiring officer, tee hee. If you're a retired army officer then I'm a Chinaman.' Nicias looked hurt 'Then you're a Chinaman,' he said.

'Huh. Now you lot listen to me very carefully…'

He had asked them to make 200 ships in two years, then he asked for them to make some weapons, i.e. swords, knives and other things like that.

So when they made them, they told Alcibiades, who then threw a huge party.

'Ladies and gentlemen, we have now twelve bottles of wine. Drink and we'll have one heck of a party!'

That night an old woman was sitting in bed knitting when she heard a noise like stones hitting a stone surface. 'Ah well, it's probably Alcibiades playing marbles with his mates,' she said. Then she carried on with her knitting.

'ALCIBIADES!'

The Athenians had gathered around the statues. They'd been wrecked. 'I know it's Alcibiades,' said a fat man with a moustache. A tall man who had just come out of his house said, 'If it is Alcibiades then we have to get 'im back.'

'Yeah,' cried everyone.

'So,' said the man, 'I want you, you, you and you to go fetch Alcibiades … go get him.'

The chase was on.

Alcibiades sat in his cabin puffing on a cigar. 'Oh those twits back at Athens really don't know what they're missing,' Alcibiades chuckled. There was a pounding on the cabin and Emillo (his navigator) popped his head in. 'We've been followed and our pursuers are hot on our tail.'

'Darn,' Alcibiades hissed. 'Then out-sail 'em.'

'Yes sir,' said Emillo, and he shut the door.

The Athenians in the boat were gaining upon Alcibiades. Emillo ran up to Alcibiades and said loudly, 'What the heck are we gonna do, they're gonna catch up.'

Alcibiades grabbed Emillo by his collar and screamed, 'Slow down.'

Emillo looked shocked. 'What are you crazy?'

'Just shut your face up and do it. Just do it!' and he threw him down so hard he was winded. The driver of the ship turned around to see Alcibiades coming towards him, before he could do anything Alcibiades had pulled out a knife and plunged it deep into the driver's neck.

'Ack,' spat the driver as Alcibiades kicked the driver off the ship. 'Now drop the anchor' called Alcibiades. His order was obeyed and the boat stopped and the Athenians looked up at Alcibiades. 'You're coming home … now,' said the leader. Alcibiades bit the inside of his cheeks. 'Who said?' he asked. 'We all did because you wrecked our lovely statues.'

'AIIIEEE,' screamed Alcibiades, as he reached for his sword. 'What are you doing, look we can talk this over can't we.' Alcibiades grinned with the sword in his hand, 'You are a stupid stuck up … bum.'

Then Alcibiades lunged forward and Nicias watched in horror as Alcibiades sliced the Athenians into one millimeter cubes. The boat filled with so much blood the boat sunk!

Alcibiades smiled and said 'They're not as they're cut up to be are they.' Then he turned on his heels and said, 'Right men let's not let some silly men spoil our invasion on Syracuse, lets go.'

Then the boat sailed on into the sunset. When they got there Alcibiades said, 'First we sleep then it's time we kick.' Nicias put up his hand and squeaked, 'Look can't we stop this altogether. I mean you've killed four men.' 'So what, I don't care,' Alcibiades grunted.

'You killed four innocent men for Zeus's sake.'

'Survival of the fittest, my dear stick insect,' Alcibiades stated. Nicias knew it was no good arguing with this psycho. Alcibiades looked proud, 'Lost for words.'

Before he could say anything Alcibiades said in a matter-of-fact voice 'If you don't want to do

this then – ' but he was interrupted by the constant moaning of the Athenians. 'Zeus it's cold.' Then he heard another load of Athenians moan about the cold. 'If it's cold I'll cut you up in one inch cubes, maybe that will warm you up.' Then the Athenians started singing.

'This is my island in the sun ...'

'I want to go to heaven,' squeaked Nicias that night.

'STOP TALKING ABOUT HEAVEN OR I'LL SEND YOU THERE.'

'Sorry.'

That night they all slept except Alcibiades who was planning something very evil ...

Back at Athens they were wondering about their search party. They hadn't arrived yet. 'So what shall we do? Send another party?' (Yes they were voting.) 'No because if we do that party might go missing.'

'Good point.'

So they carried on voting all night, but they didn't realise what was happening back at Syracuse ...

The fight had started. Alcibiades had slaughtered many of the Syracusans. But the fight wasn't getting anywhere, so the Athenians acting like chickens retreated except Alcibiades. He stayed with the Syracusans. 'Now do you want to beat the Athenians?' Everyone nodded. 'Well I've got an idea ...'

The Athenians were walking through a very dry piece of land. It was very hot. 'When I was moaning that it was cold I meant it, but the heat here is ridiculous.'

Nicias was panting like a dog. 'Yes it is rather stuffy here isn't it,' he squeaked rather dryly.

They were approaching a deserted old quarry with huge gates. The Athenians were going to search in the quarry when Nicias suddenly squeaked, 'Water, water over there quick.' They all ran towards the water and dived, some took all their cloths off and oh how they drank. They gulped down gallons of fresh spring water. Nicias heard some foot steps behind him. He turned around and there was a woosh and a long blade of a sword came down and cut Nicias in half. They all turned around as Alcibiades and the Syracusans came storming into the lane slicing everyone in it.

But Alcibiades stopped them, 'You know I really hate fast deaths. We will starve 'em in that there Quarry.' Alcibiades snapped his fingers and the Syracusan grabbed the men and took them to the Quarry.

The Athenians sat in the quarry in the baking sun. Alcibiades had left them in the hands of the Syracusans. But their freedom lies in one man. The gates opened at noon and three men stormed in.

'HALT!' screamed the one in the middle. Then the other guards saluted. 'I've decided to give you stupid bunch of spineless entrails a chance,' he said. 'If any of you can recite two lines of Euripides I haven't heard, repeat haven't heard, I'll set you free,' he said rather proudly. 'Who wants to go first?' One man put up his hand, 'You, guards' then the guards grabbed him and made him stand up straight.

'There was an old lady from Greece who had an enormous fleece,' then the leader said, 'It came down to her knees and attracted the bees and that was the end of the fleece,' heard that and it went on. The last man said one and they hadn't heard it before so he was set free and the others were killed.

Back at Sicily Alcibiades had his own house and he had invited a friend over called Plato, him and some other friends came by. Then Emillo dropped by, 'Emillo my good friend even though you have only been away for a week you've aged.' Emillo laughed 'So lets have some fun.' After that Alcibiades and his friends dressed up in women's cloths and started making fun of women. 'Who needs women,' Alcibiades slurred, 'I mean they just run around doing ... nothing.'

The emperor of Sicily was consulting his minister. 'Who is likely to become king when my father dies?' His minister checked his list. 'Alcibiades, a very sad man.' The king frowned. 'Kill Alcibiades.'

'Why?' said the minister. 'Because he will become king and I won't so I want to kill him.'

'Yes your majesty.'

Alcibiades had gotten drunk with his friends and they were now doing nude dances. Outside

the minister was pouring gasoline all over the house. Then he boarded up the windows. 'Bye Alci' said the minister and set the place alight. Alcibiades was naked when the smoke billowed through his bedroom door. Emillo and the rest of Alcibiades' friends were screaming and panicking.

Alcibiades grabbed them and locked them in the cellar. 'Let us out please Alci,' but Alcibiades was trying to get out of the burning house, but he couldn't get out.

Outside the minister watched the house burn, then a hole blew through the wall and a big lump of fire rolled out of it. It was Alcibiades.

[THE END]

Unit 5

Teaching and learning concepts

Jot down what idea or concept you have of King Alfred.

 ACTIVITY 5.1 THINKING ABOUT CONCEPTS

- Study Figure 5.1. What new ideas and information does it add to your concept of Alfred?
- Where do you think your own conceptual understanding of King Alfred and the thinking that lay behind Figure 5.1 came from?
- How does your concept of 'King Alfred' inform and influence related concepts, such as the 'English nation', 'patriotism', 'war of independence', 'resistance', 'the role of the church' and even 'the Vikings'?
- How do concepts such as these develop?

Concepts provide the scaffolding around which we, and our children, make sense of our world. They combine with factual information to produce a knowledge network. Meaning emerges from the links or relationships between the network's nodes (see pages 96–8). Concepts are individual to each of us. Everyone's understanding of a concept is different, but shares common elements that enable us to use the same term meaningfully. The definition of any concept is difficult, involving a set of logical defining elements. Our concepts reflect how we add and discard ideas and information, interpret and reinterpret views, feelings and judgements.

Concepts are central to knowledge and understanding. Jerome Bruner placed conceptual understanding at the centre of children's education. Bruner argued that conceptual development was a continuous, incremental process, with concepts being added to and refined throughout a course. In the 1960s Bruner built an educational programme for children, *Man A Course of Study* (MACOS), around exploring and developing the meaning of the concept 'Man'. Bruner's ideas about concepts serving as the scaffolding for the curriculum provided the starting point for an integrated British humanities project of the 1970s: *Place, Time and Society, 8–13: Curriculum planning in history, geography and social sciences* (Blyth, 1976). *Place, Time and Society 8–13* argues that subjects like history are tools that pupils can use to acquire conceptual understanding.

The historical dimension of conceptual understanding is grounded in interpretations of the past, interpretations that in themselves are based upon historical sources. Thus we can trace our concepts about King Alfred back to a single, major source, the *Anglo-Saxon Chronicle*. The *Anglo-*

Figure 5.1 A Victorian view of King Alfred
Reproduced courtesy of the Mansell Collection

Saxon Chronicle lists in painstaking detail the heroic part that Alfred played in the fight against the Vikings, from the dark days of total defeat in 878 when 'Alfred the king … with a small band moved under difficulties through woods and into inaccessible places in marshes' (Garmondsway, 1972: 73) to the triumphant end of his reign in 899 when the future of the English kingdom was secure. 'He was king over all England except that part which was under Danish domination' (Garmondsway, 1972: 91).

The accepted view of the *Anglo-Saxon Chronicle* is 'that the *Chronicle* had been compiled by a West Country magnate working in isolation and motivated solely perhaps by antiquarian interest'. If so, 'it would follow that neither King Alfred nor any member of his scholarly team had a hand in the compilation of the *Chronicle*. That in turn would have profound implications for the value of the *Anglo-Saxon Chronicle* as an independent witness to Alfred's greatness' (Smyth, 1996: 3). Professor Smyth then demolishes this interpretation of the *Anglo-Saxon Chronicle* in a magisterial and scholarly manner, proving that its account of King Alfred was written at King Alfred's court as 'a chronicle which would tell the story of the Christianisation of the West Saxons as well as anchor their history in the Antique past and tell of their triumph under the Christian Alfred over the heathen Dane.' (Smyth, 1996: 7). Propaganda, pure if not simple. How might Smyth's conclusions alter the conceptual understanding of King Alfred that you jotted down at the start of this chapter?

A network of linked concepts provides a framework for understanding the National Curriculum's History Study Units. Thus 'Life in Tudor Times' makes little sense for children if they do not develop an understanding of its explicitly stated concepts, 'Tudor, monarchy, society, expansion overseas, break-with-Rome, exploration overseas, the Armada, court life, progresses, role-of-a-personality'. Similarly for the Vikings we have concepts that include 'The Vikings, settlement and resistance'. In general terms concepts like communism, capitalism, dictatorship, democracy and imperialism also play a crucial role in children's general education. Without such conceptual

knowledge it is difficult, if not impossible, to make well-informed judgements that underpin membership of a modern democratic society.

 ACTIVITY 5.2 DEFINING CONCEPTS

- Produce a definition of either the concept 'Tudor' or 'The Vikings' in the form of a concept web or spider diagram. Put the word at the centre of the web and the ideas and knowledge linked to it at the end of its legs.
- If working in pairs or groups, compare your diagrams. What are their similarities and differences?
- Explain to each other the meaning of the elements in your diagrams.
- For each concept produce a combined diagram that reflects your pooled knowledge and changed understanding of the concept.

WHAT IS A CONCEPT?

At its simplest, a concept is a term that categorises information. Concepts range from simple and concrete words, like dog and chair, to the highly complex and abstract, e.g. god and democracy. As such, the concept will contain characteristics which all other words under that heading share, for example, under 'dog' we find spaniels, terriers, collies that all share the common elements of 'dogginess'. In defining a concept we apply a set of rules that give the concept its meaning, for example, it is a dog *if* it has a defining property or properties that endow it with dogginess. 'Research, then, has shown how concepts develop through a process of generalisation, by storing an image of abstracted characteristics and of deduction, by drawing from the stored image, adding to it and modifying it. It has indicated a pattern in the development of concepts, suggested that concepts need to be taught, and that they are best learned through discussion' (Cooper, 1992: 31).

Sharing concepts is how we make sense of the world to one another. They provide the building blocks for any discourse. Cooper's conceptual 'images' are stored in the memory as schema.

1. Schemas have variables
2. Schemas can embed, one within another
3. Schemas represent knowledge at all levels of abstraction
4. Schemas represent *knowledge* rather than *definitions*.

Perhaps the central feature of schemas is that they are packets of information that contain variables. Roughly, a scheme for any concept contains a fixed part, whose characteristics are always (or nearly always) true of exemplars.

(Rumelhart and Norman, 1985: 36)

How can we help children to build up their individual conceptual knowledge, their bank of schema? Let us take an example, 'The Vikings', starting with extracts from Professor D.M. Wilson's *The Vikings* (1987), written by an international academic for children:

Where did the Vikings come from? And where did they go? The Vikings were great travellers. They attacked many countries in Europe, and later they settled in parts of Britain and France. The part of France which they settled is called Normandy; the Normans who invaded Britain with William the Conqueror in 1066 were descended from Vikings. (p. 3)

The Vikings at home
Although they did have a few towns, most Vikings lived in the country. This is a picture of the inside of a Viking house. (p. 4)

Pagans and Christians
At first the Vikings were pagans – they worshipped many gods. Some of the days of the week in English are named after Viking gods (Freya, Thor, Woden or Odin). Can you guess which ones? Thor was a warrior god. He was also very stupid. Later the Vikings became Christians, but for a long time they still kept their old way of life. (p. 7)

The Vikings in Britain
In 793 the rich monastery of Lindisfarne in Northumberland was destroyed by pagan men who came from the sea... About 70 years after their first raids, the Vikings began to settle in Britain. The parts they settled are coloured grey on the map. Some of the Vikings who came to Britain were Norwegian, but the most important groups were Danes. They controlled a large part of north and eastern England, called 'Danelaw'. (p. 8)

(Wilson, 1987)

Professor Wilson's account depends upon and, in turn deepens, our knowledge of the concept 'The Vikings.' We bring to our reading an initial understanding of the term. Such a concept derives its meaning from its position in a semantic (knowledge) network of information that we build up in our minds. At its simplest a semantic network consists of nodes that have relationships that link them to other nodes; for example, a dog has four legs or a dog is faithful.

node	**link**	**node**
The Vikings	came from	the sea
The Vikings	destroyed	in 793 the rich monastery of Lindisfarne

A node's meaning comes from its relations' links with other subsidiary nodes. In effect these links give the central node, the concept, its meaning. The linked nodes have their own meaning, derived from links to their own subsidiary nodes. Thus to understand the phrase 'in 793 the rich monastery of Lindisfarne' we draw upon our semantic networks for rich, monastery and Lindisfarne. Using Professor Wilson's book we can work out a list of links and subsidiary nodes that build up our understanding of the concept 'The Vikings'. Figure 5.2. shows the properties of the concept as a simple semantic network.

Some nodes in this network inherit the properties of the concept 'The Vikings'. The brackets (Viking) in Figure 5.2 indicate such subsets of 'The Vikings'. The inherited properties in each case qualify the meaning of the related concept. For example, the semantic network for (Viking) towns has two elements, properties of the concept 'town' and the inherited properties of the concept 'The Vikings'. Thus when we consider a particular example, the 'Viking town of York' our schema has three conceptual elements, 'Viking', 'town' and 'York'. Combined, they provide a semantic network on the topic that represents our understanding.

Represented diagramatically as in Figure 5.2, semantic networks can explode exponentially. So, it is more convenient to list the links of nodes in the form used in Figure 5.3. What do the concepts '(Vikings) Normans' and its related concept 'Rollo' mean? Using Batey *et al.'s* authoritative work, *Cultural Atlas of the Viking World* (1994: 145), we can identify the links and nodes for these two concepts.

 ACTIVITY 5.3 ORGANISING KNOWLEDGE INTO A SEMANTIC NETWORK

You can turn extracts from school topic and textbooks into semantic networks. You can fill in gaps in the text where the author has not made explicit links in the argument, using your existing knowledge or inference.

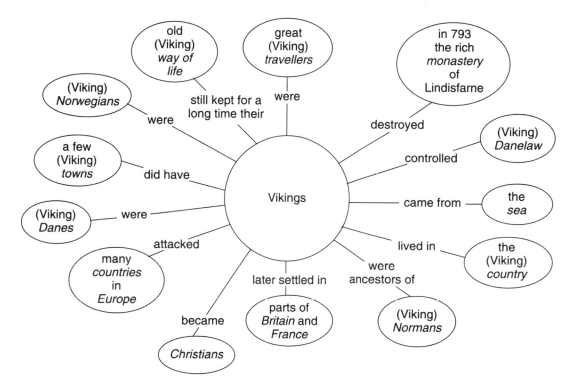

Figure 5.2 The Vikings: a semantic network

Let us take a passage from Tim Wood's Ladybird book, *The Saxons and the Normans,* to put these ideas into practice:

Viking raiders
In 789, more than three hundred years after the Anglo-Saxons had begun to settle in Britain, the first *Viking* raiders landed near Weymouth, Dorset. They did little damage but a few years later more Vikings returned. They attacked the monasteries at Lindisfarne and Jarrow, killing monks, stealing treasure from churches and capturing slaves.

(Wood, 1994: 14)

- What concepts in the text do children need to know to make sense of the passage?
- From the text we were able to construct the two first sentences below. Complete the table, adding new nodes and links to it.
- Extend the table to represent all the nodes and links in the text,

	node	links	node
1.	The Anglo-Saxons	began to settle	in Britain about 500 AD
2.	Weymouth, Dorset	is in	Britain
3.	Viking raiders	_____	Weymouth,
4.	_____	_____	in 789
5.	The Vikings	_____	_____

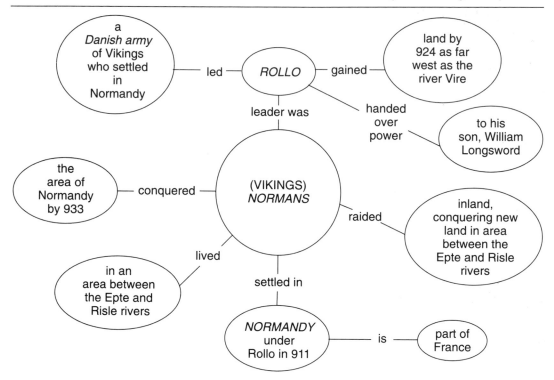

Figure 5.3 Listing of the links and nodes for the concept (Vikings) Normans

- Turn the full table into a semantic network, showing the links between the different pieces of information.
- You can create your own semantic network for 'The Vikings' (see Figure 5.3), on a sheet of A3. Add the information above to this network.

WHAT FORM DOES CONCEPTUAL KNOWLEDGE IN HISTORY TAKE AT KS2?

The History National Curriculum indicates the conceptual knowledge that 7–11 year olds should develop in three places: its key elements (HNC, 1995: 5), the study units (HNC pp. 6–9) and the attainment target (HNC pp. 15–16). We can group these concepts into three broad categories: structural, organisational and specific. As noted, what a concept means is individual to each of us, problematic and uncertain, and therefore open to debate and interpretation. Each teacher or team of teachers has to produce its own understanding of concepts and use them as the basis for the pupils to develop and extend their own conceptual understanding.

STRUCTURAL CONCEPTS

Structural concepts are the foundations upon which pupils build their understanding of the past. The structural concepts of chronology, causation and evidence are the basic tools for 'doing history', they reflect the procedures of historical study at all levels. Without an understanding of

them, it is impossible to study the past in an empirical way. As such, chronology, causation and evidence are the three structural concepts of the KS2 History National Curriculum, detailed in the key elements and the attainment target.

 ACTIVITY 5.4 MAKING SENSE OF STRUCTURAL CONCEPTS

- Either jot down a list of what you understand by the structural concepts chronology, causation or evidence, or, if working with a partner, discuss their meaning.
- Make out a semantic network for one of these concepts. To help, use the information in the key elements and attainment target.
- Consider how pupils develop understanding of structural concepts.

ORGANISATIONAL CONCEPTS

These provide a framework for historical investigation of any period. Some organisational concepts are in general use, like power and nationalism, while others relate specifically to the past and draw their meaning from their historical contexts, concepts such as settlement, colonialism, civilisation, revolution, communism and the industrial revolution. Below we give examples of organisational concepts, drawn from the History National Curriculum:

organisational concepts	**where they occur in the KS2 programme of study**
power	Tudor Monarchs (Life in Tudor Times)
autocracy	
constitutional monarchy	Victoria and the Royal Family (Victorian Britain)
conquest	The Roman Conquest (Romans)
imperialism	War and colonisation (Ancient Greece)
invasion	The Armada (Life in Tudor Times)
war	The impact of World War II (Britain since 1930)

 ACTIVITY 5.5 THE PROGRAMME OF STUDY AND ORGANISATIONAL CONCEPTS

- Take any KS2 History Study Unit (HNC, 1995: 5) organisational concept such as war.
- How would you build up your pupils' understanding of it? Think of the kinds of teaching strategies and learning activities and resources you would use.

SPECIFIC CONCEPTS

Specific concepts' meanings are drawn from the context within which they are used. As such, they usually relate to the topics of a History Study Unit (HSU). We linked our study of the Vikings to the HSU statement:

 Vikings
- Viking raids and settlement and their impact on the British Isles, *e.g. their settlement in different parts of the British Isles, King Alfred and Anglo-Saxon resistance to the Vikings*
- Everyday life, *e.g. houses and home life, work, religion*

- The legacy of settlement, *e.g. place names and settlement patterns, myths and legends, Viking remains including artefacts and buildings*

(HNC, 1995: 6)
(The plain text is statutory, italicised exemplary.)

We identified six specific concepts in 'the legacy of settlement', concepts that provided focal points for our teaching.

1. Viking – place names
2. Viking – settlement
3. Viking – myths
4. Viking – legends
5. Viking – remains – artefacts
6. Viking – remains – buildings

Children's conceptual understanding is often wrong. Thus when we asked our children to draw a picture of what the word 'Viking' meant at the start of the course, stereotypical visions emerged from the page of male warriors wearing horned helmets engaged in rape and pillage (pillage, actually!).

  ACTIVITY 5.6 A HISTORY STUDY UNIT AND SPECIFIC CONCEPTS

- Take the last History Study Unit you taught.
- List the specific concepts that it covered.
- Consider how you taught any one of these, i.e. how your pupils' understanding of it developed.
- How could you have taught it better?

CONCEPTUAL UNDERSTANDING AND TEACHING STRATEGIES

Pupils build up understanding of a concept through adding new links and nodes, modifying or discarding old ones, and organising the links and nodes into meaningful patterns and networks. A concept's links to other nodes can range from 1 to n, where n is a thousand or more. There are three dimensions to creating a concept's meaning: depth of knowledge, sophistication and coherence. These factors are reflected in the qualities noted in Level 6 of the attainment target:

- Links between different aspects of factual knowledge of a range of people, events and developments in the history of Britain and other countries drawn from the appropriate programmes of study.
- Some understanding of the relationship between distinctive features of past societies and periods.
- The selection, organisation and deployment of information, making use of dates and terms in well-structured work.
- Explanations of events, changes and developments.
- Interpretation of some events, issues, topics and personalities.
- Suggestion of lines of enquiry.
- Identification of sources of information.
- Critical use of sources to find out about specific topics.

Teaching for conceptual understanding has to actively engage the pupils' minds with the concept, forcing them to explore its meaning and to build up their own understanding of it. Crucial to this

are the teaching and learning strategies employed. Axiomatically, it is the role of the teacher to provide pupils with a learning environment for building up conceptual knowledge. Hilary Cooper (1994: 10) suggested that discussion plays a major part in concept formation. Pupils learn socially from their interaction with each other and the teacher. Verbal explanations, assimilating the spoken views of peers and the teacher, help pupils extend conceptual understanding. They test and refine their ideas against those of others, both building on each others' ideas (scaffolding) and coming to a joint understanding after initial disagreement and discussion (peer conflict).

How can children produce their own semantic networks? We use concept webs like Figure 5.2 extensively in our teaching, getting the children to build up their own and pool their ideas, either in pairs, small groups or as a whole class. The concept is placed at the centre of the web. The links are written in along the lines that connect the concept to its related information.

A second factor in conceptual development is transformation, where the pupil's mind works upon the information and re-presents it as his or her own thinking, either in the original mode of representation or in an alternative one. Here the pupil takes a schema from outside and makes it his or her own, see pp. 71–88:

mode of representation	transformation	reshaped knowledge
Iconic (visual)	through pupil's active	in one or more of the other
Enactive (active/physical)	engagement in learning	three modes of
Symbolic (written/spoken)		representation *or* reworks it
Aural (played/heard)		in the same mode.

We develop pupils' own concepts through encouraging, even provoking, them to think actively about concepts. The process is slow, messy, uncertain and difficult, because we are helping pupils push themselves to the frontiers of their understanding, constantly assimilating new information and ideas and discarding redundant knowledge. We illustrate the process through examples of how teachers on our courses taught a structural, an organisational and a specific concept, and how we taught the concepts of Viking settlement and Viking place names to our 7 and 8 year old children.

THEORY INTO ACTION

A structural concept: 'evidence'

The concept was 'historical evidence – sources'. Irene Wadding wanted her 9 to 11 year old pupils to reflect on the nature of historical evidence, and how it can be shaped in its journey from the past to the present.

    CASE STUDY 27 : TEACHING THE CONCEPT 'HISTORICAL EVIDENCE'

Starter activity

The children were each given six pieces of card. They were asked to write down any facts that they knew about the Romans (one fact per piece of card). Each child then selected their best three facts to hand in.

Pre-activity

Four children were chosen to form a panel and were briefed as to what would be expected of them. The class gathered around and the panel took its places.

The fact cards were shared out so each panel member had 22/23 cards.

The panel was offered three minutes to prepare whilst the rest of the class observed.

Child 1 sat on the chair quietly working through her cards.
Child 2 spread his cards on the floor in front of his chair.
Child 3 studied the cards to find ways in which she could 'misinterpret' the facts.
Child 4 walked around the room putting cards in 'safe' places and losing cards.

Child 1: 'Look at all these facts! There are too many, I don't want them all.' (Looked around group and made eye contact with best friend.) Child 1 started to read through each card, commenting:

'I've got your card here, I'll keep this one.'
'Ugh, look at this awful writing.' (*Discarded card*)
'Julius Caesar, I've heard of him, I'll keep this.'
'This card is bent!' (*Discarded*)
'What beautiful handwriting.' (*Kept*)
'Can't read this!' (*Discarded*)

And the process continued until half the cards were discarded.

Child 2: A cup containing the remains of a coffee had been placed by the feet of the next panel member. He carefully kicked the cup so that the coffee destroyed approximately half of his fact cards. These he binned.

Child 3: 'Look at these facts, some silly people have become totally confused. Roman facts were asked for.'

'Gladiators – a TV programme, nothing to do with Romans.' (*Discarded*)
'Baths? Is this a reminder that somebody needs a bath?'
'Coins? This person is thinking about their pocket money!'

(Cards which were repeated were discarded and the process continued until this panel member had lost half the cards.)

Child 4 (Straight into role play as Mr Forgetful): 'I know I had more cards to start with.' Told the group how he puts things into 'safe' places and then loses them – his facts are sometimes rediscovered and sometimes not.
     Teacher input 'Does anybody know anything else, any other facts, which our panel haven't mentioned?'
     The 'missing' facts were then discussed as the group became aware of how facts can get lost or misinterpreted.

Outcome

Child 1 represented bias.
Child 2 illustrated damage.
Child 3 represented interpretation.
Child 4 represented lost sources.

Irene's commentary

The children didn't recognise the term bias, but they understood what it meant. This activity was fun and was well remembered by the children. It led beautifully into the next lesson, which focused on understanding the difference between facts and points of view.

ACTIVITY 5.7 DEVELOPING PROCEDURAL CONCEPTUAL KNOWLEDGE

- In what ways did Irene's children develop their conceptual understanding?
- Why do you think the lesson was successful?
- How could you adapt this idea in your own teaching?

An organisational concept: 'The Tudors'

Alison Robson had encountered the idea of building up the understanding of a concept through 'using a selection of non-fiction books as a means of carrying out some historical fact finding and question asking.'

Alison planned to spend one lesson giving her 8 and 9 year old pupils an opportunity to select from a wide range of non-fiction books covering all aspects of Tudor life.

 CASE STUDY 28: TEACHING THE CONCEPT OF 'THE TUDORS'

Preparation

The children were asked to work in pairs and, using at least three books, were to find out five interesting historical facts about any area of Tudor life that specifically interested them. In addition, once they had completed this task they were to write down three or four questions that they would like answering. The questions could relate either to an aspect that they did not understand fully or to an area they felt they wanted to look into further.

The lesson

The children were reminded about using content pages and we talked about looking closely at illustrations and captions. The children paired off and worked for about 40 minutes.

I was very pleased by the enthusiasm shown by the children. They coped well selecting books from the range of available texts. I was able to differentiate the task to a degree, by asking the more able readers to check facts and investigate aspects more fully by cross referencing. In addition, I helped some less able readers by directing their attention to less demanding texts or by asking them to study some illustrations in greater depth.

As the majority of the class were engrossed in the task I was able to work alongside a special educational needs group. I concentrated on books with lots of illustrations and we also looked at a set of posters about Tudor times. This group was asked to describe aspects of the pictures and through this teacher-led discussion they were able to come up with some observant comments and a number of questions naturally arose from the discussion.

For example, we were looking at a street scene with lots of typical activities going on. One child commented upon the fact that the street was narrow and the houses were above the shops. Another asked, 'Why is the lady throwing water out of the window and into the street?' In addition another child commented upon a street seller who was selling water; this led to a discussion as to why they felt he needed to sell water and prompted the question, 'Did Tudor people have taps inside their houses?'

We collected together our findings during the follow-up session. Each pair were asked to share one interesting fact that they had discovered with the rest of the class. As the session progressed, children who had also discovered similar facts or could confirm the findings added their details and we built up an overview of particular aspects of Tudor life.

Once each group had contributed, the children were very eager to add more information and because of the enthusiasm we continued the discussion into the next session. We also recorded some of the questions that children had wanted to ask.

(Alison's observations and evaluation highlighted factors involved in the pupils' learning. The headings are mine.)

Practicalities

I was a little apprehensive about the practicalities of thirty-three children using the books in such a fashion. In the past I have tended to give a specific area to investigate using non-fiction books, to answer pre-determined questions or to produce some work on a restricted aspect of the topic.

Pupil choice and time limit

I found the idea of allowing the children to select from a wide range of areas exciting and I also liked the idea of providing a time limit in which they had a restricted number of statements and questions to formulate. The children were immediately placed in a position of control and the task became manageable and less daunting to them.

Purpose of the lesson

The children were provided with a meaningful purpose for using their research skills.

Collaborative learning

The activity required that they work collaboratively, both in the pair and then as part of the whole class, sharing and confirming their findings.

Speaking and listening

I was especially pleased with the speaking and listening that resulted from this activity as it was both purposeful and enjoyable. The children's concentration span was excellent and they all waited patiently for a turn and were eager to add more. The children enjoyed being in the position of providing information rather than receiving it.

Conceptual understanding

In addition to the cross-curricular aspects that were evident, I also felt that the children gained a good overview of Tudor times. The children had selected facts from many areas, including social, domestic, architectural and military. They had touched on important events like the Armada and the destruction of the monasteries. It was very interesting from my point of view to see which areas they did find interesting. It was also noticeable how much the children enjoyed recording minute detail.

 ACTIVITY 5.8 DEVELOPING ORGANISATIONAL CONCEPTUAL KNOWLEDGE: TUDOR LIFE

- What was the specific teaching strategy that Alison Robinson adopted?
- How might you incorporate it in your own practice?

Teaching a specific concept: 'Boudicca's defeat'

How can we build up an understanding of a concept like Boudicca's defeat? An insight into one of many possible teaching and learning strategies comes from Carol Merry.

Carol's class of 10 and 11 year olds had already been working intensively on Roman Britain up to the point of Boudicca's rising. Carol introduced the topic to her children through working on extracts of Tacitus's account of the rebellion (West, 1992) and reading a children's novel, a fictional story of a Celtic boy who survived the Iceni rebellion.

    CASE STUDY 29: BOUDICCA'S DEFEAT

The pupil's task

The children are to write a letter home (as either a soldier of the Roman legion led by Suetonius or a warrior of Boudicca's Celtic tribes before the final battle). This should take one to two hours.

The final draft copy could be written on paper previously aged by tea staining or slight cooking (by the teacher) and could be rolled and tied with ribbon. A wax seal using the imprint of a Roman coin could be added, with teacher supervision.

Preparation

What information do the children think they will need to do the task?

- weapons and armour
- numbers and discipline
- mental and physical state of the armies
- reasons for the battle – what is at stake?
- what is known about the enemy?
- quality of the leader, is it important?
- preparations for the battle

Discuss these or similar areas with the children to share their knowledge and identify areas for research. These could be selected in groups/pairs and the information presented to the rest of the class.

Suggested contents of the letter

1. What has happened so far? What does the writer know about the situation which has led to the coming battle?
2. Why is the writer involved in this battle?
3. What does the writer think of his or her opponents? What has he heard about them? What do they look like?
4. What is known about the writer's leader and the opponents' leader? What are his thoughts and feelings about them?
5. Will you win, and if so, why? What will you do if you lose?

Remember the date and place of writing, and use appropriate names if possible.

ACTIVITY 5.9 THINKING ABOUT BOUDICCA'S DEFEAT

- Take Carol Merry's account of her teaching, and draw up a flow chart that shows in detail how she implemented her teaching strategy.
- How might you adapt her ideas in your own teaching?

CONCEPTUAL TEACHING AND A HISTORY STUDY UNIT: VIKING SETTLEMENT

In teaching our class of 7 and 8 year olds 'The Vikings' section of the History Study Unit 'Romans, Anglo-Saxons and Vikings in Britain', we continually addressed the problem of selecting concepts to focus the pupils upon, and how to engage the pupils in developing their conceptual understanding. An example was our handling of Viking settlement, a concept that the History National Curriculum specifies.

We taught this concept as part of a course that included Viking migration from west Norway in the late ninth century (see pages 39 to 40). Our 7 and 8 year olds were in role as members of a west Norwegian valley's Viking farming, fishing and piratical community under threat from King Harold Finehair. The class had to decide whether to migrate, fight or to surrender. The children represented the valley's ten families. Their assembly or '*Thing*' voted to abandon its valley on the west coast of Norway in Sunnfjord and sail to Britain. They reached a valley on the west coast of England in what is now known as Cumbria that their Viking longship had previously raided. How could we transform an academic concept of Viking settlement into a form that children could assimilate?

The academic literature was clear as to the nature of Norwegian Viking settlements during the migration era. The Vikings formed self-contained farming communities. Professor Andersen tells us that each Viking family had its own farm, cut off from its neighbours:

> The characteristic of the Norwegian countryside was (and still is) the single farm with enclosed infields and extensive outfields for grazing herds of cattle, sheep and goats. The bonder or farmers of a local district often had at their disposal a common land in the nearby forests or in the mountains for herding, logging, fishing and hunting. The communal life of the village was unknown in Norway. Activities like fishing, hunting and herding of animals in areas outside the farm fields were necessary additional elements in the economy of the Viking farmer.

> (Andersen, 1971: 46)

How could we develop the concept that Viking settlements consisted of dispersed farms? We decided to use the strategy of a settlement simulation. The simulation was enactive, it placed the pupils in the shoes of people in the past and forced them to act out their decisions. It also used oracy, both through the explanation of the teacher and pupils to the whole class and pupil engagement in pair and small group discussion, debate and decision taking.

So, our task was to present the pupils with the problems that faced Viking settlers. Ten Viking families had sailed from Norway with all their belongings. Their ships had reached the valley (Figure 5.4), loosely based on Eskdale in the Lake District. As Viking settlers the ten families had to decide where to settle, how to plan out their valley, and the Viking names that they would give features of the landscape.

1. Introduction
    - We split the class into pairs, one pair to a table.
    - We handed out the blank maps, one to each pair.
    - The pupils shut their eyes. We told the story of the ship sailing towards land, edging closer

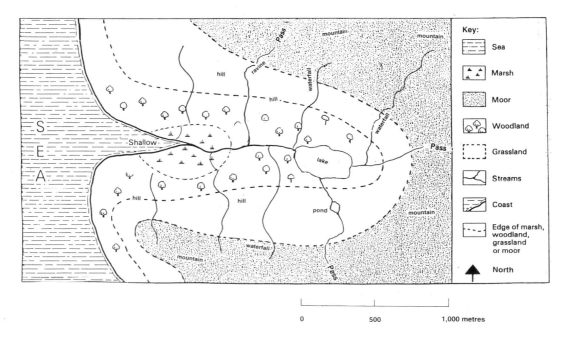

Figure 5.4 The Vikings settle the valley

and closer, features becoming clear, a long beach of sand dunes opening up into an estuary for the ship to enter, the woods and the mountains in view. The ship has sailed into the estuary of the valley. Eyes open:

- We have to go ashore to look for somewhere to land and set up camp. Looking at their map, where would each pair choose to land, and why?
- Then we will explore the valley.
- Having explored the valley we will split it up among the ten families according to the rules on their sheet.

2. Settling the valley
    - Three or four pupils came to the front. In turn we got them to read out to the rest of the class the simulation's instructions on how to settle the valley.
    - We explained fully and clearly how they should place their farms on the maps, using a map we had drawn on the board to make the point clear.
    - Then we got pupils to explain to the rest of the class what we had told them. Slowly we got there, but there was a lot of uncertainty.
    - The class set to with their scissors, cutting out their farm shapes.
    - We got each pair to discuss where they would put their farms. We made them place them on their maps, but said that they must not glue them down.
    - Going round and looking at what they had done it became clear that we had been as clear as mud in our explanation.
    - So, I asked pupils to come up to the front and explain where they would put a farm, telling the class their reasons for doing so. This was taxing. One pupil, Francis, found it exceptionally difficult. Slowly and with great care and encouragement I went through the factors, getting him to think about where he should place a single farm. After much hesitation, mistakes and confusion he managed the task. Francis whispered to me at the end of the lesson 'that was really hard', which made my day.

IN CONCLUSION

With the pupils' work all assessed and some clear idea in your mind of how well they have done in relation to the attainment target, you can reflect upon the quality of teaching and learning that history can provide. History should be an inspiring subject that gives both the teacher and the taught lasting satisfaction and a feeling of personal enrichment. If this book has helped in any way to bring this about, it will have been worth writing and, we hope, reading.

- We worked round the class until it was clear what the factors were that determined settlement.

3. Discussion and decisions
   - Each pair then reconsidered where it had put its farm. Each pair had to decide on the best place, combining their ideas and information.
   - We checked that they were in an appropriate place.
   - The pupils worked industriously away, gluing and sticking with gusto.

4. Tracks and a meeting place for the *Thing*, and a place to build the temple
   - The class next drew tracks in to join up the farms, and continued them down the bank of the main river to the sea.
   - At the point where the most tracks met they sited their temple and the place where the '*Thing*' will meet.

5. Place-names
   - We told the class that they had to give all the places on their map Viking names.
   - They could combine a personal name and the feature shown on the map, using the Viking words on the list.
   - We went through the task, with examples on the board, asking pupils to think of names for places.
   - We then got the children to work on their own maps, putting in features. They worked very hard at this, a number of them writing their names down in runic script.

All the children were on task throughout. Soon fifteen Viking valleys emerged, each different but sharing the distinct features of a Viking settlement, i.e. a dispersed settlement pattern and a valley that bore a wide range of Viking place names. At that moment a messenger arrived from the headmaster, saying that it was time for an unexpected assembly to consider the importance of Lent. Perfect timing, as the pupils had just finished their maps.

 ACTIVITY 5.10 BUILDING UP CONCEPTUAL UNDERSTANDING

- What were the different ways in which the pupils worked in order to develop their understanding of the concept of a Viking settlement?
- Add new knowledge to your semantic network on 'The Vikings' (see page 98).

CONCLUSION

The teaching strategy that a teacher adopts will influence directly the conceptual understanding of children. Teaching strategies are an element in pedagogical or teaching knowledge. Strategies are a highly sophisticated form of managing the pupil's learning, reflecting both the syntactic and substantive academic knowledge of the teacher. The appropriate strategy provides a bridge between academic history and what children will be able to learn. The teacher's crucial role is in three parts. Firstly, there is the selection of subject matter. Then comes the analysis, structuring and organisation of it in a form that can be turned into teaching subject knowledge. Finally comes the preparation of teaching and learning materials that will assist pupils' conceptual development.

History in the curriculum: teaching a History Study Unit and whole-class teaching

INTRODUCTION

At the end of our third morning of teaching 'The Vikings' to our class of 7 and 8 year olds Mo, the class teacher, said, 'I've never before had children here on task for a whole morning.' For the rest of the term the same level of engagement continued. Parents' evening revealed the involvement of mums and dads in the saga of the Vikings, for the children's interest had spilled over into their home life. Why had the class collectively become so wrapped up with the Vikings? What had made the difference? Crucially, is the essence of the teaching of 'The Vikings' transferable to other situations? And if so, how?

Our case studies in Units 3 to 5 suggest that we can all enjoy a vibrant, interactive classroom where we and our children actively bring the past to life. On page 48 we suggested that ten factors should underpin how you organise your curriculum. How did they directly affect our approach to teaching 'The Vikings' over the twelve weeks of the term? The italicised text indicates their influence.

1. Citizenship

School history centres on education for citizenship. It should meet the needs of children as members of a modern, democratic society, dealing with values, moral elements and the conceptual understanding that the responsible exercise of citizenship requires. History does this through fostering knowledge and understanding of human behaviour in the past and in the present. Pupil involvement in the process of historical enquiry, 'doing history', also develops a range of critical thinking skills needed in their lives.

Our methods of teaching 'The Vikings' reflected our beliefs about the nature of history and how it should be learned. We believe that history is a subject that relates directly to pupils' needs, as it draws at the highest level upon a range of thinking and study skills, which develops conceptual understanding about all aspects of human society. In studying the Vikings, pupils continuously confronted ethical and moral issues that provided a perspective upon their own lives.

2. 'Doing history'

History is something which children have to construct personally, under teacher guidance.

Throughout 'The Vikings' topic we engaged children in either historical investigation or in understanding problems that a Viking community faced. Thus the course opened with the pupils working as detectives investigating a suitcase that contained a child's belongings. Then we moved on to the class in the role of archaeologists excavating a Viking burial mound. The course ended with the class participating in the planning and execution of a raid on an Anglo-Saxon monastery at Exeter, thinking about the issues and problems from the viewpoints of marauding Vikings.

3. Skills

The process of enquiry involved in investigating history develops a set of skills that underpin critical and sceptical thinking, for example the ability to weigh evidence, to analyse the reasons for particular actions, to consider the possibilities open to historical agents at particular decision-taking points in the past.

The children had to draw upon and develop a whole range of thinking and investigative skills in their study of the Vikings. When preparing goods to sell in the Viking market of Dublin they used their books and resource sheets to find out the kinds of things that they would have been selling. After they had excavated the Viking burial mound they had to match the evidence that they had found with analogous information in their resources. In taking part in a Viking Thing in their valley to resolve legal disputes between the Viking families, the pupils had to weigh up the often contradictory evidence in order to reach a conclusion.

4. Social learning

The learning of history is a social activity that requires teachers and pupils to work co-operatively in the joint development of knowledge and understanding.

The teacher plays a key role. The teacher presents a topic, directs and controls the investigation, and trains children in the related processes and skills of historical enquiry. The basic approach is interactive whole-class teaching (see pages 114 to 116). Here the pupils continuously interact with the teacher and each other in carrying out a set of linked tasks that aim to develop understanding.

Throughout the period in which the children were learning about the Vikings, the pupils followed an agenda that the teacher laid down in detail for each lesson. For every new topic the teacher introduced it to the whole class. The class then worked on an activity or activities as appropriate, either as individuals, pairs or small groups. If working separately, the pupils came together to pool ideas and information in the resolution of an enquiry or activity.

The activities required the pupils to work co-operatively, forcing them to share in the development of their knowledge and understanding. Thus the whole class had to take a decision as a Viking community at its meeting (Thing) as to whether to capitulate to the demands of King Harald Finehair, or to fight, or to migrate from their Norwegian valley. Similarly, in deciding how to settle their valley in England, the pupils worked in pairs to plan out where they would site their farms and to decide what laws they would have for the running of their community.

5. Depth

'Doing history' requires pupils to understand human behaviour in the past. Such understanding is best, perhaps only, derived from study in depth.

Teaching 'The Vikings' involved five separate but linked studies in depth:

- *the Viking burial*
- *the Viking market*
- *Viking migration*
- *the settlement of the valley*
- *the Viking raid.*

The depth studies complemented and built upon each other, addressing the key question: Who were the Vikings?

6. Sources

Pupils construct their histories from using historical sources. These are both original, first-hand sources from the time, and interpretations of the topic (its histories).

The excavation of the Viking burial mound, the creation of a Viking market, the work on migration from Norway and the settlement of a valley in Cumbria were all based upon the pupils finding out about Vikings from their sources, respectively archaeological evidence, an historian's account of migration from Norway and place-name evidence from a modern map.

Authenticity

Sources should be authentic where possible.

Throughout, we went back to the original sources, for example an Arab trader's eye-witness account of a Viking burial in Russia (see page 38), and the archaeologist's account of the burial mound and grave goods found on the Isle of Man (see pages 34 to 39).

Economy

Resourcing should be economical.

- *For the burial mound we used pictures from the archaeological report and a modified plan of the burial mound.*
- *The market was based on pictures of Viking life extracted from a number of books showing the different goods that the Vikings made and used.*
- *The migration work used a single map and a picture of a Viking ship.*
- *The working out of a Viking settlement pattern entailed providing a list of place names and a map of an area the Vikings settled.*
- *In the teaching of the Viking raid we used an unedited extract from the* Anglo-Saxon Chronicle.

7. Imaginative reconstruction

'Doing history' is a creative art that involves imaginative reconstruction. Reconstruction means understanding situations that faced people in the past and how they coped with their problems. Reconstruction is based upon historical sources, both first-hand materials and the interpretations of historians, their histories. Crucially, the teacher makes the sources accessible to the pupils.

Imaginative reconstruction was the driving principle throughout our teaching. We tried to make sure that as far as possible the children would be able to see what it might have been like for the Vikings at that particular point in time, to understand the situation they faced, how it had developed and how it might change.

- *The Viking burial required the pupils to excavate a Viking burial mound, analyse the remains found and find out more about the Viking community involved. They used the evidence, source books and ancillary materials to recreate both the burial and the Viking farming, trading and military society.*

- *Trade and travel: First the class played a board game that required them to travel the Viking world, a game we found on the back of D.M. Wilson's children's book,* The Vikings and their Origins *(Wilson, 1970). Then, through taking the role of Viking traders and merchants in a Viking market at Dublin they learned about the range of goods that the Vikings produced and traded in. The list was based upon the finds in the Viking grave.*
- *Viking migration: The pupils were dramatically caught up in the problems of Viking migration from the point of view of a Viking community faced with subjugation or migration.*
- *The settlement of the valley: Here the children had to decide upon how to settle their valley. In so doing they created a Viking community. The community sprang to life when it met to deal with disputes between the different families in the valley. Place-name work enabled them to develop an understanding of settlement through using this source.*
- *The raid: My most vivid memory is the pupils all 'riding' their chairs as Viking raiders setting off on captured horses to plunder Exeter's hinterland. The* Anglo-Saxon Chronicle *tells us that this happened* (Vikings on horseback, not children on chairs!).

8. Communication

The production of a piece of history is complete when ready to be communicated. In particular, we stress the children talking about what they have learned, describing, explaining and justifying their points of view. We take great care to involve all children in public speaking, i.e. standing up and reporting to the whole class.

Of major importance was the reporting back of ideas and findings to the rest of the class; the drawings of Viking scenes in cartoon form and the writing of stories and reports. These the pupils stored in their history topic books, books that were placed on display and played a central part in the parents' evening.

9. Assessment

Assessment should be a continual process that arises naturally out of working with children. There is no need to set external tests of any kind. The best way of assessing learning is to examine the pupils' responses in the context of the actual teaching.

Thus for 'The Vikings' we continually monitored and reviewed the reactions of the children. This involved working intensively with them in lessons, discussing with them what they were learning and analysing their written, oral and graphic responses. Once each week Mo and I met in the pub in the evening to discuss how the previous lesson had gone and to reshape our teaching ideas in the light of this experience.

10. Progress

Historical education is a continuum which enables the young historian to be involved in and to initiate, plan, pursue and conclude historical enquiries of increasing complexity and sophistication.

Increasingly we have challenged our pupils and given them the chance to work independently. This term we are working on the 'Anglo-Saxons'. The course opened with a detective investigation of a body found in a Danish peat bog, Grauballe Man. The pupils had to work intensively upon the evidence and present in groups their conclusions to the whole class. The class teacher, Mo, said that such work would have been impossible a term ago.

 ACTIVITY 6.1 THINKING ABOUT THE TEN FACTORS

- Consider each of the ten factors above.
- How might you incorporate them into your own planning and teaching?

WHOLE-CLASS TEACHING

The implications of the ten factors taken together for primary school practice are serious, for they centre on a teaching style and classroom organisation that involves *active* as opposed to *passive* whole-class teaching. While accepting that there is a multiplicity of classroom organisational and teaching patterns within the context of teaching a class of children, we suggest that passive and active are the two main variations.

Whole-class teaching has been raised to the top of the educational agenda in the 1990s. A clarion call has gone out for primary school teachers to adopt this approach:

Whole-class teaching appears to provide the order, control, purpose and concentration which many critics believe are lacking in modern primary classrooms.

To a significant extent, the evidence supports this view of whole-class teaching. Whole-class teaching is associated with higher-order questioning, explanations and statements, and these in turn correlate with higher levels of pupil performance. Teachers with a substantial commitment to whole-class teaching appear, moreover, to be particularly effective in teaching the basic subjects.

(Alexander, Rose and Woodhead, 1992: 28)

Definitions

Yet, what do we mean by whole-class teaching? The term refers to a particular classroom form of organisation and the relationship between the teacher and his or her class. Axiomatically, the teacher communicates with the whole class at the same time, but not necessarily all the time. Three steps are involved:

Step 1   Introduction.   The class starts at a joint, common point. The teacher introduces the specific topic, or element of it, to be covered. The class is seated so that all the pupils can make eye contact with the teacher. If the pupils sit in groups around tables, we get them to turn their chairs round so that they are all facing the same way. Normally we reorganise the tables and chairs so that the pupils sit in pairs.

Step 2   The task.   The class works on a common task or related tasks collectively or breaks up into smaller units, i.e. individuals, pairs, small (three to four) or large (five plus) groups as the teaching and learning circumstances dictate.

Step 3   Consolidation.   The teacher draws the whole class together to pool knowledge and expertise, review and reinforce what has been learnt and present conclusions, or the class is involved in a whole-class activity, such as a dramatic re-enactment or the telling of a story.

The cycle begins again.

 ACTIVITY 6.2 REVIEW OF WHOLE-CLASS TEACHING

*   Brainstorm the points for and against whole-class teaching.
*   How would you react if the government ordered you to whole-class teach mathematics, science, history, geography and religious education?
*   What balance do you think there should be between different teaching approaches, according to varied circumstances?

Problems

Immediately there is a major problem in advocating whole-class teaching in the primary school. Overwhelmingly feedback on whole-class teaching is predominantly negative from primary teachers on our numerous in-service courses, formal interviewing of others and questionnaire surveys of teachers' opinions. We believe three factors contribute to this view:

1. There is a deeply ingrained set of personal memories of whole-class teaching as a *passive* experience that is both dull and deadly. This reflects often miserable experiences of GCSE O and A level, involving extensive note-taking and working from text books to produce knowledge to be presented in a standardised form for examination purposes.
2. Whole-class teaching is in stark opposition to the teaching and learning culture primary teachers have been trained for and work in, a culture of individualised and small group work 'that pervades not only teachers' assumptions and actions in the classroom but also how they relate to each other and to outside agencies' (Alexander, 1992: 169). This has a related problem, in that many primary teachers simply do not know how to whole-class teach.
3. For the primary classroom, there are also serious problems in transmission dominated whole-class teaching *where the pupils are a relatively passive, inert audience* disengaged from the teaching. Crucial to pupil learning is differentiation. Differentiation requires the matching of the teaching, related resources and learning activities to the wide ranging abilities, aptitudes and competences of the pupils (Alexander, Rose and Woodhead, 1992: 28). Passive whole-class teaching is undifferentiated. Here the teacher talking, working from a single textbook and setting undifferentiated tasks is the standard teaching pattern. Particularly problematic is reading, where pupils' reading ages can range from 4 to 16.

One teacher we interviewed highlighted the problems of whole-class teaching, an approach she was unused to. She was teaching 'The Victorians' and had decided to whole-class teach. In the lesson she used census material to develop pupil understanding of Victorian society. The census recorded full details of individuals, their names, addresses, occupation, marital/familial status and place of birth:

Teacher 1   *The weakness is, however you get round that, that the material does involve some reading. If I could work out a way of it not involving some reading, I think it would be better, because the less able readers were disadvantaged. I was having to fly around and make sure they were okay. But I haven't managed to think of a way round that yet, other than pairing a less able reader with a more able reader, but that doesn't always work, because you don't get the gell.*

Interviewer   *Would you change anything?*

Teacher 1   *Yes. I don't think I'd have a whole class working on it [the census material]. I think perhaps another time I would have some different activities going on in the classroom. I think I'd have some interrogating pictures or copies of photographs and just have a few groups doing that. I wouldn't have it as a whole-class activity again.*

Interviewer   *Why not?*

Teacher 1   *Because I don't think that all the children benefited from that type of lesson. I think that some would have found it easier to look at a photograph and get perhaps information from that, rather than a census return.*

ACTIVE WHOLE-CLASS TEACHING

Our solution to the problem of how to introduce whole-class teaching into the primary classroom is to make it *active*, drawing incidentally upon the best of current primary practice. What is the difference between active and passive whole-class teaching? Crucially, in an active classroom the

teacher leads, controls and directs the learning throughout making sure that the pupils are involved and focused on a specific learning task. Such teaching involves the teacher and pupils *working together* on historical investigations or in coming to grips with historical situations (see pages 31 to 36).

The teacher has to structure and organise the teaching so that pupils can develop both substantive and syntactical understanding. This means a set of dovetailing teaching strategies that enable pupils to unlock the meaning of their sources, such as census material. Oracy, talk, is vital. The spoken word is the perfect tool for differentiation, for speech makes the written word more accessible. Thus for the census material and similar documents we tape record them, and play the tape to the pupils who have the document in front of them. Question and answer, discussion and debate play a major part with all pupils participating in public sessions. Teacher support, working with individuals during single, pair or group work, is essential. Talk enables pupils to pool ideas and information in small and large groups and in pairs.

A vital aspect of whole-class teaching is the reading of documents. We treat difficult texts in the same way as teaching a foreign language. The text is for the whole class to work upon, collectively building up knowledge and understanding of words, phrases and concepts. Such teaching starts from a single, simple premise: *all children can read something in a text*. This provides the basis for reading for understanding.

Thus in our teaching of the Viking raid we provided our class of 7 and 8 year old Exeter children with an extract from the *Anglo-Saxon Chronicle* that vividly describes a Viking incursion. The account is of an attack on Exeter, as seen through the eyes of a Saxon living at the time (Garmondsway, 1972: 132–3). The chronicle has two separate but complementary accounts of the raid; we have conflated them to provide a single narrative:

1001   In this year the army came to the mouth of the Exe and so up to the fortress. They made a determined attack upon it, but were met by a solid and courageous resistance.

They then overran the countryside, and followed the usual tactics, slaying and burning.

They penetrated inland as far as Pinhoe, where they were opposed by Kola, the king's high reeve and Eadsige, the king's reeve. Vast levies of the men of Devon and Somerset were mustered [called out to fight]. They were put to flight and many of them slain.

Next morning the Vikings burnt down the manors of Pinhoe and Broad Clyst, and many other goodly manors of which we do not know the names.

Then they went riding over the countryside. Each inroad was worse than the last.

The Vikings brought much plunder with them to their ships and sailed thence for the Isle of Wight.

We gave each child a copy of the text and played a tape recording of it. The pupils had to underline action words such as *came* and *attacked* as they listened to the tape and read through the extract. Then we went through each scene in turn, discussing what it told us about the Viking attack on the Exeter area. For each scene the pupils had to produce a title. Then they drew it.

LEARNING THROUGH CO-OPERATION, CONFLICTING VIEWS AND MENTAL SCAFFOLDING

In the context of working in pairs and small groups children learn through both cognitive conflict and co-operation. Conflict is where they have different views as to a solution and have to argue through the issues and ideas, and assess the information, before agreeing on a solution or begging to differ. Co-operation means that they share their knowledge in creating a genuinely joint solution to the problem. The pairs and small groups can then come together.

Mental scaffolding occurs in active whole-class teaching when the pupils and teacher work together to build up their knowledge and understanding. Through question and answer, collective problem solving and directed discussion we pool ideas and information which all pupils share. Thus in solving the mystery of a body found in a bog each group in our class of 7 and 8 year olds

presented its conclusions and debated them, adding ideas and information to those they already held. Our whole-class Viking trial ended in genuine cognitive conflict, with the class trying to lynch a child they had found guilty of murder! He was saved by the bell…

TEACHING AND LEARNING STRATEGIES

The crucial element in active whole-class teaching is a set of teaching strategies that engages the pupils' minds. What form can such teaching take?

 ACTIVITY 6.3 REVIEWING THE EVIDENCE

- Consider the points made above in favour of whole-class teaching.
- To what extent do they answer any reservations you noted in Activity 6.2?
- Read the interview with Teacher 2 below. How does he seem to have surmounted the problems that you feel stand in the way of your whole-class teaching?

What, in reality, does the transferability of ideas about whole-class teaching mean? A teacher on one of our in-service courses discussed with a researcher a history lesson he had just taught to his class. He had adopted a whole-class approach to teach about Julius Caesar's invasion of Britain:

Interviewer   *What activities did the children do?*
Teacher 2   *Looking at a Roman galley. Yesterday the children watched a video about the invasion of the Romans, with Julius Caesar landing on the beaches of southern Britain. Today I wanted to have the children looking at a Roman galley on an overhead picture. I wanted them to look at the picture and from the picture work out how big the ship was, how wide it was, what it was used for, how fast they thought it could go, and from that information, go on to the playground, and draw the boat in chalk on the playground, and have the children pretend to be rowers and soldiers, acting out the scene as it would have been then, hopefully. OK?*
Interviewer   *Right. What was your role in the lesson?*
Teacher 2   *A multi-various role. One to be a guide, and to ask the right questions to get them thinking about what it was like at the time of the battle, what the boat was like, what it would have been used for; to keep order [chuckles]; just to really inspire them as well.*
Interviewer   *You did inspire them.*
Teacher 2   *Yes, they got very excited, you know, and enjoyed it. So it's one, to be a guide and steer the whole thing together and keep it on course, and to provide the resources, have some idea of where the lesson would go, but really to get them thinking, and enthusing, and wanting to do it.*
Interviewer   *I noticed – this isn't in the sheet – I don't want to put words into your mouth – do you think there's an element of you almost giving them a story?*
Teacher 2   *Yes. Yes. I mean the video yesterday gave them the story of the battle, but really it's just trying to get them to rethink what they've learned and go from there.*
Interviewer   *What did you want the children to learn?*
Teacher 2   *I don't know really. [Laughs.] I wanted them to think about how they would feel if they were soldiers or slaves on a galley, and what they would think and feel if they had to face an army of Celts on the beach. That's part of it. I wanted them to learn about the ship, and how the Romans fought at sea, how they had the ships, what the ships could do, how the ships would land. So, all things to do with*

	the ship. That's quite important. That was really the main focus. The whole lesson was built about, around the picture of the ship. Apart from that, it was really a kind of role-play thing, imagining being there at the time, and landing on the shore, and charging up the beach and killing people.
Interviewer	*Right. How did they learn this?*
Teacher 2	*Through role-play. Through actually going out on the playground, with the boat already drawn, acting out being slaves, and acting out being soldiers, and pretending to jump in … So the whole thing is role-play.*
Interviewer	*And they were in role. A child said to me: 'Some of the others didn't fall over when they got in the water, but I did.'*
Teacher 2	*Yes. Yes. They were really there. You saw them fighting, at the end on the beach – the grass – but to them it was a beach. It was really there.*
Interviewer	*Will you assess, or feed back to the children, their learning at all?*
Teacher 2	*Next time we come to another history lesson: I always tend to like building blocks, have one building on the other; so the next lesson, which could be, you know, invading inland and setting up camps on the British mainland – I'll always build on what they've learned already and I'll ask them questions, like: how did they land, and what did they do, and what were the ships for? And get them to tell me the story again. So rather than me saying to them: we've done this, and we've done that, and now we're going to do this, I'll ask them, well what happened last time? And where were we when we left them, the Romans? Where were they?*
Interviewer	*What organisation did you use for the children and the classroom?*
Teacher 2	*They were in groups.*
Interviewer	*They sit in groups, but it was…?*
Teacher 2	*It was a whole-class lesson. A whole-class lesson with me at the front. I suppose I asked the questions, but not… I tried to ask open-ended questions that they could think about. It's very difficult not to get a one question, one answer response kind of thing, you know, where's there's one right answer. But I asked them to think. So it was me very much at the front, talking. I wouldn't call it chalk and talk. It was more like a dialogue really. It was a conversation about what do we think this was, and how big do you think this is? That is how I would say it was organised really. And then we went out to the playground, which was different again.*
Interviewer	*Can you give reasons for your organisation and selection of materials?*
Teacher 2	*Yes. I've done it before! [Laughs.]*
Interviewer	*That's a pragmatic reason anyway.*
Teacher 2	*It's exciting. All the things I've said about making it exciting and interesting and having children involved. How I did it today, I think is the best way of getting out to them what I wanted them to have. So you start in the classroom, you talk about the picture, the children discuss it, and you move to the playground. I could have done it differently; I could have got photocopies of pages of triremes and galleys, and said: read about this and write about it, but everyone would have switched off. So I organised it so that everyone looked at the same picture, everyone focused in as one, the children discussed together what they were going to do and then we left, went down to the playground and did it there. So that's how. Does that answer your question?*

   ACTIVITY 6.4 WHOLE-CLASS TEACHING: THEORY INTO PRACTICE

• Note the teaching strategies that teacher 2 used.
• How would you have achieved the same learning effect?

PLANNING

In planning our teaching of 'The Vikings' we operated within both a strategic and a tactical framework. Our strategic planning provided us with an overview, a framework for the general shape of our teaching. In our tactical planning we responded to the day-to-day realities of the classroom and how the course was progressing. How did these principles affect our teaching of 'The Vikings'?

STRATEGIC PLANNING

Four factors were involved in our strategic planning of teaching 'The Vikings' to our class of 7 to 8 year olds:

1. Our beliefs about the nature and purpose of history teaching, contained in the ten factors (pages 110–113) that axiomatically underpin our teaching.
2. The requirements of the History National Curriculum, interpreted in the light of our beliefs. Areas involved are prescribed content and key elements, progression, differentiation and assessment.
3. Our knowledge and understanding of 'The Vikings'. In substantive, content terms we had a list of elements – the nature of Viking life and society, migration, settlement, trade, warfare and religion – that we wanted to cover. We also had in a syntactic, procedural sense knowledge of aspects of the Vikings, both in terms of sources and historians' enquiries, that we aimed to turn into pedagogic or classroom teaching knowledge through drawing on our repertoire of teaching strategies.
4. The whole school curriculum and history's role in it.

The requirements of the History National Curriculum

Content

We took the three content areas that the History National Curriculum prescribes (HNC, 1995: 6):

*   Viking raids and settlement and their impact on the British Isles
*   everyday life
*   the legacy of settlement

Luckily these topics all fitted neatly into what and how we would like to teach about the Vikings. The National Curriculum provides the loosest framework to work within, which meant our chosen topics allowed for study in detail so as to develop our children's knowledge and understanding of the Vikings.

Equally, the key elements were completely non-problematic as we would be working throughout on a range of sources that actively involved the children in interpretation, organisation and communication and which developed their range and depth of historical knowledge and understanding.

The key elements have a role in mapping out a balanced provision for the children. They provide a check-list for making certain that over a number of History Study Units the pupils have had a rounded historical education. Thus in our work on 'The Saxons' we aimed to give a fuller chronological context, relating Saxon history to that of the Romans and the Vikings, not having dealt with chronology explicitly in our teaching of 'The Vikings'.

Progression and differentiation

Progression is examined in Unit 7, page 127.

Differentiation means matching the teaching to the needs, abilities and aptitudes of individual pupils and groups, covering the whole ability range. Easy to say, hard to do. To differentiate we adopt seven main strategies. They can, of course, be combined.

1. *By outcome* Differentiation by outcome was the method we mainly used to teach 'The Vikings'. The whole class participated in a common task that pupils responded to according to their abilities. All could learn and benefit from the task, albeit at different levels. For example, such a task can involve a verbal description of a scene, children telling stories, drawing historical portraits, making models or participating in drama. Examples from our teaching of 'The Vikings':

    The Viking raid: The children drew eight scenes in sequence, having folded A4 paper into four so that they could draw four scenes on each side. The pupils provided each cartoon with a title and caption as appropriate.

    The Viking market: The class split up into pairs, each pair representing one particular Viking trade. They had to find out what a Viking craftsman would have made, then they had to draw or make their goods for sale in Dublin market and buy and sell when the market opened. All the children were able to respond to this task.

    Settling the Viking valley: The children worked in pairs, deciding where they would site their farms, where the tracks joining them up would run, where they would build their temple and hold the meeting of the valley community, its *Thing*.

2. *By resource* We provided materials that all the pupils can respond to. Visual sources are essential, particularly historical reconstructions based upon academic information. In our teaching of the Viking raid upon the monastery we used two such sources, reconstructions of the preparations for a Viking raid, showing in great detail what was involved. We took the pictures from a book that an academic expert, Professor Graham-Campbell, wrote for children (Civardi and Graham-Campbell, 1977: 10–13). Where the material is too difficult or complex in its original form we turn it into a resource that is accessible. Thus in a contemporary account of a Viking burial in Russia we reduced the length of the original and, most importantly, taped it.

3. *Graded resources* We provided graded resources for different ability levels. In our Viking work we ensured that there was a full range of visual and written materials available. The three source books were of different levels. Within them we were able to direct pupils to appropriate sources and sections. Also, we produced a range of ancillary, mainly visual, materials of scenes of Viking life.

    Thus when we were dealing with the Viking burial mound and worked out that the Viking had been buried with his farm animals we gave the children an artist's reconstruction of a Viking farm, showing the range of animals, buildings, fields and activities of a farm similar to the one the buried Viking might have owned.

    Graded resources means that each pupil has access to the historical information in a form that he or she can understand.

4. *By teaching [whole-class]* In making material accessible to all pupils, the teacher has a central role to play. Thus at each point we stopped the tape of the burial and engaged the pupils in both discussion and small-scale role-play to ensure that they all had understood what was involved.

    Whole-class teaching plays a crucial role in ensuring that the pupils, no matter what reading level they are at, have understood the text. Repetition of points and explanation in different ways help to get the messages across. Frequently we ask pupils to explain to the

whole class a particular point, checking whether all the children understand it. Thus when working on the siting of Viking farms in the valley we asked pupils to come to the front to explain to the rest of the class where they would site a farm, giving reasons. As each farm was placed on the map the class would discuss with the pupil whether it agreed that the chosen place met the criteria, and the pupil would defend his or her choice.

5. *Teacher support (individual/small group)*   Teacher support was provided according to the needs of individual pupils, to give the help they need to undertake the set tasks.

   For example, working with one SEN pupil in translating place-names to work out what the Viking society might have been like, we had to take her slowly and carefully through each step in the argument, discussing with her how to translate the Viking terms into modern English. As she wrote the translated names on her map and coloured in the particular feature her eyes slowly lit up.

6. *By stepped task*   In our teaching we also employ two other strategies, although we did not do so in our teaching of 'The Vikings'. One approach is to use a stepped task that progressively becomes more demanding. All pupils attempt the first step, those who have mastered it move on to the next one.

7. *By separate tasks*   Another strategy is to adopt different tasks and activities pitched at individual or group levels of performance.

Knowledge and understanding of 'The Vikings'

Unit 2 dealt with this at length. In planning the teaching we drew upon our knowledge as appropriate. Thus when planning out the lesson on Viking raiders, we consulted both the Usborne book *Viking Raiders* (Civardi and Graham-Campbell, 1977), as we knew it had a graphic section on the planning and execution of such a raid, and the *Anglo-Saxon Chronicle*, which has an account of a Viking attack on Exeter, the children's home town (Garmondsway, 1972: 132–3).

The whole school curriculum, and history's role in it

With history as a National Curriculum subject it is now standard for it to have an allocated place on the school's overall curriculum plan. In relation to our teaching of 'The Vikings' to our class this provided us with a term's involvement of twelve half-day sessions, extendable into the next term, which focused on the Anglo-Saxons. Specifically, we relate our teaching to the English National Curriculum.

TACTICAL PLANNING – LESSON PLANNING

Teaching is a creative, fluid activity that develops in response to factors that affect and shape the progress of the teaching and learning. Consequently we work within a very loose strategic and tactical framework, adapting and changing the course of the teaching in response to realities. Tactical planning means that we plan in detail the particular teaching strategies we intend to adopt. These are Teacher 2's 'building blocks' (see page 118). These we note down in enough detail to provide a framework for our teaching. What might a set of linked tactics look like? When we taught a combined class of 7 to 9 year olds using the 1851 local census records we:

• Discussed why the government needs to find out about us and record the information. Presented the class with a problem to solve, and asked them to think of the headings for a survey.
• Asked the children to create a census of their own family, using the 1851 census headings. (This provides a framework for understanding.)
• Pooled information in a whole-class session, using the blackboard to produce a class census.

Discussed the families, where they had come from, the number and kinds of pets they had.
- Made the sources and information the pupils need available through differentiated sources. (So, we ensured that we matched a census record or records to individual children; pupils with limited reading skills received a single record, more able children were given two or three records, and fluent readers were given a list.)
- Gave the class the original census material. (Its members recognised the shape and form of the records and related personally to them. One spontaneous comment was, 'It's a census'.)
- Asked the pupils to highlight or underline any name, word or number that they recognised, making sure that they started off with a successful, no matter how small, piece of learning. (There were great squeals of delight when a child found her family name, living in the same house! At each point we provided the knowledge and understanding that forced a pupil response to the stimuli.)
- Asked each '1851 family' to present to the whole class a mime of what their family did for a living. (Much enjoyment and not a little hilarity as the class worked out what their jobs were.)
- Each family was asked to produce a family sheet, with the number of the house, the street, the name of the family and its occupation. They could then draw a picture of the family on the sheet, showing its work.
- Hung these in order on a line, using clothes pegs.

So an 1851 Victorian community came to life. We avoided the problems that Teacher 1 encountered (see page 115). She was either unaware of, or unable to draw upon and adapt, a set of appropriate strategies. Interestingly, in terms of the reading problems Teacher 1 highlighted, she was aware of two possible whole-class teaching tactics – a booklet of differentiated resources, and using a tape:

 Teacher 1   *Maybe next year [as with materials on Thomas à Becket]… I actually put a book together, and all they had to do was turn the page and there it was; so there weren't that many worksheets flying about. They had it all in the package. Maybe next year I will spiral-bind it and do it all as a Domesday database package for them; so they don't have to fiddle about with Pritt sticks. That's probably the answer: everything to hand.*

Interviewer   *I was just going to say would you change anything?*

Teacher 1   *Yes, yes. I would. That's probably a better approach. It works with the Becket stuff which is loads of written evidence. Maybe if I do that I'll put some of it on tape, so the less able ones can be a bit more independent with it. That might work. It's giving equal access to all the children to be able to do basically the same activity. That's the thing you've got to crack in history. Sometimes it works and sometimes it doesn't.*

In our actual teaching we use the ideas listed in our lesson plan as a guide, a skeleton that we adapt, change, add to and discard as circumstances dictate. Where we are carrying out action research we record in detail what happens, either in note form or through a tape. This we then write up as a detailed account, with suggestions for improvement.

What form did the tactical planning of part of a lesson on 'The Vikings' take and how was it written up? The lesson was the last of the term, the children were to be settlers in a Viking valley who had decided to go on a raid. To go on the raid they had to build a longboat. The account of what happened is italicised.

1.   *Planning the boat*

- Gave out a picture of Viking longboat, an artist's drawing.
- Asked the children to look carefully at the picture, thinking about the shape, size, length and depth of the ship.
- The children drew a plan from the picture, in rough. They would do this as if from the top of the mast.

We handed out the book by D.M. Wilson (1970), The Vikings, *which has a picture of a Viking boat on the cover.*

Detailed observation. We asked the children to count the number of people, how many planks, how many oars, how it was steered, how it was propelled. Lots of discussion and argument about this, as we pooled information.

Drawing. We asked the children to draw a plan on rough paper as if they were looking down from the mast, a bird's eye view.

Then we asked Bethan to come up to the front and draw her plan on the blackboard, putting in how long and wide the boat was. A duck egg shape emerged, so we looked back at the picture and tried to get her to alter the shape to match it.

Through question and answer, looking at the men in the picture to get some idea of scale, we were able to work out how long, wide and deep the boat might have been. An important point was to count the oars, allowing enough room for a man to sit and row at each one.

We decided the boat would be 3 metres wide in the middle, 14 metres long and 3 metres deep. It would have eleven oars on each side.

We asked the class how the Vikings would plan out a boat, working round to the idea of them pegging the shape out on the ground.

2. *Planning the boat*

- Took the kids into the hall, taking their rough plans with them.
- Worked out a plan of the ship on the hall floor, using string, marking the length, keel, bow and stern, mast, shape of sides, place for oarsmen to row, steering oar.

We went into the hall with a ball of string that we had bought and a metre ruler.

We lined the class up along one wall, and told it that we were going to plan out the boat, using the string.

First, we paced out how long it would be. We worked out that there would be a long piece of wood, the keel, along the bottom. The 14 metres took up the whole length of the hall.

Terri was placed at the bow; we paced out 14 metres and put Joe at the stern.

The mast was next, so we asked Stephanie to stand where it would be, in the middle of the keel.

We did some creaky mental maths to sort out how wide the boat would be from the centre. 1.5 metres was the answer, this we paced out with a stride and a half.

Now we created a long arc, with children holding the string. This we placed on the floor to give us the shape of one side of the boat. We decided the bow would be more pointed than the stern, and altered the string accordingly.

We followed the same procedure for the second side.

We asked questions about why they needed oars
– putting out to stop being swamped in a storm
– rowing in and out of port
– when no wind
– in battle

I also told them stories of Viking warriors running along the oars.

3. *Synchronised rowing*

- Got the class to row, showing them how to do this in time.
- Called out the commands and the rhythm.

We had to work out where the eleven oars would be on each side. To do this we spaced the children out so that they could sit down and swing forward.

We asked about where and on what they would sit; the idea of using their sea-chests arose.

The class chose a steersman, and the remaining pupils looked after the sails.

Now for the synchronised rowing!

4.   *Life on board*

• What was life like on board?

We asked them to think about living in their space for a week or more, and what it would be like to go on a long voyage. We focused on the senses of feel, taste, touch.
Luke commented that life would be very hard, Michael that it would be cold while Natalie said that there would be the taste of sea salt in their eyes and mouth.

 ACTIVITY 6.5 TACTICAL PLANNING

• What were the benefits of teaching about the Viking ship in the whole-class approach described above?
• What drawbacks can you think of?
• Would it have been possible to teach the class about building, sailing and rowing a Viking boat in an equally effective, non-whole-class way, and if so, how?
• Take any single topic you think would be suitable for whole-class teaching, but which, before reading this unit, you would have been unhappy to teach in this way.
• Consider in detail the steps you would take to teach the topic to the whole class.

Assessment

WHAT IS ASSESSMENT?

Assessment measures pupil performance both during and at the end of a history course in terms of both substantive and syntactic knowledge. Thus assessment provides an index of improvement, as it shows the progress of each pupil. Improvement is evaluated against the pupil's own previous performance, the relative performance of peers and what can be expected from children in that age group nationally and internationally.

WHAT IS ASSESSMENT FOR?

Quite simply, its main purpose is to improve teaching and learning. It gives the teacher information about how individual pupils are performing, and pupils an understanding of how well they are doing and how to progress.

It should also be sensitive enough to be diagnostic, showing pupils how they can improve through indicating both their qualities and factors that may be inhibiting their performance. As such, it should help teachers and pupils both put things right and build on achievement.

Assessment should encourage and sustain learning through being positive and supportive. Merited praise and appreciation can give the pupil a great boost, and encourage increased and sustained application.

WHO IS IT FOR?

Assessment is for each pupil individually and other pupils collectively to see how well they are progressing; it is also for parents and guardians; for the teacher, other teachers and the school and for external consideration as and when appropriate, for example, a new school, social services.

WHAT IS ASSESSED?

Assessment is not only of cognitive and affective (emotions and feelings) development, but also of social development, or how well the pupil can function as a member of a collaborative group

and develop interpersonal skills and qualities. Assessment is of the overall, holistic quality of a pupil's thinking and understanding in relation to the subject. It should therefore draw upon a range of techniques and approaches and be the outcome of a process that extends over sufficient time to produce as accurate a picture of the child as possible.

WHAT DOES THE HISTORY NATIONAL CURRICULUM ASSESS?

The basis for assessment in the History National Curriculum is the Programme of Study (PoS), with its key elements and study units. Combined, they embrace both historical skills and processes (as laid out in the key elements), and historical content (the study units). Thus assessment of National Curriculum History should cover pupil progress in both syntactic, procedural (know how) and substantive, propositional (know that) knowledge.

ASSESSMENT AREAS OF THE NATIONAL CURRICULUM AND AN ALTERNATIVE – A PROFILE OF HISTORICAL LEARNING

The History National Curriculum (HNC) presents areas for assessing learning in history in its key elements. Taken together they provide a profile of historical learning. You can use the key elements for formative assessment, after diagnosis, to inform and shape future pupil learning. One alternative to the key elements of the HNC is that assessment should reflect seven factors involved in historical learning (Fines, 1994). The seven elements of the Fines model are:

1. *Basic skills*
   Reference skills, selection of evidence and debate, without which there can be no engagement with the subject.
2. *Questions and questioning*
   Questions are raised about the subject matter under study –by children as well as by the teacher.
3. *Sources and evidence*
   The search for evidence in the sources.
4. *Meaning*
   Connection and comparison in the evidence accumulated, to see whether there are any emergent groupings or patterns.
5. *Explanation*
   Explanation that makes sense and illuminates the question or subject.
6. *Informed explanation*
   Explanation that takes account of all the evidence available.
7. *A sense of period*
   This is 'that constant understanding that the past is a foreign country and that they do and think differently there' (Fines, 1994).

HOW SHOULD WE ASSESS?

Assessment should reflect as closely as possible what pupils can do. The form that assessment takes is therefore crucial. Central is the concept of minimising the gap between the results of an assessment task and actual performance, to ensure that the assessment provides a true reflection of the child's qualities.

Children between the ages of 7 and 11 can think both logically and imaginatively, using a range of genres and registers. However, they may not do this spontaneously. We can assist children to produce high quality work through:

- supporting them in their asking and answering of real questions
- helping them in working on sources
- providing a framework for presenting their findings
- supporting and directing them in their work from early drafts to the final presentation.

The history children write will reflect the task set. So, if asked to do a low-level task they will function at a low level. Assessment tasks should challenge pupils to think at the leading edge of their capabilities. Because much assessment is of written work, on pages 86 to 88 we have given some ideas for using writing frames so that pupils can produce high quality written work.

Assessment tasks should also reflect:

- Time: children need time to complete assessment tasks properly – some need more time than others, and should be given it, so they can show what they can do.
- Normal work in history: assessment tasks should seem no different to the children from those they usually experience.
- Different methods and media: it is essential to use a variety of approaches. Otherwise we disadvantage children who perform best through a different method from the one chosen. Some children perform best enactively through drama and role-play, others through a visual medium, some through writing, and others through oral expression. For an example of assessment of oral work, see Acts to Save your Head, pages 135 to 136. Only by employing as full a range as possible will your assessment accurately reflect the pupils' attainment.

Self-assessment

One aspect currently being developed is self-assessment, whereby pupils assess their own learning in history. We can add such evidence to their portfolios (see below). To help their self-evaluation we can give children a range of statements and questions, such as:

I have used these sources…
From them I learnt that…
I believe my account/conclusion is right because…
or
I have found out that…
How I know is/The evidence for my conclusion is…

Questions children can ask themselves include:

Have I understood what I have to do?
What sources of information have I used?
How reliable are my sources? Have I checked my evidence against other sources?
What is the most likely explanation, taking all the evidence into account?

PROGRESSION

Having defined the qualities involved in historical learning, the adult historian's conception of the domain, we can relate these to a set of criteria that indicate pupil progress. Progression is a difficult word to handle in terms of children's historical learning. Progression implies linear progress, with the mastery of ideas, concepts, skills and processes, smoothly ascending a ladder from the pit of ignorance to the Elysian fields of academia. But, it ain't like that.

We can recognise progress through time, with pupils slowly building up skills, competencies, knowledge and understanding in relation to tackling historical topics. The crucial element in

progression is a continuous pattern of reviewing and reflecting upon the class's progress, adapting and refining ideas and approaches in response to circumstances.

Progression: the History National Curriculum view

The History National Curriculum attempts to measure progression through its Attainment Targets (AT). The HNC defines progression as a hierarchy of eight holistic levels, each of which describes ever-more complex historical knowledge, understanding, skills and processes; the final level, eight, reflects the mentality of the mature historian. The AT is primarily for summative assessment at the end of each key stage. Levels 2 to 5 are intended to cover the 7 to 11 age range.

The attainment target – problems

The AT draws on the key elements. Each key element usually has a related sentence within each level description of the AT, although that sentence does not cover the different aspects of each key element. The AT takes the key elements' areas and shows how understanding of them develops. For example, in terms of key element 4b, 'To ask and answer questions about the past', the AT's levels are:

AT level 1 'They (pupils) are beginning to find answers to questions about the past from sources of information.'
AT level 2 'They answer questions about the past, from sources of information, on the basis of simple observations.'
AT level 3 'They find answers to questions about the past by using sources of information in ways that go beyond simple observations.'

At this point questioning disappears from the equation!

The attainment target model of progression is extremely problematic. No research into the assessment of 7 to 11 year olds' learning underpins the hierarchies and structures of levels 2 to 5. The evidence for placing qualities in specific levels related to the age of children is simply missing: the AT is untested in terms of historical learning.

Worse, the AT's structure and organisation are deficient, for it is not comprehensive, failing to cover each factor of the key elements at each level and show how they progressively become more demanding and sophisticated. Thus, in the case of questioning the AT fails to include a crucial aspect of historical learning that is mentioned in key element 4b – children *asking* (as opposed to answering) questions.

The AT also introduces new factors and omits others on an *ad hoc* basis.

Even more difficult, there is no explicit concept of progression, in terms of changing qualities of thinking that reflect cognitive development. Implicitly the attainment target assumes that once a descriptor is mentioned in a level it is then mastered. This negates progression, denying the concept of the incremental development of that skill over time – thus in the case of questioning, what kinds of questioning do we expect from children in levels 4 to 8?

A final, related problem is that the AT's levels do not reflect subtlety and complexity in pupil thinking. Thus the AT would not register the complex understanding two Year 6 (10–11 year olds) pupils, John and Aelfred, revealed in discussing their involvement in a historical drama:

John   *We actually thought what people thought in those days.*
Aelfred   *I didn't. In 1066 I thought what I think now, not then, it's impossible.*
John   *But he gets you into the place, so you think like they would have done.*

A wide-ranging discussion then followed, in which Aelfred insisted that people in the past had fundamentally similar ways of thinking as people in the present, although much of their thinking would appear to be different because of the historical context.

Making sense of the AT

Accepting the simple fact that we have to use the AT for assessment, how can we make it operational?

 ### ACTIVITY 7.1 WRITING AN ASSESSMENT SCHEME

Taking the key elements and the Fines scheme (page 126), you can produce your own model for progression to cover levels 2 to 5 for 7 to 11 year olds. The Fines scheme headings are in *italics*:

Take any one point. Under it produce, from examining your pupils' work, an analysis of what kind of thinking, knowledge and understanding you would expect them to have for each level. Then consider how the whole assessment scheme might appear.

1. Chronology
(a) sequence
(b) common words and phrases

2. Range and depth of historical knowledge and understanding
(a) aspects of the past
(b) causation
(c) consequence
(d) difference
Meaning
Connection and comparison in the evidence accumulated, to see whether there are any emergent groupings or patterns
Explanation
Explanation that makes sense and illuminates the question or subject

3. Interpretations of history
Different ways the past is interpreted
Sources and evidence
The search for evidence in the sources

4. Historical enquiry
(a) finding out about the past from evidence
Basic skills
Reference skills, selection of evidence and debate without which there can be no engagement with the subject
Sources and evidence
The search for evidence in the sources
(b) to ask and answer questions about the past
Questions and questioning
Questions are raised about the subject matter under study – questions raised by children as well as by the teacher

5. Organisation and communication
(a) handling historical information
(b) using of historical terms, for example court, monarch, trade, industry, law
(c) communication of knowledge and understanding
Informed explanation
Explanation that takes account of evidence available
A sense of period

This is 'that constant understanding that the past is a foreign country and that they do and think differently there' (Fines, 1994)

The assessment triangle

Because of the AT's deficiencies, we need an approach to assessment that enables us to assess all aspects of the key elements. In our analysis of pupil work we have identified three common criteria – coherence, sophistication and depth – that enable us to to determine the extent and quality of pupil learning. These factors produce an assessment triangle. On the basis of the judgement made on the three criteria we can then see where is the best match with the statements in the attainment target.

Coherence

The ability to produce a coherent account or explanation is relative. At one extreme we have a set of unrelated statements, at the other an explanation that is presented as an integrated whole that makes sense and is plausible, with elements pulled together, different pieces of evidence reconciled and contradictions explained.

Sophistication

Sophistication has two facets, the process and skills of enquiry and the quality of thinking involved as revealed in the use of language, concepts and ideas. Pupil work provides us with evidence of developing understanding, the result of continuing debate, discussion, challenge, practice. The child shows the ability to handle complexity, to understand and take different viewpoints and to present interpretations based on the processing of historical evidence of increasing complexity and extent.

Depth of knowledge

This is the extent and range of the propositional and conceptual knowledge that the pupil displays in historical work. It develops through focusing on a selected number of events/situations and investigating them thoroughly. In turn, learning in depth leads to a sense of period through relating an understanding of the particular context to its overall development.

MEASURING PROGRESS

How can we measure the progress that pupils make in the three areas? The first step is diagnostic: we need to have some idea of a pupil's capabilities at the start of the process. This involves a review of their previous historical work, of the knowledge and understanding they already have. The review in turn provides the basis for a programme to enable the children to make progress from their starting points. The second step is the assessment of the teaching and learning, continuously reviewing and reflecting upon progress and adding to the pupil's portfolio.

RECORDING

Historical learning is not a smooth continuum, a seamless rail of progress. Pupils respond to contrasting tasks and challenges in different ways; one piece of work will differ markedly from the next. Where demands are made that draw upon discrete areas of thinking and different types of response, the learning outcomes in turn are understandably variable. So, the recording of

progress should be incremental, built up over a period of time according to context and circumstances. The resulting rich and varied record enables you to make an holistic judgement, based upon what you consider to be the pupil's real level of performance.

Judgements of children's learning depend on your knowledge of each pupil, and on the background to each assessment task and how it was introduced and supported. To understand your assessment later it helps to note the background, the context and the resources available on each piece of work recorded as evidence of learning.

A photocopy of the attainment target for each pupil

The attainment target can provide a running record of pupil performance through keeping a photocopy of the AT's level descriptions for each child in a class. Whenever a piece of work is assessed, the teacher underlines the sentence in the level descriptions which best fits that piece of work. Each underline can be colour coded or dated, to check whether progression is constant and linear – a highly unlikely outcome. At the end of the key stage, each child is assigned a level according to which level description has the most underlines.

However, after level 3 the AT's level descriptions are difficult to relate to detailed, in-depth work such as Andrew's description of the finding of Tutankhamun's tomb and the poems praising Eirik Bloodaxe (see pages 133 to 137).

Pupils' portfolios

In our own teaching, our pupils create their own history books that include all the history work they do. These provide an excellent source for judging pupil progress, with annotation of separate elements so as to build up a holistic picture. In turn, the pupil book can contribute towards a pupil portfolio which contains exemplar materials of progress over four years in different areas. As the portfolio builds up over time, a clear picture emerges of what each child can do. It is impossible to assess a child on one piece of work alone: first, and obviously, because any given task is highly unlikely to target all the key elements; second, because it is only over a long period of time and over a range of tasks that we can judge performance and track progress in historical thinking and knowledge. The portfolio should include not only evidence of children's written and art work from their history books, but also the teacher's observation notes recording pupils' oral performance.

REPORTING

The History National Curriculum allows maximum flexibility to teachers in reporting children's progress. All they *must* do is report to parents once a year. *How* they do this is entirely up to them. At the end of key stage 2 teachers do not even have to assign children an AT level, although if they don't they may have to justify this to OFSTED, who are required to look at how teachers' planning relates content (PoS) to the key elements and reflects level descriptions.

If our reporting system does not make sense to children and their parents, to other teachers, the governors and the community, it will be worth nothing. And, of course, reporting to children – i.e. feedback on their progress – should be a regular feature of your teaching. Such feedback should be both positive and comprehensible to the pupil.

Reporting on performance should concentrate on what the pupil can do. Pupils should also be clear about what they need to do to improve their performance. For this reason, the children must know and understand the criteria on which they are being assessed. One way to do this is by giving pupils self-assessment prompts (see page 127). Another is to reword the key elements in 'child-speak'; for example, key element 2b could be rewritten thus: I can say why something happened and I know what happened afterwards.

CHILDREN'S WORK ASSESSED: THEORY INTO PRACTICE

How, in practice, can we apply the assessment triangle approach – sophistication, depth of knowledge and coherence – to assess pupils' historical learning in terms of the five areas of the key elements? In assessing pupils' historical learning we advocate three steps:

1. Identification of the aspect or aspects that you are judging, taken from the key elements.
2. A judgement of the quality shown according to the three dimensions of sophistication, depth and coherence.
3. The mapping of this judgement on to the attainment target and the recording of the assessment in a portfolio.

Below we analyse examples of work – from our Vikings course taught over five weeks to a class of 10 to 11 year olds and from the pupils of teachers on in-service courses we have run. The level attained was marked on the pupil's copy of the attainment target and the work and comments were added to the pupil portfolio. The assessments relate to a range of key elements as each pupil's work draws on several.

Assessment 1: Lian and the work of the archaeologist

A Year 6 mixed ability class in a Leeds primary school worked through two archaeological activities at the start of a unit on Ancient Egypt. The teacher, Claire, introduced the children to: the role of archaeology in developing understanding of the past (key element 4a – historical enquiry: range of sources of information about the past); how and why archaeologists work; and prepared the class for investigating Carter's discovery of Tutankhamun's tomb. The HNC requirements for studying a past non-European society, that the unit should cover 'the use of archaeology in finding out about the people and society' were satisfied, while at the same time the children were introduced to archaeological processes.
    The two initial activities involved were:

1. Digging up pottery remains from a sand tray divided into a grid with string, and recording the position of each fragment on an overhead transparency of the grid – a whole-class exercise. The children then raised questions about and discussed archaeologists' purposes, tools and methods.
2. Groupwork, with each group digging up its own pottery fragments, recording their positions and reassembling the finds.

    After the first activity Lian wrote:

> Archaeologists discover the past. They dig for evidence that something has happened such as tombs, they find the tombs and the pictures inside the tombs, that tells us about the Egyptian that is dead's past. To dig something up they have to divide it into sections so that they can record exactly were it is and so they can put it back. An archaeologist has to be very patient, they dig with a trowel and when they hit something they brush away the soil or whatever until they get to the object. When they reach the object they have to dig round it and put a board underneath it, and pull it out being very careful. Archaeologists have to wear plastic gloves and masks. They label the objects as soon as they come out of the ground. When the object has been studied it might go to a museum.

Assessment of Lian's response

Lian's account demonstrates that through participation in simulating the methods of archae-ologists, and subsequent questioning and discussion, he has acquired knowledge and under-

standing of the process, methodology and purposes of archaeology. He has satisfied key elements 4 and 5.

The assessment triangle

How does Lian register on the assessment triangle?

Coherence   The account is extremely well constructed, with each part following on logically from the next.
Sophistication   A clear indication of the work of the archaeologist – a good level of sophistication shown. The use of correct terminology, an idea of how a dig proceeds, the destination of objects are all correctly understood.
Depth   A good depth of knowledge.

Relating the three criteria (coherence, sophistication and depth) to the AT

The problem of 'fit' raises itself. Our analysis suggests that, in terms of reporting, Lian is operating at level 7, showing an ability 'to select, organise and deploy relevant information to produce well structured narratives, descriptions and explanations, makng appropriate use of dates and terms.'

Assessment 2: Andrew and the tomb

After the archaeological preparation activities, the class had a Tutankhamun discovery day. Afterwards, Andrew communicated his understanding in two forms: a grid showing the position of the finds in the tomb's antechamber, and a description of the finding of the antechamber by Carter.

The Antechamber
Howard Carter was chipping a hole in the door to the antechamber and he was so apprehensive he couldn't say a word. In the room there was food, statues, a toilet, a chest, a chariot's body, and beds with animals on. There was a lion bed a typhon bed and a cow bed. After peering into the room he went in and saw all the things. There was a rotten, musty smell and dust kept falling off things. The statues were statues of Tutankhamun and they were stood opposite each other in a guard sort of way. The toilet was very poor and it was battered in. Then suddenly he saw an entrance which had been covered up then opened up and then covered up again. One of the team said Look there's some finger prints on the objects and on that wall. Then they looked more closely and it was true. There were finger prints. 'Look over there' Some of the gold leaf had been stripped off the beds and the chariots were smashed and part of the jewellery were taken. Robbers must have been in the tomb.

Assessment of Andrew's response

Andrew's work satisfies key elements 2, 4 and 5, as he has used various sources of information to produce his grid and description. He has also selected and recorded relevant information, organised it and communicated it in a structured narrative.

The assessment triangle

Coherence   Logical and well-argued account, clear description and sequence of events. A convincing narrative.
Sophistication   Clues (fingerprints, damaged and stripped artefacts) presented as evidence that robbers had been in the tomb. Inferences made – statues standing 'on guard'.
Depth   Wealth of detail. Imagination informed by knowledge, for example dialogue, description

of Carter's state of mind as he broke into the tomb. Deep knowledge of archaeological processes, for example his drawing of antechamber goods; close and detailed observation of objects and drawing inferences about the past.

Relating the criteria to the AT

The three criteria suggest that Andrew is working at level 6, where pupils can 'select, organise and deploy relevant information to produce structured work, making appropriate use of dates and terms.'

Assessment 3: Viking burial

The assessments which follow arose from a topic of half a term on the Vikings, one afternoon a week (ten hours in total). The key initial activity was a historical enquiry: digging up a Viking burial mound on the Isle of Man, working out what the finds could tell us about Viking society, then comparing our archaeological finds with an eye-witness account of a Viking burial in Russia. The follow-up activity was to write an archaeologist's report on the excavation. The first example is Richard's archaeologist's report; while the second example is an extract from a story by Rachel. This story was written two weeks later, as a result of an investigation into Viking settlement in Yorkshire, using placenames work. She had incorporated into her story of a Viking family's journey to settle in England a description of a Viking burial – applying the knowledge acquired from the archaeological investigation of the first session. It is worth a lot to acquire knowledge. It is worth more to apply that knowledge in other situations. This Rachel has done in her settler's story.

Richard (Year 6): archaeologist's report on the Viking mound excavation

My archaeologist's report
I think that the decayed wood would have been the remains of an old coffin. He must have been a warrior as he was buried with his sword, shield and two spear heads also he could have been a farmer as on the second level there were lots of animals. I think that the slave woman was in the mound and the Warrior/Farmer wanted her to look after him in Valhalla.

Richard shows aspects of key elements 2, 4 and 5 in constructing his report. He also demonstrates that he can draw conclusions based on evidence from more than one source (evidence from the burial mound, and the not-quite-matching evidence from Ibn Fadlan's account). He has made inferences from the evidence to create a plausible explanation – a sophisticated skill not explicitly acknowledged in the NC history order.

The assessment triangle

Coherence   The report is clear; all the threads are pulled together to create a convincing picture of the man buried in the mound.
Sophistication   Demonstrates good skills of enquiry, and presents a sound conclusion based on evaluating several different pieces of evidence.
Depth   This is a straightforward account, showing depth of knowledge about this burial, but no more.

Relating the criteria to the AT

As ever, fit is a problem with the AT, but in relation to reaching conclusions based on evidence, Richard can be said to be operating at level 7: 'They are beginning to reach substantiated conclusions independently.'

Extract from Rachel's story (Year 5)

 But before they reached the next village an upsetting sight met their eyes.

There had been a war over who should own the land and there was a Viking burial of an important warrior. He was on a ship with his servant lying next to him.

His belongings were richly decorated in gold and blue and his ship's figurehead was very finely carved. Many spearheads and knives lay about him ready for his next life in Valhalla. He was dressed in his best clothes and his hair was brushed and the angel of death had washed his hands. Then his nearest relative set the ship on fire and all that was left at the end was a pile of ashes.

Rachel's account shows evidence of key elements 2a (features of past society, including beliefs), 4a and 4b (the account draws on her earlier use of written and archaeological sources about Viking burial practices), and 5a and 5c (she has recalled, selected and organised historical information and communicated her knowledge in a structured narrative).

The assessment triangle

Coherence   The account is coherent, but no more.

Sophistication   The level of sophistication is less developed than her knowledge in depth here. Her introduction to the episode (*an upsetting sight*) and her use of the word *Viking* betray her as a twentieth-century child, rather than the Viking settler she supposedly is.

Depth   Rachel's extract demonstrates knowledge in depth – she includes a wealth of detail about a Viking burial ceremony.

Relating the criteria to the AT

We have assigned this work to level 4: 'Pupils demonstrate factual knowledge and understanding of aspects of the history of Britain and other countries'. Her factual knowledge of Viking burial ceremonies is the major determining factor here.

Assessing groupwork

Groupwork forms an intrinsic part of learning in most primary schools. Group activities can be assessed, as the example below demonstrates. In assessing individual contributions to a group's efforts, the teacher can either rate each group member on the same level, or, by judicious observation of pupils as they prepare the group's work, can identify individual pupils' contributions.

Assessment 4: Acts to save your head

Imagination is germane to historical understanding: we can investigate the past using our cognitive skills, but we cannot enter it except via our imagination. The role of imagination is not made explicit in the HNC's key elements, although it is implicit in the phrase 'knowledge and understanding'. What is the relationship between imaginative activities like storytelling and simulation, and activities which can be assessed? In short, the story or simulation brings children into the past, they are then imaginatively engaged and ready to pursue the topic, doing work we can assess.

For example, during the Viking topic we drew the children into the past by telling them the story (from Egil's Saga) of how Egil Skallagrimson fell into the hands of Eirik Bloodaxe, King of Yorvik (York). Bloodaxe and Egil were deadly enemies, and Egil was in danger of being killed immediately. Fortunately for him, his friend Arinbjorn, who was also one of Bloodaxe's henchmen, pleaded successfully for Egil to be given one night's grace before being brought before Bloodaxe

again to meet his fate. Egil had only the hours of darkness to think up some way of saving his neck. At this point we broke off the story, to groans of disappointment all round, and told the class to take the role of Egil and come up with a convincing plea or act that would save them. The children worked in groups of three, and after fifteen minutes, during which we arranged the classroom to look like Bloodaxe's Great Hall, the different Egil groups walked up the length of the hall, knelt to us – in role as Bloodaxe and his wife Gunnhild – and made their bids for life.

The purpose of this exercise was to put the children in the position of people in the past, facing decisions they faced. We can assess the children's bids in terms of the understanding they demonstrate of the tenth-century political, cultural and social world of the Vikings. At this point the Viking topic was in its fourth week. The previous three weeks had been spent digging a Viking burial mound; establishing, through placename research, the pattern of Viking settlement in Yorkshire; and investigating different aspects of Viking life.

The children's strategies, 'Acts to save your head', were:

1.   A fake conversion to Christianity: this group came forward bearing a cross and intoning Christian prayers for forgiveness.
2.   Bribery, with offers of jewels and silver in return for life.
3.   Bribery again, but more cunning: 'If you spare my head, I will give you half my land and all my belongings when I die naturally.'
4., 5.   Pleas for forgiveness, appealing to the king and queen's better natures.
6.–8.   Poems, two appealing to the pair's past friendship; another a praise poem to Gunnhild (an extract: 'Oh Queen/you are/such a/delight/You make/the whole/kingdom/come to/light. You are/a mother/of gracious/warriors…').
9.   A combination of the above: 'Would you like cargo with jewels and gold? And maybe we could give you some of our land in Iceland. And maybe my lord might be interested in some stories for when you drink and talk with your men.'
10.   An offer of single combat, and when this was scornfully refused by Bloodaxe, a breathtakingly astute second offer: to kill King Athelstan of England (who trusted Egil) and make Bloodaxe king of all England in Athelstan's place.

The strategies show a wide variety of historical thinking. This ranges from the naive and unlikely strategies of 4 and 5 to the highly plausible, politically aware offer made by group 10.

We select just two of the above examples for assessment: groups 1 and 10.

Group 1 show knowledge and understanding that the Viking period was characterised by conversions to Christianity (key element 2a). Group 10 also satisfy key element 2a, with their knowledge about the wider political power situation in England.

The assessment triangle

Oral tasks like this one are more difficult to analyse in detail than is written work. The Christian conversion strategy of group 1, while coherent in itself and conceptually quite sophisticated, lacks plausibility in terms of its likely effect on Eirik Bloodaxe. It therefore lacks true historical depth or conviction. In contrast, group 10's head-saving offer is entirely convincing in the context of the Viking world. It shows a high degree of political acumen, knowledge of the power structures pertaining in that world and understanding of the size of the bribe needed to change the mind of a hard man who has you in his power. On the coherence, sophistication, depth ladder group 10 is several rungs higher than group 1.

It is with activities like this one that the limitations of the National Curriculum become obvious. The children's role play cannot be explicitly assessed in terms of the AT, yet such role play is a perfect vehicle for helping children to develop that sense of period which constitutes true historical understanding.

Assessment 5: Viking praise poetry

The two children below, both in Year 6, have entered imaginatively into the Viking past, showing evidence of both cognitive learning and full affective engagement with the Viking world.

Vicki's poem to King Eirik Bloodaxe, written in his praise after he granted Egil his life:

To Eirik...

As Eirik stalked the battle field
The moaning cry,
The broken shield.
Many a soul hath asked him why
They now dead, their sorrows sigh.

As Valkyries swooped
And sword did smote.
As foes did fall unto the spear
Did Eirik Bloodaxe laugh.

The Yorvik water ran red
As blood flew.
And in Odin's name to strike
The axe came unto neck.

As Eirik sat at home,
A battle won
Drinking mead, a bright red sun
Shone through glass

And stained the light to blood.

Anna's praise poem to Egil's best friend and blood brother, Arinbjorn, who helped him to save his life:

A perfect friend

Your open hand I did not doubt,
On battle field you exchange the glance,
An enchanting look of fate.
Let all points and blood red suns,
Protect your men till journey's end.

The name 'Arinbjorn' sounds the waves,
From shore to shore they know your name.
They know you of your wonderful wins,
They fear you in their frozen hearts.

The clash and clatter of swords and shields,
Odin looks upon those you have killed,
And knows overall the fate,
That your bows and arrows are the sharpest.

You are the most lavish man I've met,
This poem is for you my friend,
So let our friendship ring out through all lands.
The light of you is the strongest.

In relation to the key elements, the poems are underpinned by information gained from a range of sources (key element 4a) and show a depth of understanding about the ideas, beliefs and attitudes of people in the past (key element 2a). Vicki and Anna recall, select and organise historical information (key element 5a) and communicate their knowledge and understanding in a structured way (key element 5c). They also represent and interpret their view of the Vikings (key element 3) through their poems.

The assessment triangle

Coherence   The three strands of form, content and structure unite in these poems in a satisfying and convincing manner, giving a high level of internal coherence.
Sophistication and depth   These poems show historical understanding of a high order. They convincingly capture the spirit of Viking praise poetry. The value the Vikings placed on success in battle, on generosity to friends and allies, on reputation and fame, all are reflected here. The reference to Odin and the Valkyries shows integrated understanding of Viking religious beliefs.

Relating the criteria to the AT

The poems score high on all three coherence, sophistication, depth criteria, placing them at level 6 in the AT: 'They select, organise and deploy relevant information to produce structured work, making appropriate use of dates and terms.'
    As we have stressed throughout this book, history and language are inextricably linked. Anna and Vicki's poems demonstrate their ability to write in the Viking poetic form, to use metaphor to excellent effect and to deploy new words (for example mead, lavish, Valkyries) vividly and appropriately. The praise poems are securely at level 4 of the English level descriptions for AT3 (Writing), and are moving towards level 5. To quote from AT3, level 4, 'Pupils' writing in a range of forms is lively and thoughtful. Ideas are often sustained and developed in interesting ways and organised appropriately for the purpose and the reader. Vocabulary choices are often adventurous and words are used for effect.'

 ACTIVITY 7.2 ASSESSING PUPILS' WORK

1. Take the history work of three pupils who are judged to be:
    - extremely able
    - average
    - poor
2. Select up to four different pieces of work that they have all done and which show them working in different ways and contrasting genre. Assess each piece:
    - First use the three dimensions [COSOD]:
        Coherence
        Sophistication
        Depth
        Write down your comments.
    - Then assign each piece to its level, using the attainment target. Underline the element in the attainment target that you feel the pupil has attained.
    - Finally, on the basis of your assessment, place each pupil in a level for the attainment target.

References

Aldrich, A.(ed.) (1991) *History in the National Curriculum*, London: Kogan Page.

Alexander, R. (1992) *Policy and Practice in Primary Education*, London: Routledge.

Alexander, R., Rose, J. and Woodhead, C. (1992) *Curriculum Organisation and Classroom Practice in Primary Schools: A Discussion Paper*, London: Department of Education and Science.

Andersen, P.S. (1971) *Vikings of the West*, Tano: Sandnes.

Anderson, C.W. (1991) 'Policy Implications of Research on Science Teaching and Teachers' Knowledge', in M.M. Kennedy (ed.) *Teaching Academic Subjects to Diverse Learners*, New York and London:Teachers' College Press.

Batey, C., Clarke, H., Page, R.I., Price, N.S. (1994) *Cultural Atlas of the Viking World*, New York: Facts on File Inc.

Bennett, N. and Carré, C. (eds) (1993) *Learning to Teach*, London and New York: Routledge.

Bersu, G. and Wilson, D.M. (1966) *Three Viking Graves in the Isle of Man*, London: Society for Medieval Archaeology.

Blyth, A. *et al.* (1976) *Place, Time and Society: Curriculum Planning in History, Geography and Social Sciences*, Collins.

Borlase, W. C. (1878) 'A Visit to Dr Schliemann's Troy', *Fraser's Magazine*, no. 17, February 1878.

Bourdillon, H. (ed.) (1994) *Teaching History*, London: Routledge.

British Museum, The (1986) *The Romans, Activity Book*, London: The British Museum.

Brooks, R., Aris, M., Perry, I. (1993) *The Effective Teaching of History*, London: Longman.

Brown, S. and McIntyre, D. (1993) *Making Sense of Teaching*, Milton Keynes: Open University.

Bruner, J.S. (1960) *The Process of Education*, Oxford: Oxford University Press.

Bruner, J.S. (1966) *Towards a Theory of Instruction*, Cambridge, Mass.: Harvard University Press.

Calder, W.M. (1972) 'Schliemann on Schliemann: A Study in the Use of Sources', *Greek, Roman and Byzantine Studies*, 13: 335–53.

Carré, C. and Ovens, C. (1994) *Science 7–11*, London and New York: Routledge.

Chaffer, J. and Taylor, L. (1975) *History and the History Teacher*, London: Allen & Unwin.

Civardi, A. and Graham-Campbell, J. (1977) *Viking Raiders*, London: Usborne.

Collingwood, R.G. (1946) *The Idea of History*, Oxford: Oxford University Press.

Coltham, J.B. and Fines, J. (1971) *Educational Objectives for the Study of History* TH35, The Historical Association.

Cooper, H. (1992) *The Teaching of History, Implementing the National Curriculum*, London: David Fulton.

Cooper, H. (1994) 'Children's Learning, Key Stage 2: Recent Findings', in P. John and P. Lucas (eds) *Partnership and Progress: New Developments in History Teacher Education and History Teaching*,

University of Sheffield: The Division of Education.

Cooper, P. and McIntyre, D. (1994) 'Teachers' and Pupils' Perceptions of Effective Classroom Learning: Conflicts and Commonalities', in M. Hughes (ed.) *Perceptions of Teaching and Learning*, Clevedon: Multilingual Matters Ltd.

Dawson, I. (1996) 'Standards of Living in the Middle Ages', *Teaching History*, 82: 27–30.

Dean, J. (1995) *Teaching History at Key Stage 2*, Cambridge: Chris Kington Publishing.

Department for Education (1995) Key Elements of the History National Curriculum.

Dickinson, A. and Lee, P. (1978) *History Teaching and Historical Understanding*, Oxford: Heinemann.

Elton, G.R. (1969) *The Practice of History*, London: Collins/Fontana Library.

Farmer, A. and Knight, P. (1995) *Active History in Key Stages 3 and 4*, London: David Fulton.

Fines, J. (1994) 'Progression – A Seminar Report', *Teaching History*, 75: 27–8.

Finley, M.I. (1977) *The World of Odysseus*, London: Chatto and Windus.

Foote, P.G. and Wilson, D.M. (1970) *The Viking Achievement*, London: Sidgwick & Jackson.

Fraser, A. (1970) *Mary Queen of Scots*, London: Panther.

Garmondsway, G.N. (ed.) (1972) *The Anglo-Saxon Chronicle*, London: J.M. Dent.

Glasfurd, G. (1993) *The Future for the Past of the Former Soviet Union*, Department of Independent Studies, University of Lancaster (unpublished paper).

Grossman, P.L., Wilson, S.M., Shulman, L.S. (1988) 'Teachers of Substance: Subject Matter Knowledge for Teaching', in M.C. Reynolds (ed.) *Knowledge Base for the Beginning Teacher*, Oxford: Pergamon Press.

Hexter, J.H. (1971) *The History Primer*, New York: Basic Books.

HMI (1991a) *Training Primary Teachers for the History National Curriculum*, London: DFE.

HMI (1991b) *Reports on History and Geography in Selected ITT Institutions*, London: DFE.

HMI (1991c) *Impact of the Secretary of State's Criteria (Circular 24/89) on the Planning for Arts/Humanities Courses in the Initial Training of Primary School Teachers*, London: DFE.

HNC (1995) *History in the National Curriculum*, London: Department for Education.

Homer (1951) *The Iliad*, trans. R. Lattimore, Chicago: University of Chicago Press.

Husbands, C. (1996) *What is History Teaching?*, Buckingham: Open University Press.

John, P. (1991) 'The Professional Craft Knowledge of the History Teacher', *Teaching History*, 64: 8–12.

John, P. (1992) 'Preparing Students for the History Classroom: Issues in Lesson Planning', in P. Lucas and R. Watts (eds) *Meeting the Challenge: Preparing Tomorrow's History Teachers*, University of Sheffield, Division of Education.

Jones, G. (1984) *A History of the Vikings*, Oxford: Oxford University Press.

Kennedy, M.M. (1991) 'Merging Subjects and Students into Teaching Knowledge,' in M.M. Kennedy (ed.) *Teaching Academic Subjects to Diverse Learners*, New York and London: Teachers' College Press.

Knight, P. (1991a) 'Teaching as Exposure: The Case of Good Practice in Junior School History', *British Educational Research Journal*, 17, 2: 129–40.

Knight, P. (1991b) 'Good Practice and Teacher Education: A Study of History in Key Stage Two of the English National Curriculum', *Journal of Education for Teaching*, 17, 2: 201–12.

Lee, P. (1991) 'Historical Knowledge and the National Curriculum', in A. Aldrich (ed.) *History in the National Curriculum*, London: Kogan Page.

Lewis, M. and Wray, D. (1996) *Writing Frames: Scaffolding Children's Non-fiction Writing in a Range of Genres*, Exeter: Exeter Extending Literacy Project.

McNamara, D. (1991) 'Subject Knowledge and its Application: Problems and Possibilities for Teacher Educators', *Journal of Education for Teaching* 17, 2: 113–28.

Magnusson, M. (1980) *Vikings*, London: Bodley Head.

Olsen, O. and Crumlin-Pedersen, O. (1978) *Five Viking Ships from Roskilde Fjord*, Copenhagen: The National Museum of Copenhagen.

Reeves, M. (1954) *The Medieval Town*, Harlow: Longman.

Reeves, M. (1980) *Why History?*, Harlow: Longman.

Rogers, P.J. (1979) *The New History: Theory into Practice*, London: Historical Association.

Rumelhart, D.E. and Norman, D.A. (1985) 'Representation of Knowledge', in A.M. Aitkenhead and J.M. Slack (eds) *Issues in Cognitive Modelling*, London: Lawrence Erlbaum Associates.

Schank, R.C. (1985) 'Reminding and Memory Organisation', in A.M. Aitkenhead and J.M. Slack (eds) *Issues in Cognitive Modelling*, London: Lawrence Erlbaum Associates.

Schliemann, H. (1869) *Ithaque*, London: John Murray.

Schliemann, H. (1875) (ed. Philip Smith) *Troy and Its Remains: A Narrative of Researches and Discoveries made on the Site of Illium, and in the Trojan Plain*, London: John Murray.

Schon, D. (1987) *Educating the Reflective Practitioner*, San Francisco, CA: Jossey Bass.

Schools Council (1977) *Schools Council History 13–16 Project*, Edinburgh: Holmes McDougall.

Schwab, J.J. (1978) *Knowledge and the Structure of the Disciplines.*

Shulman, L. (1986) 'Those who Understand: Knowledge Growth in Teaching', *Educational Researcher*, 15/2: 4–14.

Shulman, L. (1987) 'Knowledge and Teaching: Foundations of the New Reforms', *Harvard Educational Review* 57: 1–22.

Smyth, A. (1996) 'The Anglo-Saxon Chronicle', *The Historian*, 2–7, The Historical Association.

Traill, D. (1995) *Schliemann of Troy: Treasure and Deceit*, London: BBC Publications.

Treece, H. (1955/1969) *Viking's Dawn*, London: Bodley Head.

Trevelyan, G.M. (1930) *Clio, a Muse and Other Essays*, London: John Murray.

West, J. (1992) *Classroom Archives*, Huntingdon: Elm Publications.

Wilson, D.M. (1970) *The Vikings and their Origins*, London: Thames & Hudson.

Wilson, D.M. (1987) *The Vikings Activity Book*, British Museum Press, London.

Wilson, S.M. and Wireburger, S.S. (1988) 'Peering at History Through Different Lenses: The Role of Disciplinary Perspectives in Teaching History', *Teachers' College Record*, 89: 525–39.

Wood, M. (1985) *In Search of the Trojan War*, London: BBC Books.

Wood, T. (1994) *The Saxons and the Normans*, Loughborough: Ladybird Books.

Index